THE GLASS STATE

THE GLASS STATE

The Technology of the Spectacle ❃ Paris, 1981 – 1998

ANNETTE FIERRO

THE MIT PRESS ❃ CAMBRIDGE, MASSACHUSETTS ❃ LONDON, ENGLAND

This book was set in Minion and Corporate by Achorn Graphic Services, Inc.
Printed and bound in the United States of America.

Library of Congress Cataloging-in-Publication Data

Fierro, Annette.
    The glass state : the technology of the spectacle, Paris, 1981–1998 / Annette Fierro.
      p. cm.
    Includes bibliographical references and index.
    ISBN 0-262-06233-X (hc : alk. paper)
    1. Glass construction—France—Paris. 2. Public architecture—France—Paris—20th century. 3. Architecture and state—France—Paris—History—20th century. 4. Symbolism in architecture—France—Paris. 5. Mitterrand, François, 1916– 6. Paris (France)—Buildings, structures, etc. I. Title.

NA1050 .F53 2002
721'.04496'094436109048—dc21

2002024448

TO MY PARENTS, **ALEJANDRO** AND **MARIA TERESA**

CONTENTS

Preface: The Details of the Discourse

Poor Narcissus: Irresistibly compelled by his own image, finally opting to be kept at bay rather than risk the prospect of imploding his beloved reflection. In this study of glass building, the Greek myth lends more than psychic phenomena associated with reflection. Architectural inquiry, particularly of any length and speculative dimension, is always a multivalent endeavor, but never moreso than when confronting the topic of glass. As one approaches this quicksilver subject, with every step forward, it grows, finally threatening to expand infinitely just as the final touch suggests possession.

At first glance the topic of this study seems, however ambitious, also finitely limited—the monumental glass buildings of contemporary Paris, most of which are in the program for the *Grands Projets* of François Mitterrand, president of France between 1981 and 1993. A factual recount of the conception and building of these immensely significant projects in the cultural and political spheres of Mitterrand's Paris is more than enough to endow an enormous study. However informative, this type of study would still be hardly adequate to addressing the proper scope of the subject matter. The imposition of transparent and technologically motivated monuments prominently with a public Parisian urban domain inevitably instigates multiple domains of history: vast physical histories of Paris and Parisian architecture as well as vast intellectual histories, in many different disciplines, that have addressed issues of transparency and technology.

But the danger of Narcissus immediately harkens: the amount and different types of literature devoted to glass attests to our propensity to be fascinated, seduced, and compelled by it. Technological studies of glass architecture typically represent it as the forefront of invention, the extreme edge of structural investigation and material innovation. This presumption is not an exaggeration. Since the Gothic cathedral, glass has been coupled with the birth of the structural frame, arguably the most significant development in architecture in the last millennium. With the rise of the structural frame in the late nineteenth century, glass construction, particularly curtain wall assembly systems, have followed suit; together the two systems have dominated contemporary large-scale construction. Most recently, the association of glass with highly advanced technology was illustrated once again in Paris, where the structural properties of glass itself threw into imbalance all previously existing hierarchies between structure and cladding.

As the vanguard of technical progress, the use of glass has appropriately incited a number of historical studies. Numerous authors dwelled on the tremendous effect of glass architecture in the nineteenth century in provoking new building types such as train stations, arcades (Geist), and exposition structures (Giedion). In the modern era, issues of glass and transparency assumed a pivotal role in new heroic architecture. Developments in glass manufacture in the 1910s and 1920s made it possible to enlarge pane size and the degree of its transparency, advances that prompted modernist dissolution of the building's exterior envelope. Transparency also assumed a central metaphorical role for the modernists, serving as the guiding principle for generating the building form out of the expression of its structure, a system of legitimization for the new architecture that realized Renaissance ideals of centuries past (discussed at length in chapter 1). From the Gothic, to the modern, to the most contemporary of recent work, glass has transformed the most basic principles of architecture, from structural and formal morphologies, to programmatic types, to fundamental material, spatial, and philosophical conceptions.

Of all building materials, glass also incited the most provocative departures outside proscribed architectural discourse. It is frequently found, for example, as a central metaphor in the fine arts and art history. Remarkable in its capacity to be employed in diverse media, most striking is the fluid potential of glass to suggest and assume widely divergent meanings. An idiosyncratic few, for example: in film classics such as Jean Cocteau's *Orpheus,* the reflective surface of the mirror is used as a literal metaphor for the duality of psychic realms between life and death, a psychological exploration of the mirror. In an entirely different vein, in Jacques Tati's film *Playtime* the reflectivity of glass serves as a vehicle to critique the imposition of modern architecture onto everyday life. In sculpture, at one extreme, artists such as Christopher Wilmarth and James Carpenter employ different types of glass almost as a conventional material, although residing in the particular paradox of its physical properties. Wilmarth explores in his translucent cast glass and steel structures of the 1970s and 1980s the contradictory impulses found in glass of weight and weightlessness. Carpenter's recent explorations using new technologies of diachroic coatings on glass emphasize its holographic potential. As the position of the viewer shifts, the spectrum of color and opacity at the surface changes radically, hyperbolizing the effect of glass reflection and its dependence on a particular point of view. On the other hand, in more conceptually oriented art, the physicality of glass (or lack thereof) has functioned to represent its very absence. Through the use of glass, Duchamp's seminal "definitively unfinished" *Bride Stripped Bare of Her Bachelors Even* (or *The Large Glass*) exhausts the question of pictorial temporality and its representation. Glass in contemporary artist Dan Graham's work serves as the vehicle to destabilize the context of the artistic work within and outside the museum proper; an ambition that synopsizes the direction of much contemporary artistic production since the 1960s. Graham uses glass to reframe contemporary social spaces by situating viewers unexpectedly against reflected environments (see chapter 3). Hovering between material and immaterial, glass is quintessentially an *open* medium, sustaining often paradigmatic shifts in structure and type, material and metaphor.

Philosophy and psychology have been especially unable to resist the provocative interpretations offered by glass. As an agent of vision and light, glass is encumbered by overarching discourses that begin in Greek philosophy. Tethered to systems of Greek idealization that imparted to light the authority to make form visible and therefore known, glass gave architecture the same pure light: glass architecture is known predominantly as rational architecture.[1] Equally, it granted architecture the capacity to view from inside to outside, but also to gaze, charged in various critiques with the capacity to control. The analogy between vision, as a system of order and control, and architecture, as absolute knowledge, became most explicit in Michel Foucault's discourse on punishment and Georges Bataille's writings on occularcentrism.[2]

In its reflective capacity, the topic of glass also absorbs psychoanalytical as well as philosophical questions instigated by the mirror. Allen Weiss recounted the essential properties that incited the provocation of Freud and Lacan: "Symbols of narcissism *and* alienation, of the self enrobed in its image and the self lost in the *other,* mirror images offer a vast series of poetic and rhetorical effects transposed onto the visual realm."[3] In the medieval era, the mirror was considered either the reflection of God or an instrument of the devil.[4] In seventeenth-century Baroque, the catoptric mirrored device, an aristocratic toy, served as the philosopher's muse for such seminal figures such as René Descartes and Jean-François Niceron. Writings of Gilles Deleuze on the profound instability of the mirrored surface in Carroll's *Through the Looking Glass* have been enormously influential, not simply in philosophy, but across many fields of creative production.

In the field of architecture, the use of glass over the last few centuries has been equally diverse, also inspiring notable explorations in theoretical debates. These ranged from Paul Scheerbart and Bruno Taut's call for crystalline social utopias (which provided, for this study, a potent history of ideological implications), to Frank Lloyd Wright's association of the mathematical perfection of glass to the idealized product of the "humanized machine."[5] In more contemporary theory, Anthony Vidler invoked Freudian and Lacanian interpretations of mirrors to problematize the translucent surface in OMA's entry to the Paris Bibliothèque Nationale competition (see figure 5.2).[6] To address the translucent surface, Terence Riley cited ideas of literary critic Jean Starobinski, who himself referred to writings of essayist Michel Montaigne and philosopher Jean-Jacques Rousseau.[7]

The study of glass is as elusive as the material itself, uncontrollably branching into speculations from many different directions, many different disciplines. Serious readers of external disciplines will possibly be disappointed by the cursory treatment of their respective interests in this book. This is admitted out of both necessity and design. A full historical, political, theoretical, and technical explication of the Grands Projets is exactly akin to the dilemma of Narcissus's reflection: although suggestively accessible as a finite set of buildings, when given the added weight of history and the multiplicity of tangential discourses, a full study is unattainable perhaps by definition. It is notable that given the enormous significance of the projects, a full discussion has never been attempted, and perhaps never will. I too retreat, both from the naiveté of attempting a totalizing depiction, as well as the dire inadequacy of only one type of description. Rather, a large part of my endeavor is to constitute a particular frame of reference from which the matrix of issues from different disciplines might emerge and be cultivated together.

For the glass buildings of Mitterrand's Paris, I chose the most local frame of reference possible. For whereas the buildings sit squarely enmeshed in complex issues of politics, urbanism, technology, material and figurative symbolism, phenomenology, psychology, philosophy, and the fine arts, manifestation of these issues is attempted with the most insubstantial of expressive means. With the exception of the Eiffel Tower, the buildings examined in this book are typically simple geometric forms, primary elemental volumes. In these buildings, the flirtation of transparency with its host of incumbent associations is registered primarily by the nuance of the construction of the surface and the spaces disposed in front and behind. Architect Rafael Moneo, in reference to a range of contemporary transparent architecture that he similarly characterized as formless, noted: "Construction becomes the sole means of expression. The continuity between form and matter becomes the most important issue, and the transition from the material to the almost nonexistent form is the passage that these architects celebrate."[8]

Intrinsic to the emergence of Mitterrand's glass buildings in Paris is a political concept: that physical construction might be endowed with the potential, through the medium of transparent skins, simultaneously to heighten, transcend, and make literal a politically construed metaphor of accessibility; an agenda proposed anew by Mitterrand after earlier efforts in the 1960s to open previously closed cultural institutions to the general public. For Mitterrand, primary elemental forms lined in refined details of glass and steel symbolized the most grandiose aspirations of the French leftist state. Laden with subject matter questionably beyond their capacity to convey, the glass buildings of Mitterrand's France pose an opportunity to observe the contradictory impulses of expressive intents and resources: in the very thinnest of surfaces, in the most nuanced configurations of glass to details of support, the most lavish of meanings were attempted. It is this stark dichotomy that compels this study. As the meanings incumbent in the glass accrue out of control, the physical elements are simultaneously pared down to their most minimal. Very centimeter between glass and support, every decision to weld rather than screw, every chemical additive to the surface coating of the glass becomes extravagantly significant.

As its primary goal, this book proposes the formation of a discourse of detail, where detail assumes a status typically accorded to other conventionally primary aspects—planimetric syntax, spatiality of the interior, or structural order, for example—in configuring and describing the entity of the architectural work. In this proposed discourse, the details of Mitterrand's buildings become doubly tied to prevailing social orders, if one regards the process of building production itself as the culmination of negotiations at all levels, from political state to general public, from architect to engineer to local fabricator. As Rosalind Krauss put it, the facts of material building, especially in transparent construction, evidence the "technological and economic production that has structured the building's social field," giving them inherently political overtones.[9] The detail, as the final outcome of this expanded definition of production, crystallizes into a physical manifestation the complex set of cultural conditions that surrounded the building's design and production. Marco Frascari tells us that in the detail one can see the process of signification, the attachment of meaning to man-made objects.[10]

The first evidence of this discursive structure is found in the organization of the chapters of this book. The first introductory chapter is the only exception, and attempts to place in context the urban component of the Grands Projets in Paris as well as the appearance of transparency as a resurgent expression in the city's history. Subsequent chapters are more closely configured along the lines of the main intention of the book; each is posed as a case study of a building or set of buildings relating a element of structure or detail to its political, theoretical, and urban contexts. Chapter 2 examines the precedent of the Pompidou Center, and its own precedent, the Eiffel Tower, as benchmarks of "ideological construction." As the exposed monumental frames and their method of fabrication and assembly are exaggerated and exposed, they generate a new spatial and occupational prototype for public space.

In chapter 3, Jean Nouvel's two Parisian institutions, the Institut du Monde Arabe and the Fondation Cartier, are examined for the potential of contemporary curtain wall construction to assume the mantle of cultural representation. Chapter 4 traces the development of a set of glass details designed by engineers Rice Francis Ritchie (RFR) across the most highly charged symbolic landscapes of contemporary Paris; from I. M. Pei's Grande Pyramide du Louvre, through the utopian park projects at La Villette and André Citroën (collaborations of RFR with architects Adrien Fainsilber and Patrick Berger, respectively), to the final Louvre inverted Petite Pyramide, all of which are Grands Projets. Finally in chapter 5, the last and most recent Grand Projet, Dominique Perrault's Bibliothèque Nationale de France, illustrates the counterpoint to the ideological construction of the Pompidou Center, foregrounding Mitterrand's role, ultimate ambition, and final achievements in the Grands Projets as a whole.

This book examines at length the often prosaic construction and constructional processes of the most prominent transparent buildings in Paris. They are considered from the moment of initial conception, through material and structural execution, to pertinent associations and histories of materials and structures, and finally, to the effects rendered by surfaces and their construction. It is this last point that is most salient to beginning the reading of this text, which is ethically committed to going beyond simply tracing historical and academic referents and the preconceived political intents, and engaging the actual effects of physical structures when implanted prominently in the public domain; hence essential forays into commentary from popular sources. The implicit concept of the built surface in this study is that its effects perform with definitive social ramifications, as well as symbolize socially and politically inspired aspirations.

Given the multiplicity of domains that this topic encompasses, basing this frame of examination around the questions of material details may seem contrived and limited to some. Perhaps. Yet I chose the Grands Projets as a case study because they provide and extremely rare opportunity: to examine a finite set of buildings, all constructed of similar materials, all constructed in a specific urban landscape in the same period of time, all engendered with related ideologically expressive missions.

This quest to examine the multiple consequences of materiality and construction is positioned between two current vastly divided architectural climates. One on hand, the virtuality afforded by three-dimensional digital generation has fulfilled the avant-gardist pursuit of the immaterial, demoting all issues of material to the rank of hopelessly nostalgic.

At the other extreme, calls from a group I loosely term the "tectonists" for generation of form by the terms of construction alone also were tremendously influential, expecially for the built sphere of architectural practice. In this quest, presumably to recuperate architecture from the ravages of poststructural excesses of the late 1980s and early 1990s, questions of theory and criticism have been relegated to near extinction. A discussion of these issues is broached in the epilogue, which addresses the discourse of the tectonic in the wake of discussions of the Grands Projets. Suffice for now to say that it is within the middle ground set up by these two seemingly irreconcilable discourses that this study proposes to occupy, outside rhetorical exclusions proposed by either extreme and within the possibilities of the acts, effects, and thoughts involved in building.

Acknowledgments

Support for a first book comes in many forms. In making possible the circumstances which prompted the initial interest in this topic, I first thank H. Randall Roark at the Georgia Institute of Technology and Peter McCleary of the University of Pennsylvania, both of whom had the long-sightedness and wisdom to encourage young faculty to teach and study in foreign locales. Financial support for the project was provided primarily by University of Pennsylvania in the form of a Research Foundation Fellowship grant, as well as from the continuous aid of Dean Gary Hack and Richard Wesley at the Graduate School of Fine Arts. Richard Wesley I thank especially first for acknowledging the contradictory realities that a substantial teaching career imposes on scholarly production and then combating countless policies in gaining time for such production.

For the formative inspiration that has been brewing for many years, I credit two mentors: Henry Smith-Miller, who trained me in both the facts and ultimate significance of the detail, and Peter Waldman, who taught me that to work, one must play. For more recent generosity of time and specific critical import, I thank David Leatherbarrow, Edward R. Ford, Peter McCleary, and John Stuart and two other anonymous readers for MIT Press (surely they know who they are), all of whom provided extensive and thorough remarks. At MIT Press, I thank Lisa Reeve, designer Erin Hasley, editors Sandra Minkkinen and Sarah Jeffries, and of course Roger Conover, for considering the unsolicited manuscript in the first place. Various other readers also contributed to pieces of the text or added crucial encouragement at particular points: Harris Dimitropoulos, Joseph Harriss, Jennifer Bloomer, Ben Nicholson, Margaret Crawford, Lindsey Falck, and Franca Trubiano. To all of the architects and kind members of their staffs, thank you for the generous time given in interviews to an unknown American: Dominique Perrault; Brigitte Metra and Didier Brault in Jean Nouvel's office in Paris; Giorgio Bianch in Renzo

Piano's office also in Paris; Michael Flynn and John Neary at Pei, Cobb, Freed and Partners in New York; and Jean-François Blassel from Rice Francis Ritchie's office in Paris.

My trusty research assistant Ufuk Ersoy I thank for countless hours in dusty pursuit spent away from his own research on glass as he dug for facts, images, and popular lore on buildings for which there were volumes of useless information. The original technical drawings were products of student labor, and I thank now generally and later specifically, Charles McGloughlin, Marvin Rodriguez, Amity Kundu, and Robert Trempe, Jr. For technical help in producing the text and images, I thank Greg Finnson at Penn. Scattered throughout the text are also ideas from legions of other students who knowingly and unknowingly made contributions, in research seminars as well as design studios, and who I hope will recognize their own voices as they read through my words; particularly my thanks go to Kevin Cannon, Alfred Dragnani, Beck Feibelman, Katherine Gibson, Ron Henderson, Carey Jackson-Yonce, Marlene Krawczyk, Amity Kundu, Harry Marks, Charles McGloughlin, Brian Milman, Natasha Ruiz-Gómez, Wayne Verspoor and Scott Walters. The list of remarkable students from both Georgia Tech and Penn who inspired certain thoughts might go on indefinitely.

My final thanks go to three essential individuals who contributed in disparate degrees but imparted similar effects. When this was all a rough and vague amalgam of ideas delivered in a lecture at Columbia University, Mary MacAuliffe provided one late-night statement of support that was essential to initiating this study. I thank her posthumously for the inherent generosity in her trademark commitment to incise sharply and truthfully, which made her brief words of encouragement all the more substantial. I thank my husband Richard A. Ashworth who supported me in all ways from prosaic to profound, from giving me time from our precious children, to carrying camera equipment throughout Paris, to reading through the manuscript and making remarks that both reduced the opacity of the writing and nuanced the technical facts. Finally, my thanks to Andrea Kahn for slugging through countless rough drafts, never relenting in giving criticism of the staunchest integrity yet therapeutically lacing it with ther never-failing sense of humor. If the honesty and laughter of these three people are not reflected in my actual words, it is to their tough love, given to me and to others around them, to which this book is dedicated.

We have to realize that art and life are no longer separate domains. Therefore the idea of "art" as illusion unconnected with real life has to disappear. The word "art" no longer means anything to us.

—Theo van Doesburg and Cornelis van Eesteren, *Towards a New Collective Building* (1923)

1

✿ Paris, The Grand Projet

IN 1998 THE INTERNATIONAL PUBLIC was presented with the completed Bibliothèque Nationale de France, culmination of the *Grands Projets* of François Mitterrand. These projects, comprising not only a number of individual buildings but also the urban design of significant portions of peripheral Paris, are attributed to the will of Mitterrand himself, much in the way that the last great reorganization of Paris carries the name of Haussmann (however originally envisioned and presided over by Napoleon III). Compelled by creation of a symbolism monumental both at the scale of the individual building and at that of the city, the projects were motivated almost entirely by the French president. Although conceived and executed under a system of democratic governance, they entailed a decisive implementation on Mitterrand's part that often meant circumventing typical legislative procedures or political compromises that might have threatened to obstruct their progress. And thus appropriately, the Grands Projets will indeed remain a legacy, imbued with great possibilities of authoritative vision but tainted by the disquieting presence of authoritarian rule.

An American political sensibility might dismiss the series of building projects as phenomena of a lingering monarchist sensibility of power. Although this would probably be an accurate assessment, the first distinction to be drawn in France is in the very different historical value accorded to a paternalistic notion of state. Termed *dirigisme,* the traditional role of the state is not limited as an unqualified representation of its citizenry, but exists as its benevolent protector, guarantor of its wealth, and securer of equality among its citizens. *Dirigisme,* translated literally, connotes not only management but also guidance. This distinction is a legacy in France, where an expansive concept of state developed as democratic structures introduced in the French Revolution joined with paternalistic leanings of Louis XIV's *ancien régime*. Evolving most recently under the consolidation of presidential power of Charles de Gaulle's constitution of the Fifth Republic of 1958, the leader of state was granted authority to make sweeping changes in parliamentary structures and elections, effectively giving presidents decisive control over a number of government offices and policies.

Many historians believe that of all recent French presidents, François Mitterrand assumed the mantle of Charles de Gaulle, his old political enemy, in assuming the mythic *politique de grandeur*.[1] Like de Gaulle, in the new bipolar structure of world power inherited from World War II, Mitterrand tenaciously maintained a notion of France as independent, however secondary. Under him, the public sector in France was also enlarged significantly; upon assuming office he nationalized thirty-six banks and a host of industrial companies, and expanded the nation's elite rail network. However debatably unsound economically, however vehement the calls for reform issued by the United States and other European countries, the legacy buttressed by Mitterrand is maintained zealously: in both public and political spheres, an expanded public sector is held in high esteem.[2] The idea of a beneficent state thrives in France, fortified ethically, and tenaciously, against the liberalism of competitive private economies elsewhere.

If we are to believe recent intellectual scholarship, the unrelenting French notion of state is complemented by an uncommon sense of the public (at least of those native French) of the collective whole of their society and culture. A consensually held amalgamation of cultural beliefs is at the core of the mythical national French persona, *la France éternelle*.[3] Under such a value system, the relationship among the state, its leadership, and its citizenry is, despite the complexities and intrigues of a multifarious system of modern political parties, vaguely familial. The fluidity of identity between governing entities and their public constituency becomes of central significance when examining the Grands Projets, which were instigated by Mitterrand but had the intention of representing Paris, which had the historical mandate of representing all of France.

Most of the Grands Projets were built, to some degree, of glass. It is the contention of this study that the transparency of the projects presumed to express, yet simultaneously challenged, the implicit continuity between an expression of state and an expression of the public, an agenda embedded in Mitterrand's newly ascended leftist government. Predictably, these enormous monumental projects, as political statements brought into physical form and overlaid on the capital city,

ɪ.ɪ Johan Otto von Spreckelsen, the Grande Arche de La Défense, 1989, north flank.

were enveloped in controversy. The most prominent buildings were greeted with national and international protests. Although Mitterrand and his committee deftly maneuvered successfully through the worst of these, building nearly all the projects proposed, his activities hardly exemplified the benevolent transparency proposed rhetorically as the new leftist relationship between the public and its government.

Surrounding these relatively local dilemmas is the larger crisis of monumentality itself, particularly in France. The oldest of European states, the nation's descent to secondary status after World War II is being steadily amplified by the cultural drain of international globalization. French intellectuals portray their traditionally hegemonous culture as under attack in all terms economic and cultural.[4] Glittering in their glass skins and technological garb, Mitterrand's insistently transparent monuments present the beguiling desire to disappear, rather than to assert France's mythic presence.[5]

The most debated of Mitterrand's projects—I. M. Pei's Grande Pyramide du Louvre and Dominique Perrault's Bibliothèque Nationale de France—went beyond extolling the use of glass and steel; they were statements about the nature of transparency itself. The emergence of transparency was given added emphasis by the host of other prominent, although more politically benign, examples in the projets that also use glass—greenhouse structures (Les Serres) at the Cité des Sciences et de l'Industrie in the Parc de La Villette (1986) and at the Parc André Citroën (1992) designed by Adrien Fainsilber and Patrick Berger, respectively, in collaboration with engineers Rice Francis Ritchie (RFR); Jean Nouvel's Institut du Monde Arabe of 1987; and Pei's second, less controversial Petite Pyramide at the Louvre Carrousel of 1993. This book examines each of these Grands Projets as well as Nouvel's Fondation Cartier, completed in 1993, whose prominence in the public sphere grants the building relevance for the discussions at hand. These contemporary examples are set against two less recent works that establish precedents for monumental transparency in Paris: the Pompidou Center of 1977, by Piano and Rogers and Gustave Eiffel's tower for the Exposition of 1889.

Two other Mitterrand Grands Projets attest to the singular appearance of transparency at a monumental public scale, but since this book undertakes the study of transparency primarily as a material phenomenon (see Preface), they are not included. They are, however, significant to the scope of the transparent operation in Paris. The first, Johan Otto von Spreckelson's l'Arche de la Défense of 1989, establishes an emblematic precedent for the transparent antimonument; opposite to

I.2 Bernard Kohn et Associés, subway head, Métro Météor, 1999.

Pei's Grande Pyramide du Louvre, at the other end of the Voie Triomphale, the arch is seen through rather than focused upon.[6] The second example, the last of Mitterrand's Grands Projets, was never built. Parisian architect Francis Soler's Centre International de Conférences was to be located along the Seine near the Eiffel Tower before cost overruns of Perrault's Bibliothèque Nationale quelled enthusiasm for the project. If it had been completed, Soler's visionary structure would have been a culmination of many of the themes posed by the other transparent Grands Projets. An international diplomatic meeting facility, replete with large facilities for the press, would be housed alongside a contemporary garden in enormous double-shelled glass boxes. Political events would be intermingled with huge trees and exotic birds, all of which would be open to view—and considerable interpretation—by the general public.

Although plans for this building were abandoned, Nouvel's Musée du Quai Branly, unbuilt at this writing, is intended for the same site. It will house existing collections from the National Museum of African and Oceanic Arts and the Musée de l'Homme. This latest museum, instigated not by Mitterrand but by his successor and long-time adversary, Jacques Chirac, was dubbed by the popular press as Chirac's own Grand Projet. Once again, it will continue the lineage of the contemporary Parisian monument: it will be built almost entirely of glass. Taken together across the public landscape of Paris, these buildings have been vehicles for a new symbolism. Despite Chirac's late rush to contribute his own transparent legacy, doubtlessly glass and technological imagery in Paris's monuments will be historically attributed to Mitterrand and, by extension, ascension of the Left to momentary power.

Anecdotes tell of Mitterrand's private obsession with *la transparence.* It was he, after all, who defended Perrault's glass towers against an international onslaught of (well-grounded) criticism. In the face of strikingly obvious problems associated with housing France's literary archives under glass, Mitterrand tenaciously justified the material's use by arguing for its cultural symbolism—accessibility of knowledge to all. And in a recent counter-gesture whose irony was not lost on many, the library, besieged from its opening by tremendous operational problems, was posthumously renamed by the succeeding rightist government la Bibliothèque Nationale de France *François Mitterrand.*

The proliferation of glass, however tempting to dismiss as Mitterrand's personal folly, is wedded in a far more complicated way to a contemporary international material zeitgeist. Initiated debatably by the French projets in the 1980s, particularly Pei's pyramid, the use of glass and advanced technology pervades much architectural production in the present day, especially in buildings of British High Tech (Richard Rogers, Nicholas Grimshaw, Norman Foster, et al.) as well as more contemplative work in Switzerland of Peter Zumthor and Herzog and de Mueron. Despite the prominence and prevalence of contemporary glass, critical examination has been sparse at best; the most comprehensive overview occurred in a 1995 exhibition at the Museum of Modern Art in New York heralding "Light Construction." Here, curator Terence Riley equated attainment of lightness, most often through the use of translucent glass, with ambitions paralleling the rise and fall of architectural postmodernism. He wrote: "They [the projects in the exhibition] likewise reject the strictures of post-modernism, which have alternated between invoking, as inspirations for architecture, a suffocating supremacy of historical form or arid philosophical speculation."[7]

In France the ubiquitous appearance of glass in the 1990s hardly indicates interest in academic architectural polemics, although it follows Riley's suggestion that the emergence of transparency is largely self-propelled. Despite being advanced by the public scrutiny of the Grands Projets, the invasion of glass into realms of both public monument and commonplace vernacular suggests a popular movement with motivations beyond Mitterrand's political symbolism. Glass can be found in numerous recent commissions at all scales and degrees of civic significance completed by a variety of lesser-known French architects—Christian Hauvette, Frances Deslangier, Haumont and Rattier, Brunet and Saunier, Phillippe Gazeau, and many others.

In 1997, the pervasive presence of transparency in specifically Parisian architecture prompted a large exhibition sponsored by the Pavillon de l'Arsenal—the architecture and urban history center of the contemporary city—entitled "*Paris sous Verre: La Ville et ses Reflets*" (*Paris under Glass: The City and Its Reflections*), which chronicled the development of glass from its earliest appearances to the latest ubiquity. Beginning its documentation with examples of Gothic cathedrals of Saint Denis and Sainte Chapelle in the twelfth century, and tracing its proliferation in late nineteenth-century in department store atriums, train stations, arcades, and exposition halls, the exhibition ends its view of the latter day with the pervasive use of glass in modernist work of the 1930s and 1940s. The intent is apparent: if contemporary French architecture seems besieged by glass, history suggests that this is only a resurgence of a material that seems oddly wedded to Paris.[8]

This suspicion is borne out by examining the significant history of glass manufacturing in the city that dates to the fourteenth and fifteenth centuries.[9] Considering the exorbitant price of glass at that time, importation of the fashionable
commodity from Venice represented a significant economic loss for France. For
several centuries France contrived to steal glass-making secrets and artisans from
the Italians, granting immigrating glass-makers special noble status, although
exposing them to risk of punishment by death if found out by Italian authorities.
It was not until the seventeenth century that French glassmakers perfected a technique for casting glass on metal tables, which granted them the international market for the large sheets of flat glass eventually known as plate glass. In 1700, Louis
XIV granted the manufacturer of this new product complete monopoly over its
production. The company, Manufacture Royale des glaces de France, evolved over
the centuries into the Saint Gobain Vitrage, S.A., now located in the Parisian sub-
urb of Courbevoie and still the country's preeminent glass manufacturer. Indeed,
in most of the projects presented in this book, Saint Gobain Vitrage played a considerable role, researching and engineering new methods for producing and con-
structing with glass.

French preeminence in glass manufacturing was confirmed in the widespread
emergence of new building typologies employing the material in its capital.
Whereas the most recognized nineteenth-century glass exposition building is Paxton's Crystal Palace of 1850 in Hyde Park, the most pervasive appearance and evolution of the building type was in Paris. In the world expositions of 1855, 1867, 1878,
and 1889, the serial building of the great *Galeries des Machines* continuously challenged previously known structural concepts and scales of enclosed spaces.[10]
These buildings went beyond heralding new technologies of iron building. Constructed to house displays of consumer goods, they were meant to dazzle and
seduce an increasingly large and undifferentiated public, influencing civic opinion
in favor of governing entities responsible for the expositions.[11] Glamorizing the
power of the state, the glass exposition buildings anticipated the definition of the
spectacle that was to obsess Guy Debord and his band of Situationists a hundred
years later, in another very Parisian phenomenon.

The presence of glass in Paris also had another precedent in a seamier locale
to which Debord was far more sympathetic: *les passages couverts,* arcades built in
the earlier nineteenth century. Largely destroyed by Haussmann's reconstruction
of the city in the 1860s, their demolition elicited protestations by such figures as
Louis Aragon, who in *Paris Peasant* described a very different aura of a glassed

space: "My attention was suddenly attracted by a sort of humming noise which seemed to be coming from the direction of the cane shop, and I was astonished to see that its window was bathed in a greenish, almost submarine light, the source of which remained invisible."[12] For Aragon the glassed arcades were both frames for supernatural visions as well as venues for subterranean existence, imaginative life-lines for surrealists and dadaists.

In these two very different urban structures, the presence of glass signals especially relevant, if contradictory, associations for the latter day. The arousing presence of the exposition buildings indicated the state's full knowledge of the seductive power and expressive potency of advanced glass technology. Conversely, for surrealists, glass's alteration of light and image incited a fantastic thrall that was conceived as a form of resistance to that same state; in this case, the hegemonizing tendency of Haussmann's urban development. Both of these aspects of glass, firmly embedded in Parisian urban sensibility, unite to construct a paradoxical subnarrative, a conflicted "text," in which the meanings of the new Grands Projets must operate, whether or not they were conceived in such terms.

THE CITY RESTRUCTURED

In beginning to address the Mitterrand projects and their presence in the city, it is first necessary to go further in understanding a more conventional sense of the historical urban context in which they were envisaged. No city in the world has been deployed as a symbol of national identity to the same degree as Paris. Since Le Nôtre followed Louis XIV's command to extend the Tuileries axis down the Champs-Elysées in the seventeenth century, the city has served as an unparalleled laboratory for architects and urban designers. This willingness to experiment with the image and structure of the city at the grandest scale imaginable continued as recently as the 1960s, when Georges Pompidou, like Mitterrand, attempted his own transformation of Paris to address the demands and imagery of a contemporary technological city (see chapter 2).

Of the many periods of redevelopment, none is more instructive to revisit, however, than the precedent-setting Haussmannian era in the mid–nineteenth century. Certainly, issues raised in these earlier *Grands Travaux* served as the point of departure for contemporary critics and historians interpreting the effects of the Grands Projets.[13] One particular distinction raised by Haussmann's intervention parallels the intent of Mitterrand's building program: while developing ambitious pragmatic solutions to an explosion of the city's population, both regimes were

1.3 *"Plan général de Paris, au point de vue des promenades,"* A. Alphand in "Les Promenades de Paris,"
1867–1873. Courtesy Bibliothèque de la Ville de Paris.

also actively involved in discovering urban and architectural devices through which to transform the city into a monument. In their similar missions to intervene in extant orders of monumentality, the two eras forced changes to the expression of national identity and drastically altered the mnemonic order of the city.

Haussmann's legacy first established an overwhelming physical setting within which the Mitterrand projects would have to resonate. Although Haussmann's reorganization of the urban fabric was motivated by a number of highly complex infrastructural features, its most memorable characteristic was permeation of that fabric with a comprehensive system of grand axial boulevards. Conceived to provide increased mobility through the congested medieval city, particularly by providing for an east-west axis along the Rue de Rivoli and a north-south axis along Boulevard Saint Michel and Boulevard de Sébastopol, the boulevards also instigated a number of highly potent visual devices, connecting new and existing foci across the scale of the entire city, establishing a visual and physical connectivity at a scale that would augment how Mitterrand's transparent monuments would be individually situated and perceived.

In terms of physical and economic interventions, the two urban projects were of course markedly different. Georges Eugène Haussmann, Prefect of the Department of the Seine from 1860–1870, was commissioned by emperor Napoleon III to implement a variety of measures, primarily to augment existing and new infrastructures: streets, parks, and services, particularly sewer systems, as well as buildings associated as urban focal points. Haussmann's interventions provided specific remedies to insalubrious conditions, from introduction of a network of subterranean storm sewers to addition of substantial green spaces throughout the city. Among his additions to Paris are the Parc des Buttes-Chaumont, the Parc Monceau, and the two "lungs" of Paris, the Bois de Boulogne and the Bois de Vincennes.

Napoleon III and Haussmann's shared desire for a new monumental order was augmented by reconfiguring the existing context of the city to complement the new arteries. Vernacular buildings pierced by new boulevards were refaced with highly regularized façades. Existing street, plaza, and monument façades were thoroughly cleaned. Trees were planted throughout the city. Various significant existing buildings were given new squares in front of them; by freeing them from the mesh of urban fabric, these buildings acquired new status in the city. Most important of these was the Cathedral of Notre Dame, which illustrates

1.4 Place de la Bastille, with Carlos Ott's Opéra de la Bastille, 1989.

Haussmann's typical methods. By both augmenting the frontality of its façade with the new parvis and liberating the sculptural quality of its flanks and back toward the Seine, Haussmann distinguished it as the symbolic center of the Church in Paris. Similarly sited new monuments were added as well, most notably the Opéra Garnier, typical of the new types of cultural institutions demanded to accommodate the burgeoning and increasingly powerful upper middle class.[14] According to Haussmann scholar Howard Saalman, the mere presence of these prominent institutions had a decisively political intention. For the struggling regime of the second empire, this new grandeur in the city's buildings provided evidence of a stable and powerful political order—a "symbolism of governability."[15]

Prior to this great scheme, Paris had never been surveyed comprehensively. As Haussmann's Paris marked the first consideration of a city as a single organism, it also marked the birth of urbanism as a disciplinary study. For Mitterrand, president of France from 1981 to 1993, the precedent of the Haussmann project first established the viability of reorganizing the order of the entire city. Yet the morphological order of the city represented only the partial agenda of visions of Haussmann and Mitterrand's Grands Travaux. Instigated in a time of perceived malaise, both sets of projects set out to establish a new image for Paris through which France's prominence in the current world order would be revitalized. In both the nineteenth and twentieth centuries, the new image of the city was intended to insinuate France into the first order of technologically advanced countries.

The specific devices employed by the Mitterrand projects in reordering and reimaging the city were distinctly different from those of Haussmann. Buildings and urban spaces of the twentieth century were to be legible as new construction, in decided contrast to older monuments and fabric. Rather than manipulating the order of the city to emphasize existing monuments, the Mitterrand projects strategically deployed provocative technological imagery in new public buildings and spaces. This program of creating a new aesthetic was meant to rejuvenate the entire city's celebrated nineteenth-century grandeur.

Whereas the Grands Projets did not encompass the connective urban strategy associated with Haussmann's boulevards and infrastructural services, one intervention across the scale of the city particularly recalled the axial boulevards. Terminating the Voie Triomphale at the Grande Pyramide du Louvre and simultaneously building the new Opéra at the Place de la Bastille (by Canadian architect Carlos Ott, 1989) effectively extended Le Nôtre's western axis across the entire city

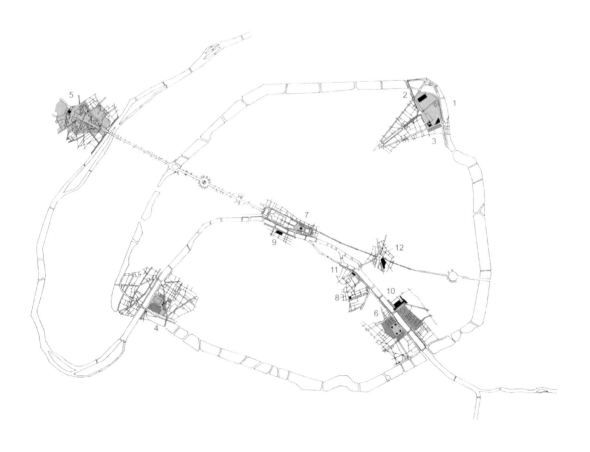

1.5 François Mitterrand's Grands Projets, Paris, 1998. (Drawing: Ufuk Ersoy.)

1.6 Paul Chemetov and Borja Huidobro, Grande Galerie du Musée National d'Histoire Naturelle. (Renovation, 1995)

(see no. 12 in figure 1.5), an alteration of tremendous significance for Paris' urban history.[16] In addition, the two large open green spaces at Parc de La Villette and Parc André Citroën specifically recalled the Haussmannian parks of Monceau and Buttes-Chaumont, particularly as they similarly provided amenities to peripheral working-class neighborhoods.

Mitterrand's projects also used Haussmann's device of the isolated monument to provide focal points at numerous discrete areas. In planning large swaths of peripheral Paris, typically an architectural setpiece was prominently located within the boundaries of larger areas of renovation, granting each development a sense of identity through its own local spectacular building. Thus the three projects at La Villette—the Parc de La Villette of 1987–1991 by Bernard Tschumi (no. 1 in figure 1.5), the Cité des Sciences et de l'Industrie by Adrien Fainsilber of 1986 (no. 2), and the Cité de la Musique by Christian de Portzamparc of 1992–1994 (no. 3)—recharacterized a segment of the nineteenth arrondissement that included new housing built over the defunct slaughterhouse district. Equally, Patrick Berger and Gilles Clément's Parc André Citroën of 1992 (no. 4) marked a large area of housing and institutional building in the fifteenth arrondissement over remnants of the old Citroën automobile-manufacturing yards. For this comprehensive development, the area was designated as a *Zone d'Aménagement Concerté* (*ZAC*) under provisions set up to circumvent typical regulatory authorities and transform marginal or peripheral lands in urban regions.[17] If Johan Otto von Spreckelsen's arch of 1989, looming over the enormous new development at La Défense (no. 5), is the earliest example in the history of the Grands Projets of the use of an architectural set piece to focus a large development area, the latest is the new Bibliothèque Nationale of 1998 (no. 6), surrounded by an extensive development in the twelfth and thirteenth arrondissements, areas also designated as *ZACs*.

Other Mitterrand Grands Projets, all but one a cultural institution, follow Haussmann's precedent even more closely in terms of being single entities monumentally sited in distinction to the urban fabric. In contrast to the large urban developments, as single buildings they are limited in engaging a relative degree of active urban planning. Their isolation is also largely due, however, to the relationship of individual projects to preexisting institutions; most of them were initiated out of urgency to redress drastically outdated facilities. Of these there are three types: renovations of existing institutional buildings, relocations of existing institutional entities, and entirely new cultural institutions.

The challenge to architects of institutions remaining on their former sites consisted of both reordering highly complex existing facilities and reinvigorating already highly monumental buildings. The most prominent of these were the Grande Pyramide du Louvre by Pei and Partners of 1989 (no. 7, figure 1.5) and the Grande Galerie du Musée National d'Histoire Naturelle (no. 8, and figure 1.6), a renovation by Paul Chemetov and Borja Huidobro of an original building of 1889 by Jules André. Another Grand Projet that might be included with these was the Musée d'Orsay of 1986 by ACT Architecture and Gai Aulenti (no. 9), a renovation of the Gare d'Orsay (Victor Laloux, c. 1900) undertaken by former president Giscard d'Estaing to house the substantial Impressionist collection previously held at the Jeu de Paume.

Relocations of other existing institutional entities were undertaken primarily because of inadequate space at the original locations. One of these is the Ministère de L'Economie of 1988 (no. 10), also by Chemetov and Huidobro, a building mandated by the Louvre's incorporation of its north wing, the ministry's previous home. Now prominently relocated extending into the Seine on the Right Bank in the twelfth arrondissement, it joins a constellation of new building in the Bercy-ZAC Rive Gauche area. The Bibliothèque Nationale itself can be similarly characterized; the project included the Olympian task of relocating existing national archives and research facilities previously housed adjacent to the Palais-Royal in a complex notable for the famous Labrouste reading room of 1868–1869. The final category of projects, representing entirely new cultural institutions on new sites, was even more akin to the bourgeois monuments built during Haussmann's era: certainly, the Opéra Bastille, designed as the focal point of various axial boulevards at the Place de la Bastille, but also to some extant the Institut du Monde Arabe of 1987 by Nouvel (no. 11), poised across the Seine from Notre Dame.

Whereas Mitterrand's first pragmatic motivation in replanning the city was, like Haussmann's, to accommodate a burgeoning population expanding in various directions outward, planning for latter-day projects explicitly addressed the destructive effects of decentralization resulting from Pompidou's recent expansions toward the *banlieues*. Outward growth was complemented by insistence on maintaining the density of inhabitation at the core, regarded as a crucial component of the city's urban character.[18]

The general attitude toward urban intervention exhibited neither the comprehensive nor coherent precision of Haussmann's projects. Nevertheless, the Grands Projets were conceived holistically. Rather than Haussmann's surgical infrastructural incisions, they present a diffuse strategy of rehabilitation by evenly distributing projects of spectacular dimension throughout the city. Especially for projects located in economically troubled peripheral areas, the capital gain from tourism was expected to revitalize and regenerate those areas. This explains their support by conservative mayor Jacques Chirac.[19] Rather than merely signifying accrual of symbolic power, as in Haussmann's era, reimaging of the city in Mitterrand's era was also expected to sponsor significant economic gains.

THE CITY REVISUALIZED

Although Haussmann's Parisian boulevards legitimately improved circulation and indeed initiated the rapid passage characteristic of the modern city, the boulevard itself proved to be the central facet of symbolic reinvestment of the city's fabric. The effects of the arterial axis were multivalent. Walter Benjamin notes that the widened boulevards in the *plan voyant* provided a ventilated locale for the Parisian promenade, a practice in drastic contrast to the *flânerie* of the previous era that had been associated with the poetic reverie of the passages couverts.[20] Yet these two urban practices had marked similarities. Constituted by forms of passage and movement, both were also dominated by the overabundance of images of consumable goods and crowds they attracted. Balzac described the passages as *"la gastronomie de l'œil,"* a quality shared at a different scale and density by the boulevards.

On the boulevards, the newly affluent, many of whom had been made wealthy through real estate speculations during the Haussmann era, could display themselves to each other. Equally, newly produced commodities (available to a wider spectrum of population through mass production) could be shown in ground-floor shop windows. Embodied as an arena of display for the bourgeois, boulevards provided a physical manifestation of social relationships developing among the newly stratified society. Indeed, the accomplishment of nineteenth-century Parisian urbanism was to render society itself as a spectacle.[21]

Two distinct effects to the extant monumental order thus emerged in Haussmann's new city. The first, based in the infinite one-point perspectival vista had already been inscribed in the city's sensibility by Le Nôtre's Louvre axis and his gardens at Versailles.[22] Haussmann's boulevards, however, implemented within Paris across similarly vast distances, terminated on discrete monuments rather than open vistas, monuments that had been largely known previously within intimate physical constructs. Haussmann's axes had the effect of turning formerly stable popular symbols into floating *signs,* whose shifting meanings were dependent on the eye of the beholder.[23]

In eighteenth-century Paris known for the rise of capitalist culture, the image of these monuments at the end of their vistas also became agents for propagandizing the city as a tourist destination. If earlier glass exposition halls had exploited technological imagery as a spectacular device, the Haussmannian boulevard followed this precedent in terms of consciously manipulating the city's images: existing sites of particularly cherished popular import were appropriated by the state purely for their values as images, in another anticipation of the Debordian spectacle, replete with his apprehensions of modern alienation.

By virtue of the very length of the boulevards, however, very often monuments at the termination of axes were simply too far away to be seen. Subsumed into a Paris recomposed of vast boulevards, the monuments' status was preempted emphatically by the city itself. Benjamin reported that the buildings along the boulevards were draped in canvas en masse and unveiled on completion. Rather than commemorating a specific event or providing a legible institutional function, the boulevards themselves became permanent, iconic testaments to a collective historical moment, significantly different monuments than objectified buildings or markers.

Rather than a static entity set prominently within the city fabric, these boulevards were composed of a fabric that was dynamic and volatile, a composition of vehicular and pedestrian movement set in the foreground against the highly regulated neutrality of buildings' elevations.[24] Sometimes as long as three miles, the boulevards constituted the flanks of an endless perspectival stage in constant motion. Particularly for Piano and Rogers's Pompidou Center (chapter 2) as well as Nouvel's Institut du Monde Arabe and Fondation Cartier (chapter 3), this dynamic redefinition of the urban flank provided a seminal point of departure for the concept of façade in a contemporary Parisian setting; not only was the action of the city to be foregrounded against the building, but the face of the building itself was to become actively involved as a dramatic component. At the Pompidou, the transparency of the building's façade was conceived to unite the actions of the building's occupants to the city, creating a seamless condition that followed Haussmann's sense of the boulevards' flanks against the active city. At the Cartier, the image of the street in constant motion was reflected back to the city on Nouvel's glass façades. In a manifesto of cultural representation, the façade is made possible

1.7 Ricardo Bofill, Place du Marché, 1998.

not only by reflective glass, but by Haussmann's precedent in raising street traffic to a preeminent component of urban constitution.

For dwellers and shop owners disenfranchised by Haussmann's appropriation of property, boulevards represented the state's right to seize entire terrains of the city indiscriminately. Yet as a visual device, the boulevard not only represented the state's authority at that particular moment, but was implicated in a lengthier historical representation of power. Recalling Le Nôtre's imposition of perspectival vistas for Louis XIV at both the Louvre-Tuileries axis and at Versailles, representations of power in Haussmann's era were nevertheless different. As noted by Allen S. Weiss, the perspectival vista imposed onto the seventeenth-century garden was directly correlated with the gaze of the king and operated at two scales.[25] At the scale of Le Nôtre's landscape, the western-extending axis enjoined his reign with the divinity of the setting sun; within his court, the gaze of the king was a local device to disempower his subjects. Stripped of the literal presence and representation of the king at the termination of the axis, the boulevards constituted a secularization of the perspectival vista appropriate to representations of power in a postrevolutionary republican society.

The fundamental mechanisms inherent in the perspective as a visual device were equally powerful, however, in affecting relationships among inhabitants of this newly configured city, particularly when regarded in a theoretical sense. Art historian Norman Bryson illustrates the consequences of encounters across such dynamic geometric fields by recounting Sartre's scenario of the "watcher in the park" (from *Being and Nothingness*). As the solitary watcher's field of vision—its horizon, its implied lines of convergence—is broken by another (the Other, an intruder), Bryson contends that shifts in vanishing points from center to tangent pull the scene away from the watcher to "where he is not." This shift constitutes Bryson's thesis of the "annihilation of self-possession," a modern *decentering* of the subject, a phenomenon he poses as the norm, rather than the exception, of perspectival space.[26]

If we apply Bryson's conjecture to Haussmann's Paris, the consequence of imposing vastly scaled perspective fields continuously across different scales and reaches of the city becomes evident and terrifying: not only did the morphology of the city shift in conforming to the order of the gaze, so did the profound order of relationships among its inhabitants. With scalar distortions and imposed mechanisms of observation in the boulevard came disintegration of an urban intimacy

1.8 Rue de Rivoli, looking east, 2000.

that had previously comprised "self-possession" for its inhabitants. If not unitary in a purely theoretical sense, this self-possession was certainly the fundamental element in the constitution of personal privacy within an urban domain.

The gaze of the new bourgeois public in Haussmann's Paris was to have as its subject a new class of inhabitants unfamiliar to them. As boulevards cut across the city in unrelentingly straight lines, they provided a sectional slice through quartiers that had been closed to view. Immediately behind the regulated facades of the boulevard, neighborhoods of the lower classes could be seen, and their constituents had full access to the city's major thoroughfares. Consequently, boulevards provided an arena for the display of the bourgeois not only to each other, but to a wide demographic mix of economic classes and nationalities. In the face of irresolvable social and economic difference, the gaze of the public became anonymous, passive, and truly modern in its alienated disaffection.[27]

Various writers have commented on similar aspects of the boulevards. Particularly for Engels, the now modern crowded street was abhorrent: "The greater the number of people that are packed into a tiny space, the more repulsive and offensive becomes the brutal indifference, the unfeeling concentration of each person on his private affairs."[28] Situationists, in a similarly Marxist vein, were even more damning, identifying Parisian boulevards as primary agents of the mechanistic workings of the city, providing the setting for the "artificial imperatives of speed, making savings on capitalized time, rushing toward sites of alienated production or consumption."[29] Only Benjamin found some grace, however ambivalent, in the axial boulevards and the crowds they generated. Reflecting on Baudelaire, he noted that the crowds were also to present an enervated setting for the poet's *flâneur* to become enraptured, but as well disfigured, within the modern cosmopolitan setting: "the stigmata which life in a metropolis inflicts upon love."[30]

As a consequence of Haussmann's work, the city inherited by Mitterrand was resoundingly modern, dismembered by boulevards hurling crowds and traffic across the vastly scaled landscape toward landmarks themselves transformed into vaporous mirages. By virtue of the boulevards, the new bourgeois city was also transfigured as a relentless arena for display—the entire city a temporal vitrine. When characterized in these evanescent terms, the imaginary quality envisioned by Mitterrand of his sparkling crystalline monuments seems a contextual response to Paris itself, a city pulsating radiantly with forces of alienation as well as light.

TRANSPARENCY, SURVEILLANCE, RATIONALIZATION

The Haussmann network of arterial streets and green public spaces was motivated by a more tangible sinister agenda, as Sigfried Giedion and Benjamin, among others, noted. Amelioration of public space and introduction of light and air were also meant to quiet the discontent of the masses, whom Haussmann disdainfully admitted into the ranks of the public. In the event that these measures proved inadequate, the widened boulevards, especially in the eastern working-class section near the new Bois de Vincennes, provided that the lower classes spilling out onto the boulevards could be seen and presumably controlled. The boulevards' width now not only provided a means of surveillance, they also facilitated transportation of troops in quelling popular unrest, which had last been witnessed in 1852. Rather than Mitterrand's ambition to gather crowds (particularly of well-heeled tourists) at key points in the city, in nineteenth-century Paris the dominant goal was their dispersal.

Just as Haussmann's projects were tainted with disquieting undertones, so too were Mitterrand's projects overshadowed. Both eras of Grands Travaux encountered resistance to the idea of a single governing entity imposing their whims across the scale of the entire city. Often Mitterrand was accused openly of pharoanic impulses in dictating almost entirely by himself the conception and execution of the Grands Projets, and often for his own political gain. This authority over the city granted to the president was historic. After the city's right to self-governance was rescinded in 1871 following the revolts of the Paris Commune, it was not until 1975 that the municipality of Paris once again had an independently elected mayor. Responsibility for the city had been long considered a national priority, and subject to the rule and desires of the president, or monarch. In Mitterrand's era, despite the election of Jacques Chirac as mayor, little changed in the role of the president in establishing major agendas affecting the city. Planning of programs, sites, and competitions for various Grands Projets was accomplished primarily by Mitterrand, and his minister of special projects, Emile Biasini, with a select committee of four: Paul Guimard, a writer; Jacques Lang, Minister of Culture; Robert Lyon, cabinet head and advisor to the president; and Roger Quillot, Minister of Urbanism. Repeatedly the concentration of power compelling enormous public issues was called into question by the popular press.

The aesthetic goal of the projects to modernize Paris overtly was also certainly a great point of contention. To the general public, initial proposals of a glass and

1.9 Tour Société Générale, La Défense. (Architect unknown)

steel pyramid in the heart of the seventeenth-century courtyard of the Louvre complex seemed preposterous stylistic arrogance. Yet even the harshest critic will today admit that the discontent and controversy of the pyramid quelled considerably since its completion. Indeed, in many separate instances involving prominent glass construction in the Grands Projets, public outrage quieted on growing familiarity with the built fact. In the new buildings, the presence of highly advanced glass technologies, both in support systems and the material qualities of glass itself, perhaps provided enough distance from preconceived objections anticipating the glass box skyscraper as it proliferated in the 1970s. The new systems and surfaces are characterized by technical inventiveness, rather than technological homogenization.

Equally, newer glass construction is now far more responsible to a variety of environmental factors that in previous eras were the basis for strong financial objections. These technologies, particularly in surface modifications and methods of coating applications, have substantially improved the performance of glass and reduced the cost of interior climatological systems. In the 1970s the glass skyscrapers of La Défense were vastly underpopulated; newer glass constructions in the same area are now fully occupied.

The most lasting objections to glass architecture might be drawn from higher levels of critical discussions, which, as in the case of the perspectival boulevard, implicate the material with the discourse of vision. Martin Jay, in his comprehensive *Downcast Eyes,* outlines the repeated appearance of "ocularphobic" critiques weaving through twentieth-century French philosophy, from Bergson and Foucault to Derrida and Lyotard. Jay notes the profound suspicion on the part of these writers to the hegemonic role of visual metaphors in French art and intellectual discourse. And yet Jay himself also notes that the actual urban culture in Paris, in which many of these philosophers produced their treatises, seems remarkably indifferent to their critiques. The "City of Lights," is renowned, after all, for cultural forms predominantly visual in nature—fashion, cinema, and architecture.[31]

The relationship of glass to these discourses relies on a fundamental supposition: the glass window provides a bipolar viewing frame from within and from without, a picture plane that is intrinsically related to the painted canvas, the perspectival plane, or, perhaps more closely, the filmic image. From within a disengaged interior the ability to capture the surrounding scene and to reflect on it introspectively is nothing but another version of the very same problematic gaze.[32] The mandate of economic constraints to enclose interior space environmentally

1.10 View from within Sirvin et Associés, the Maison de la RATP, 1996.

further supports the analogy. Vision typically separated from all other sensory activity renders the external world available for review, isolating it, objectifying it, and giving the viewer the opportunity to control it by means of distanced abstraction. In painting, as theories go, the subject's disengagement from alternative sensory modes ultimately produces disembodiment, reduces the erotic and even the *narrative* constituent of the viewed space (and its participants) as apprehension is limited by purely visual parameters.

Recent critiques come to this: as the subject is rendered transcendent and the object of view inert, the ethical boundaries, which previously governed relationships between the two, disintegrate. As Michel Foucault noted in his work on the evolution of disciplinary institutions, architecture has the capacity, far more than painting or other representational media, to make literal the most disturbing aspects of vision. By either allowing or occluding vision, constituent elements of buildings—windows, doors, corridors, spaces transform hierarchical relationships between those being viewed and those viewing, between those being surveyed and those surveying. According to Foucault, this transformation happens particularly when the actions of the body are controlled. Foucault's ideas extend not simply to those positioned in the privileged points of power but implicate the transformation of a vast network of relationships: in this hyperbolized visual world, everyone would be complicit in some way, everyone would be surveyed by someone else. In an effort to escape attention and maintain circumspect neutrality under such a prospect, Foucault surmises that the final effect on a population would be the systematic normalization of all behavior.[33]

This troubling potential becomes doubly problematic when considering large public works. As the discrete mechanism of the framed window is enlarged to the enormous glass wall, the building is posited symbolically and literally to structure relationships between individuals and national culture. A frequent complaint reported in the popular media from scholars anticipating the experience of working in glassed spaces of the Bibliothèque Nationale de France was the prospect of being constantly on display, "animals in a zoo," exposed to scrutiny from a general public who were too distant for the scholars to engage reciprocally and meaningfully.

If the bodies of the viewer and the viewed are de-eroticized through the mechanism of the sealed window, the body of the building is equally prey to the ravages of vision.[34] The Renaissance idea of transillumination posed that the metaphysical implications of light—the divine *lux*—was truth, ultimately the will

1.11 Aymeric Subléna, Direction de l'Action Sociale, Ville de Paris, 1992.

of God. The eighteenth century's fascination with optical instruments and the mathematical properties of light and optics represented an attempt to recover the geometrical purity of nature, therefore divine guidance. For architecture the origin of these principles was in the Renaissance, founded particularly in the transparency implied by anatomical studies of Leonardo da Vinci. Yet the full fruition of this divine illumination came again in the period of the high modernists, fortified by principles inherited from the Enlightenment. In a gesture that was equally endowed ideologically, the building—its structure, its mechanical systems, its constructional processes, and its very skin—was violently disrobed, revealing its previously hermetic inner workings. This disrobing was to engage intelligence; the revelation was intended to be moral as well as didactic. The imperative of authenticity added impetus to rendering concurrently developing systemization of building legible, ensuring not only that the building be rationalized technologically, but that its rationale also be apparent—or *transparent.*

This ever-encroaching impulse to rationalize figuration in building shares much conceptual ground with that of perspectival depiction; unchecked, both have the capacity to sublimate all aspects of building and/or scene to the rationale imposed by the gaze. For both, the manifestation of this rationale occurs in geometric terms, either in the mathematical construct of the perspectival cone of vision, or in the imposition of a regularized module on a building's structure and constituent systems.[35] The most problematic extension of this effect would be, again, on the body; not the literal bodies of visitors, but on the larger metaphor of the building itself as a body. Suggesting the infiltration of emerging biological sciences into eighteenth-century Ecole des Beaux Arts pedagogy, the Ecole's idea of *transparaître* provided building enclosure with the analogy of human skin: just as the presence of internal organs is legible on the skin's surface, so interior spaces might be evidenced by buildings' external massing. Specific correlations are numerous in this analogy; not only does the enclosure of the building equate with the body's skin, but so does the building's structure with the skeleton and its mechanical systems to circulatory networks. Operating in this metaphor, transparency at the exterior boundary is fundamentally unsettling. Not only are the building's basic physical properties overturned, but they are also controlled, subjected to a rationale of logical empiricism. Critic Gerhard Auer wrote:

> Leonardo dissected the body in order to acquire the secret of its beauty; Alberti and others defined that invisible spatial grid of proportional geometry

which could be used to impose universal rules on buildings. Filarete showed in his anatomical drawings what later was postulated by Filibert de l'Orme: the fact that inner structures manifest themselves in an outward appearance. And yet it was only the Enlightenment (and the progress of science) that the myth of transparency reached its peak: material no longer remained tangible between heavy and light, solid and airy, opaque and transparent. Its contradictions fused into an infinite structure to be made legible by the X-Ray gaze of empirical knowledge.[36]

According to Auer, a transparent, "objective" condition at the exterior boundary implied that through disintegration of the exterior skin as the *physiographic* boundary of the body, rationalization of the human body itself would be complete.

In contemporary Paris, two agents of vision merge to form a multiply layered display of the urban spectacle (in the historical spectrum of urbanism, perhaps *the* manifestation of the spectacle). At the head of the Haussmann boulevard an imaginary perspectival plane frames emptiness, if not empty signs—distant floating monuments disconnected from their cultural locales. Located somewhere in the infinite beyond, this perspectival plane is framed by the dynamic flanks of the city's vernacular fabric, as if the lines extending outward from the frame had become miraculously embodied by the urgent life of the city. In this context, Mitterrand placed his signature glass architecture as if to challenge the perspectival paradigm of the earlier era with his own. As in the case of the Louvre, or the Grande Arche, or even the Opéra Bastille, when Mitterrand's monuments are placed directly on urban axes, their transparency becomes wedded to the emptiness that predated them. Located on the urban flanks, his transparent buildings engage, indeed attempt to *become*, the life of the city.

As the bodies of visitors and general public are displayed and surveyed through the translucent skins of monumental buildings, so are the bodies of buildings themselves, replete in all previously undisclosed and shadowy inner domains. Haussmann's perspectival boulevards add the final context to the unrelenting mechanisms of vision in an enormous and multifaceted display of the potential reach of the rational gaze. One needs only the example of the Pompidou Center to admit a convergence of such speculations. And yet, this reading of the building's relationship to its surrounding is incomplete without an account of the complex social dynamic of the same transparent condition (see chapter 2).

TRANSPARENCY, ACCESSIBILITY, POLITICS

Mitterrand said of the national library in 1995, "The second imperative was entirely new: it involved the accommodation of a huge public, people of all ages trained to all kinds of different professions and callings; people eager to deepen their knowledge, to enrich their culture, and to gain access to the documents necessary for their work."[37] This suggests a basic intention on the part of the state. Indeed, the dominant idealism of many of the Grands Projets was based in a principle of accessibility, an opening of a previously closed and therefore elitist French culture to the general public.[38] This agenda was consistently reiterated throughout the conception and planning for all of the Grands Projets; their success was to be measured in the general public's interaction with the various cultural institutions. And indeed, dispersal of various forms of public culture throughout the capital since the inception of the projects has been impressive.

New and renovated museums provide vast amounts of public exhibition space allowing the display of substantial permanent collections previously held in storage. The Louvre renovation eased circulation and provided new public galleries, some even fully visible from exterior public thoroughfares (figure 1.12). In the sciences, several new important educational facilities were created; many in decay were rejuvenated. Despite controversies associated with it, the new national library provides desperately needed public access to material long sequestered for scholarly use. The new performance halls at the Opéra Bastille, through their sheer capacity to accommodate large numbers, have the ambition and the potential to make classical opera popular.[39]

Yet the galvanization of popular public access was intended to occur not simply through literal access but through symbolic connotation.[40] If Haussmann's boulevards provided a literal visual and physical connectivity at an urban scale, Mitterrand's buildings were to interpret transparency as a metaphor at the scale of the building, the metaphor of accessibility tied to the leftist government and symbolic democracy. It is noteworthy that the use of glass toward this end was not conceived initially, but rather acquired potency as the various buildings were realized and a group of glass monuments emerged to identify Mitterrand's influence.[41] Neither the Grande Pyramide nor the Institut du Monde Arabe—both early projects—overtly used glass as a device symbolizing political intentions. Yet by the time of the national library competition, glass had accrued a significance that was increasingly deployed to prompt a particular political signification.

1.12 I. M. Pei and Partners, Passage Richelieu, Musée du Louvre 1992.

The contemporary association of literal accessibility through architecture, and particularly transparent architecture, to symbolic democracy did not originate with Mitterrand. As recently as the 1960s this metaphor was propelled into public consciousness by de Gaulle and André Malraux's (then Minister of State for Cultural Affairs) visualizations of "open institutions." It culminated in the building of the Pompidou Center, a cultural center encompassing various functions from public library to cinema house to contemporary arts center. In the 1960s, however, the primary gesture in opening official culture was oriented toward the French provinces; it implied decentralization away from Paris, having the exact opposite effect of the Grands Projets.[42] Indeed, the Grands Projets are as conspicuous an endeavor to glorify and centralize the capital as were the projects of Haussmann's era.

In consciously using architecture as a vehicle to embody specific ideological expression, the agenda of the state remains a point of public contention. The last decades have seen Mitterrand's transparent architecture become entrenched as a national focus of political discord between the conservative Right and the progressive Left.[43] This is due certainly to recalcitrance of the Right to accept the imposition of a set of monuments on Paris that would forever stand as a visible legacy of a Socialist regime. This is also due, however, in no small part to disproportionate expenditures by Mitterrand on public architecture, which were held partially accountable for the national economic duress of the 1990s—*la crise*. Whether they are reasonable or not, these claims undoubtedly influenced public reception of the new architecture, particularly in the case of the national library.

The association of the Grands Projets with leftist politics exists at several levels. First, the programmatic concept of state-sponsored projects might be itself regarded as a demonstration of Socialist principles, an illustration of the state's responsibility and potential to advance culture over and above that of private enterprise. Equally significant is the first gesture of Mitterrand in extending the axis of the Voie Triomphale eastward to the poorer sections of the city—an enormous symbolic gesture to the commitment of the Left to disenfranchised segments of the city.[44] Similarly, as has been mentioned, the two parks of the Grands Projets were located contiguous to working-class areas. Whereas they certainly represent political appeasements to significant voting blocks, the highly used parks are uncontestable amenities, and provided without the hidden agenda in the Haussmann era of placating discontented workers.

1.13 View from Masa Yuki Yamanaka and Armstrong Associates, Maison de la Culture du Japon, 1997.

Despite Mitterrand's desire to represent these socially minded gestures as phenomena of leftist rule, many of them were rooted in practices established by the French Revolution. Indeed, in many ways the Socialist enterprise for the Grands Projets included the blatant appropriation, and overt public projection, of Revolutionary values. Architectural historian William J. R. Curtis noted of the Mitterrand projects, "Of course, it so happens that the Left is in power for the commemoration of the Declaration of the Rights of Man, which is publicized as a charter of universal human relevance with, we are told, an inevitable future trajectory in world events. History is thus telescoped to suggest that the current Left is the heir to all that is most idealistic about the revolution."[45]

The Grands Projets, inaugurated in 1989, were in themselves a 200-year commemoration of the Revolution. The three actual memorials were institutions located along the Voie Triomphale—the Grande Arche de La Défense, the Grande Pyramide du Louvre, and the Opéra Bastille. The connection of the monarchist axis to the Bastille, the most symbolic site of the Revolution, is confirmation enough of the projects' homage.[46] Programming the projects as cultural centers also stemmed from the Revolutionary zeal for democratic institutions. Even the expressive use of progressive technology was characterized by fervor for all things Revolutionary: the projets of 1989 followed a legacy established by the centennial of 1889, an exposition whose buildings included the indelible Eiffel Tower. In Paris monumental technological expressionism, of which glass and steel construction is a primary component, is inextricably tied to the symbols of the Revolution.

Most important for this study, transparency was a theme inherited directly from the Revolution, primarily through the influence of Swiss naturalist philosopher Jean-Jacques Rousseau. For Rousseau, transparency was a fundamental metaphor expressing a utopian state for humans. When each person's innermost feelings and thoughts were absolutely open, the deceptive outer appearances (to which Rousseau assigned the greatest evil) would disappear, leading to a pure expression of inherent goodness. Writes Jean Starobinski on this pervasive theme in Rousseau's writings: "Evil is veil and obfuscation, it is mask, it is intimately bound up with fiction, and it would not exist if man had not the dangerous freedom to deny, by means of artifice, what is given by nature."[47]

Rousseau's extension of his theory of artless transparency to principles of social order was profoundly significant to revolutionary political constructs. Suggesting popular sovereignty governed by a self-imposed law of reason, his advocation of the *honnête homme* was projected into a utopian political state where governance by the people would emerge spontaneously from concern for the common good. This idealized state could be reached only by the absence of separation between government and public. Thus the rhetoric of accessibility of both Pompidou and Mitterrand urban projects was informed principally by a lingering sentiment of Rousseau's romantic transparency. As a subtext of the doctrine of the Revolution, the concept of transparency had been universally influencing French thought for several centuries.

Transparency, even in the days of the Revolution, was not without flagrant conflictions. As it was transferred from a utopian hypothesis into an actual set of social practices, these contradictions would become terrifying. R. J. Sierksma wrote, "The French Revolution demanded it [complete transparency] and gave it political force. Solitude would become anti-Revolutionary. Privacy would be suspect."[48] The "popular sovereignty" advocated by Rousseau would become a form of popular justice that was essentially a police state composed of the masses. Evidenced in the infamous September massacres of 1790, newly anointed citizens were sanctioned to "cleanse" society, murdering anyone even slightly suspected of harboring secret royalist sympathies, as well as prisoners deemed a threat to the new republican purity. Applied to architecture, the transparent metaphor was equally burdened. After the Revolution, Danton authorized indiscriminate "domiciliary visits"; surprise late night or early morning searches through residences for incriminating evidence against the Republic.[49] Inhabitants were also required to post on their exterior walls lists of visitors. In the name of transparency, no secret was to be kept from the populist government; even the solid walls of houses were to reveal potentially damaging information living within.

In appropriating the values of the Revolution to characterize his tenure, Mitterrand's government carefully chose those of its early, less controversial, stages to emphasize primarily the Revolution's proclamation of universal human rights.[50] Mitterrand's adoption of transparency to symbolize dissolution of boundaries between state and public seems as selective, given the conflicted history of the concept from the Revolution. If the goal of the projets was to express accessibility, surely a more benign metaphor was available.

TRANSPARENCY, MODERNITY

Whereas transparency has particular associations in France, it has also been implicated into the more universal developments of modern architecture. Transparency, both literal and phenomenal, as well as metaphorical, pervaded the entire modernist architectural oeuvre, from Le Corbusier to Mies van der Rohe and Rietveld, to the later work of Richard Neutra and Gordon Bunshaft. Indeed, the modernist project was noted by Vidler to be "haunted" by the idea.[51] And while early modernist architecture was not consistently engaged with the actual use of glass, its central characteristics include peripheralization of space and concurrent disintegration of the exterior boundary. These characteristics suggest the definition of another form of transparency, most eloquently understood by Colin Rowe and Robert Slutzky.[52] Theo van Doesburg, whose de Stijl manifestoes proposed expansion of dematerialized space into the realm of everyday (proletarian) life, provided the accompanying reformative ideology.[53] Presumably through a denigrated exterior boundary, a purified aesthetic realm would escape and proliferate into the vernacular landscape. As the de Stijl aesthetic spread it would rehabilitate the general population as well. Common people would live better, freer, and more honest lives in such unfettered surroundings.

The aesthetic revolution heralded by van Doesburg did not happen through the rarified language and short-lived production of the de Stijl architects. Instead, "objective construction" was manifested primarily in France, indelibly inscribed in the vernacular landscape by Le Corbusier and his imitators in hundreds, if not thousands, of buildings interpreting his aesthetic and spatial investigations.[54] This proliferation happened essentially in terms of transparency; not one of glass construction, but manifested as volumes of space and solids in a tense relationship with an exterior container. In Le Corbusier's early career, this container comprised the signature white skin of the international "machine" phase of his works, whose paradigmatic products, the villas at Poissy and Garches located just outside of Paris, were tremendously influential in France. Indeed, Le Corbusier's work realized most palpably van Doesburg's heroic calls for universal aestheticization. That is, until the latest and debatably even more effective excursion into the vernacular by the proliferation of glass.

As ubiquitous as the influences of Le Corbusier and the latest appearance of glass might be in France, neither can be credited with the type of societal reformation found in either Rousseau's romantic naturalism or in the modernist merger of politics and aesthetics in which both utopian metaphors of transparency are considerably burdened. As critiques of modernism have long demonstrated, prophesies of societal reformation were at best naïve, hopelessly confused between the literal properties of architecture and its associated metaphors.

1.14 Renzo Piano, Agence de la Propreté. (City Cleaning Department, 1988)

Three fundamental tensions thus undermine the implementation of a contemporary symbol of transparency in Paris. The first is the ill-considered Socialist operation to reinstitute the conflicted metaphor of the Revolution, which is burdened by the events of the Terror. The second is the problematic tie of transparency to the failed aspirations of the modern movement, an equally naïve desire to infect the world with the aesthetics and social moralism tied up in the movement. The third is in the theoretical affiliation of transparency with mechanisms of control. In the obsession to reveal, transparency is fraught with problematic capacities of vision from sublimating the behavior of architecture's human inhabitants to provoking methods of technological rationalization in the design of buildings and public spaces. These tensions have been discussed only perfunctorily in relation to the Mitterrand projects; perhaps their very obviousness makes commentary unnecessary. Yet they are undoubtedly at the core of the indifferent intellectual reception to the Grands Projets.[55]

This book neither attempts to justify nor invalidates the buildings according to these expansive terms, which are limited not by their accuracy but by their generality. Through an extensive examination of the buildings situated in their particular context, with their particular ambitions and histories, the effort is to discover the parallels and divergences from these fundamentally problematic conditions of transparency. Through the nuances of each specific condition, these buildings have established their own coherent precedent, altering and contributing substantially to the body of history surrounding the deceptively simple but ultimately elusive term known as transparency.

✿ Populist Frames: Eiffel and Pompidou, Again

Finally I came to the *émetteur à étincelles soufflées* designed for the Eiffel Tower, for the emission of time signals between France, Tunisia, and Russia, the Templars of Provins, the Paulicians, the Assassins of Fez. (Fez isn't in Tunisia, and the assassins were in Persia, but you can't split hairs when you live in the coils of Transcendent Time.) I had seen it before, this immense machine, taller than I, its walls perforated by a series of portholes, air ducts. The sign said it was a radio apparatus, but I knew better, I had passed it that same afternoon. The Beaubourg!

—Umberto Eco, *Foucault's Pendulum*

DESPITE THE VAINGLORIOUS CLAIMS of Mitterrand's Grands Projets to the expression of progress, advancement, and sociopolitical accessibility, evident in the last chapter was the much longer and more complex historical lineage of the many different ideas embedded in the metaphor of transparency. This chapter focuses on extensions to the construct of transparency posed in the most recent (and notorious) examples of French monumentality predating the Grands Projets. In Renzo Piano and Richard Rogers's Pompidou Center of 1977, transparency emerges with marked similarities to the Mitterrand projets in the political rhetoric surrounding conception of the building as well as many of its physical characteristics. The cultural center might even be thought of euphemistically as the first Grand Projet, despite having been created by Georges Pompidou in the 1970s, rather than François Mitterrand in the 1990s. The second example, the Eiffel Tower, gives the quintessential precedent for the Pompidou and, endowed by a legacy of critical theorization, provides a redefinition of transparency in the modern monument that is indispensable in understanding Mitterrand's projects.

In these two monuments specific characteristics emerge that echo resonantly into the present day. First, transparency is employed on a gargantuan scale with the intention of dwarfing and/or emphatically expressing difference from the surrounding fabric. Second, in these enormous monuments advancing technology is an essential part of the expression of their transparency above and beyond that called for by the demands of structure. And third, the overwhelming popularity of these buildings, both as public sites and as iconic images, problematizes the concept of their transparency with issues of contemporary spectacle. Rather than continuity presupposed by the ideal of transparency, the spectacle, at least as defined

2.1 Georges Garen. Lighting of the Eiffel Tower at the Universal Exposition of 1889. Engraving. (Photo: Jean Schormans) Courtesy Réunion des Musées Nationaux/Art Resources, New York.

by Guy Debord, raises the potential of disempowering the very public that it proposes to embrace.[1]

In the Eiffel Tower and the Pompidou Center, glass is not necessary for transparency, at least not the expansive definition of monumental transparency at the heart of this book. Instead, what merits attention is the articulation of the structural frame as the primary constituent. At issue are the frame's exaggerated scale, the spectacular appearance of its technological derivation, and the characteristics and occupation of the spaces contained within and outside its interstitial domains. Historically, as the skeletal frame (the traditional partner in the development of glass) emerged from the confines of the previously inert masonry wall, it challenged the way the building's physical entity was perceived, from stable solid mass to ambiguous void space.

As the hyperbolized frame in the Eiffel Tower and the Pompidou Center provided the expression of their monumentality, this ambiguity was extended; the monument as an inert marker was also a dynamic boundary, the symbolic object also a space to be occupied, the commemorative work also a display of technological advancement. The issues inherent in the gargantuan frame layer constructional and structural concerns with conditions of program, occupation, and monumentality, providing the benchmark for a sense of ideological construction as it is to unfold throughout this book.

LE MILIEU POMPIDOU

The conception of the Pompidou Center was entangled in the 1970s sociocultural milieu that the building has come to mythify. Between the postwar 1940s and the 1960s, a long period of economic expansion known as *les trente glorieuses* lulled France into an unprecedented sense of prosperity and growth. By May 1968, however, changes in traditional French society and increasing disaffection of French youth prompted a large general strike and street riot by students, intellectuals, and workers. The event attained legendary status in contemporary French history, palpably affecting political sentiment, if not actual policy, for several decades to follow.

By 1969, after dissolving the National Assembly, President de Gaulle dismissed Prime Minister Pompidou, only to see Pompidou succeed him as president after de Gaulle's resignation later that same year. In the years of his presidency, Pompidou embarked on a massive campaign to reform the lethargic French economy, devaluing the franc and launching enormous public works projects to modernize Paris, including massive investments in transportation systems. It was Pompidou's era that initiated the regional rail system known as the RER and the British tunnel connection, as well as rehabilitating France's chronically dysfunctional communication system. The president also implemented several substantial building programs in and around Paris. To address the drift of nearly half a million of the city's population to the suburban banlieues, Pompidou built five new towns in the region surrounding greater Paris. Ever the Manhattan enthusiast, he also embarked on building the high-rise district on the periphery of the city known as La Défense.

Accompanying Pompidou's programs of reformations and modernizations was a rhetoric that, once again recalled the Revolution, and thus also foreshadowed Mitterrand. Pompidou's promise of a new society was in distinction to the extant society, which he called "blocked." His commitment to reform was through open dialogue with citizens. In his own claim to his government's transparency, Pompidou dedicated himself to communicating primarily by means of direct addresses at press conferences or on television.[2] These claims, however, were largely rhetorical; Pompidou relied as much on presidential autonomy as de Gaulle had done. Pompidou's urban initiatives were also hardly exemplary; his encouragement of skyscrapers within the city enabled erection of the Tour Montparnasse in the fourteenth arrondissement, still a source a lingering resentment. The towns that he built in the banlieues have been the sites of some of Paris's most significant racial and economic conflicts in the recent past.

The era of simultaneous expansion and disaffection of 1970s France gave rise to the Situationist group of which there has already been much mention. Led by Guy Debord, the group was blatantly skeptical of the type of official representation of modernity and urbanism, supported by big business and government interests, engrained in Pompidou's hyped conception for the Pompidou Center. In his book, *The Situationist City,* Simon Sadler commented that the Pompidou Center represents ". . . one of the purest and most refined forms of spectacle."[3] Jean Baudrillard was even more damning of the center's relationship to the public, in a rant written upon the museum's opening: "Truthfully, the only content of the Beaubourg is the masses themselves, which the building treats like a converter, like a black box, or in terms of input-output, exactly like a refinery treats a petroleum product or a flow of raw material."[4] The paradox of the Pompidou Center, or Beaubourg, as it is popularly known, continues.

When Piano and Rogers began designing the competition entry for the center, their goal was blatantly to challenge the fixed monumentality of the conventional notion of a cultural institution. The two architects, together with their engineer collaborators, Ove Arup and Associates, were swayed toward the idealism of "institutionalized spontaneity" proposed by the 1968 revolution, which had been recently replayed in Situationists' protest against the elitism of the recently completed Charles de Gaulle Airport and the commercial development at La Défense. The response of the two unknown architects and their engineering team underscored an essentially political inclination: "The image of culture is static and elitist; our problem is to make it live to both entertain and inform, not only for tourists and specialists, but for those who live in the neighborhood, a neighborhood in crisis."[5] In this spirit, Piano and Rogers advocated eliminating aesthetic qualities in favor of functionalist and technological imperatives, a practice seen as paramount in purging elitist culture for societal good.

Although this positivistic line of thinking belonged to a continuous lineage from the canonical modernist doctrine of the 1920s, it lacked its sobriety. Rather, Piano and Rogers's sensibility was informed more directly by the 1960s British pop architectural movement, Archigram, with whose members they were much more closely affiliated in London than with the more literary French Situationists. At the core of the disparity between the two counter-cultural movements was Archigram's optimistic embrace of advanced technology as an activator for urban life. Advanced technology for Archigram was emblematic of contemporary existence and would provide forms that would project the energy of industry and science. By offering literal elements of flexibility and interchangeability in exaggerated, overscaled architectural forms, architecture would grant the city opportunities for choice in actual mechanisms as well as metaphorical presence. This sense of choice, combined with the raw power of industrial forms, would imbue the city with unforeseen creative energy.[6]

Certainly the Situationists were equally invested with setting off the creative impetus of the city, but this would necessarily be located in subterranean terrains, in subversive practices—ambient "drifts" against all conventional orders and places of the city.[7] For Guy Debord and his gang, advanced technology would always be indicative of the activity of the state to glamorize itself, an activity consisting essentially of manufacturing of wonderment to conceal the exploitations of capitalism to an unsuspecting public.

Despite the saturation of the particular sociopolitical context around the Pompidou Center driving these conflicts, to a large extent, nearly one hundred years earlier across the city in the fifteenth arrondissement, the Eiffel Tower had been embroiled in the very same discord regarding technological expressionism. These issues were addressed by Walter Benjamin, Emile Zola, Guy de Maupassant, and a host of other more contemporary writers and artists, especially Roland Barthes in the 1970s. In many ways, the Pompidou Center's claim to iconoclasm was largely deluded. To recall Eco's excerpt, it is the Eiffel Tower that functions more as *émetteur à étincelles* than the Pompidou in the enduring French passion to signal the passage of time and history by building enormous technologically driven monuments. For a thorough understanding of the issues at hand in the Pompidou Center, as well as the Grands Projets, it is thus to the Eiffel Tower to which we must digress; not to general descriptions, but to the most intimate acquaintance of the tower's physicality, which has been the origin of its extensive theorizations.

DELIRIOUS SURFACE: THE EIFFEL TOWER

Just before the Eiffel Tower was to be erected, Maupassant circulated a strident petition signed by twenty prominent literary figures protesting the structure and submitted it to Alphand, minister of public works. Given the larger context of strife caused by the effects of rapidly introduced industrialization in fin-de-siècle Paris, it is amazing that anyone even took note. The social and historical paradigmatic shift accompanying the industrial revolution at the end of the century was profound, much more so than in Paris of the 1970s. For architecture, the birth of iron construction in this period was revolutionary in spatial, representational, and as well technological terms, particularly given the implications of radically changing methods and scales of production. As evidenced by the World Expositions of 1855, 1867, 1878, 1889, and finally 1900, new iron technology was also complemented by new technologies of artificial light.[8] These enormous expositions, the first spectacles of "the heavenly city," did not merely display developing technologies, but offered them to the general public as phantasmagorias, insinuating glimpses of futuristic utopias yet to come. The expositions both represented and exploited the societal trauma accompanying industrialization, and were at once terrifying and irresistibly seductive.[9]

As an engineering feat, the Eiffel Tower is well known in the history of iron construction, far exceeding the technical achievements of the Pompidou Center.

2.2 Eiffel Tower, typical joint.

Designed to surpass in height all previous manmade structures and attain the 1000-foot mark (an altitude mystified by popular engineering lore), Gustave Eiffel conceived the monument primarily in terms of lateral deformations encountered with wind loading at heights never directly observed before.[10] This was his first attempt to study such forces in the vertical dimension; for several decades his experiments had concentrated on their effects in long-span bridges. Coupling his interest in lateral stressing with a contemporary enthusiasm for building in iron, Eiffel designed the structure as an experiment in both the strength of the material and the new construction practices it provoked. He realized that a transparent iron construction offered an opportunity over solid masonry. Rather than countering lateral force with immutable mass, he could configure the primary structural components—built-up wrought-iron lattice trusses—so wind would simply pass through the voids.

The remaining lateral demand—the force of wind against iron—was dealt with in three ways. First, the curvature of each straddled leg was determined by geometric addition of the vectors of force from wind and gravity loads. Second, the two intermediate visitors' platforms were conceived as lateral bracing elements. Third, as part of the design, Eiffel verified the nascent concept of the modulus of elasticity developed in 1807 by Thomas Young, a ratio measuring stresses within the iron members caused by physical deformation of the structure as it bent with the wind. Eiffel's calculations eventually proved highly accurate; during either strong winds or high temperatures, the top of the tower deflects less than ten centimeters.

This artless play to the demands of nature was reflected in several devices invented for the building process. In the massive foundations, Eiffel employed pneumatic caissons to allow continual leveling of the four different foundation structures, since water levels and soil conditions varied greatly over the tower's enormous footprint relative to the distance of each leg to the Seine. Indeed devices for adjustment were found throughout the structure during construction. Eiffel used pistons inside the shoes at connections between the foundation and primary columns and sand-filled weights at the top of supporting wooden pylons to constantly adjust the height and angle of the four piers. Under construction separately, they had to come together exactly—at a tolerance of 1/10 of a millimeter—at the level of the first platform. Eiffel raised the construction process and its materials to unprecedented heights with his design of "creeper cranes," whose tracks later accommodated the famous diagonally moving elevators. During construction, the

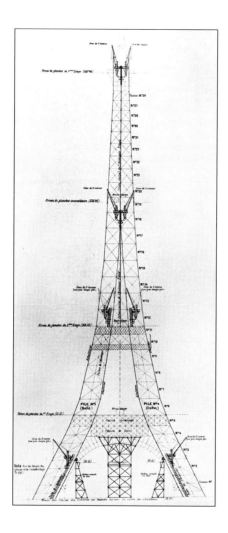

2.3 Eiffel Tower, adjustable wooden pylons and creeper cranes used during construction. Illustrated in Joseph Harriss, *The Tallest Tower: Eiffel and the Belle Epoque* (Boston: Houghton Mifflin, 1975, 62). Courtesy Joseph Harriss.

tower was more than a technological metaphor for the age of the machine; very much like the Pompidou Center, it was itself a machine, an enormous self-gauging apparatus that adjusted itself incrementally in minute movements.

Mounted for the 1889 World Exposition, the tower's future on the Champ de Mars site was uncertain. Its 18,038 components, each drawn exactly by Eiffel and his associates, were prefabricated; all 2.5 million rivet holes were predrilled precisely for final erection on site. Two-thirds of the rivet holes were set in place in the shop, substantially decreasing on-site assembly time. This system not only accommodated a compressed construction schedule; with the vociferous early protest accompanying the tower's initial construction, it was also ideal for the likely prospect of its dismantling.

Given the tower's tremendous scale as well as its enduring iconographic presence, the first paradox is found in its accommodation to movement and its impermanent state of completion—its transiency is present at all scales of construction and levels of conception. The state of the tower as simultaneously inert and mobile can be perceived visually in the constructed elements. To accommodate the changing curvature required for the lateral thrust, each of the twenty-eight trussing panels varies in dimension from top to bottom. When viewed from below at an oblique angle, the delicate opposing members of the three-dimensional boxed truss parallelograms never appear coincident. This optical effect (viewed from near or far) makes the trusses always seem slightly out of focus. Although Eiffel's use of statics and materials ensured that the tower would move only minimally, it nonetheless appears to move constantly.

Venerated by leagues of artists, from Delaunay to Rousseau and Seurat to the surrealists, the tower's import was not confined to the ranks of engineering society. Even its processes of mass assembly prompted Walter Benjamin to examine it as an epistemological object, simultaneously technological and discursive. Susan Buck-Morss speculated that the tower inspired the structure of Benjamin's *Passagen-Werk* (*Arcades Project*), regarded by many historians as a definitive revision of philosophical history. Organized around Benjamin's observations on Parisian material culture in the early part of the twentieth century, the text was organized as an amassing and categorizing of commonplace elements, an analogue Benjamin derived from the tower's "extremely small, extremely effective forms."[11] Wrought-iron assemblage, as interpreted by Benjamin, became montage, the guiding formal principle with which he characterized modernist space. Thus the specific details of

2.4 Eiffel Tower, southeast pier.

2.5 Eiffel Tower, from underneath.

the tower and the implications of their method of assembly provoked his influential observation on the definitive shift in paradigmatic space.

Roland Barthes's famous 1964 essay on the Eiffel Tower inscribed it in the pantheon of erudite Parisian monuments, while providing further insightful observations on the significance of its detail. Barthes outlined the tower's multiple perceptual and intelligible effects on visitors, and consequently on their perception of the city of Paris.[12] Describing the tower's enticing paradox, he elaborated on its simultaneous existence as object to be seen in the landscape and device in turn allowing the city to be seen and reseen. This particular inversion has another consequence found in the monument's interior spatiality. The tower can be comprehended only partially when viewed from a distance. As Aragon observed, its complementary effect is understood only as one approaches and passes underneath into an enormous bowel of purely feminine anatomical space: the phallus regendered.[13] As visitors move up into this feminine space, the final engagement occurs within the space of the structural components.

Eiffel marveled that the age of iron marked the advent of rationality over the muddled lack of quantification characteristic of masonry construction. According to Barthes, this force of intelligence is engaged incrementally as the vast structure is encountered at closer and closer distances. He noted that the visitor's psyche is manipulated continuously between intellectual and sensible engagement. While the visitor is mystified by the tower's sheer scale and sense of advanced technology, this mystification is coincident with rational appreciation, as the particular configuration of the structure and the method of assembly of its constituent pieces become apparent. He wrote, "and for anyone who takes the stairs, there is the enlarged spectacle of all the details, plates, beams, bolts, which make the Tower, the surprise of seeing how this rectilinear form, which is consumed in every corner of Paris as a pure line, is composed of countless segments, interlinked, crossed, divergent: an operation of reducing an appearance (the straight line) to its contrary reality (a lacework of broken substances). . . ."[14] If the tower's details for Benjamin spawned the condition of modernist spatial collage, for Barthes they provided the mechanism that conflates two diametrically opposed states of the observer's consciousness—mystification and rational engagement.

This conflation occurs in an equally fissured physical space. The tower is unlike earlier benchmarks of iron construction—great exposition halls, train

2.6 Eiffel Tower, from the inside.

stations—where internal spaces, although seemingly infinite in scale, were nonetheless contained and perceived within a unitary figure.[15] Giedion observed that inside the tower there is a strong presence of "continuously changing snippets of landscape." These potent slices of the city's view from dizzying heights destabilize the tower's exterior boundary, challenging the interiority of its space. As the geometries of its irregular trapezoidal trusses are overlaid, interstitial spaces project across the interior, gathering views of the exterior surround within the spatiality of a three-dimensional collage. Just as the construction method is marked by a process of assemblage or montage, so is the resulting interior space.

This spatial collage is amplified by the overwhelming physical materiality of the iron construction, where the filigree of thousands of plates, angles, and rivets enhances the disorienting effect. In this multiply fractured space, the visitor's experience is perceptually and temporally dislocated. The tower fulfills Benjamin's definition of modernist space; it is multivalent and kinetic in perception, ultimately challenging the unitary disposition of the observer.

Caught in this destabilized interior, the visitor is drawn into an even stranger intimacy, Barthes's "little worlds" of vendors and restaurants.[16] As these are discovered, the monumentality of the giant structure disintegrates. The final understanding of the tower is as the scaffold for a series of small carnivals, accommodating the quotidian activities of eating, drinking, and strolling for which Parisian culture is renowned. Here again we are reminded of Benjamin's fractured modernist space—an ambulatory procession, surrounded by familiar distractions, through which walkers would wind their way, occupied by nothing more significant than the everyday act of strolling. Within the Eiffel Tower the public becomes enmeshed—literally—with iconic transparency by being able to enter and, most important, move within the enormous structure as if within any other urban space. The tower becomes once again transparent, both *in* the city and *to* the city.

The way the tower is occupied by everyday activities, from strollers to vendors, bears considerable resemblance to Victor Hugo's account of life within the bounds of Notre Dame Cathedral. In *Notre-Dame de Paris,* the tracery of the building sets the stage for the actions of its shadowy inhabitants, whose turbulent emotions are defined by daily life. All three protagonists actually live within the spaces of the cathedral. The cathedral is in constant tension as a protective shelter, a literal asylum. It is also, however, the instrument of the state, the dwelling of the

2.7 Eiffel Tower. Life in the Tower. From René Clair's "Paris qui Dort," 1921. Courtesy Réunion des Musées Nationaux/Art Resources, New York.

2.8 Eiffel Tower post office, 1998.

libidinous archdeacon and symbol of the king's domain. The monument simultaneously connotes the paternal power of the state and the maternal body for its constituents. The corporeal connection between the public and its monument extends beyond literal bodily inhabitation and becomes visceral during the story. When attacked wrong-headedly by its own misinformed public, the body of Notre Dame effuses liquid as Quasimodo pours hot oil from its famous spouted gargoyles onto the crowds below.

The search for the transparent monument's ultimate referent leads to Notre Dame, with which the Eiffel Tower shares many attributes. The cathedral's construction was equally a vanguard of advancing technology and a historical moment equally significant in the development of the structural frame over load-bearing masonry. By increasing the height of the nave well beyond previous limits, the outward thrust was accommodated by reinforcing the bearing walls with a series of parallel transverse vaulted walls, rendering the lateral walls, containing the nave space, as infill. This early wall-frame system was augmented later in the thirteenth century by the cathedral's famous flying buttresses, which realized the full manifestation of the frame as individually defined elements in space.

Art historians have long claimed that the buttresses were added to increase the amount of glass and light into an overly dark interior (as the amount of glass increased, the amount of wall surface available for structural support decreased). Yet as architectural engineer Robert Mark theorized, the addition of these members was also provoked by observable material failure due to wind loading. He noted that Notre Dame represents the first "tall building," encountering the structural demands of a new environmental realm, that of lateral stresses produced by winds at higher elevations.[17] Both Notre Dame and the Eiffel Tower were forays into unprecedented vertical heights, and both prompted progressively externalized, lightened structures. In their day, both were also appreciated as technological markers. Indeed, as in the case of the Eiffel Tower, in the twelfth century the motivation for building even higher church towers was largely the result of competition among cities.[18]

Equally, the technological invention of the cathedral was motivated by a higher quest for dematerialized physicality pervasive in High Gothic symbolization.[19] By extracting the structure to the outside of the building and stretching and thinning all the enclosing interior surfaces, the church's ceilings were to be perceived as a heavenly domain; like the Eiffel Tower, the effect was intended

2.9 Notre Dame, exterior structure.

primarily to mystify. This ascription of mysticism was upheld by leagues of future artists and writers, from Ruskin to Monet, Debussy (*La Cathédrale Engloutie*), and Huysmans. For clergy and nobility, this mysticism was coherent to an understanding of the cathedral as the ultimate expression of the Roman Catholic spiritual faith.

Similar to conflicting interpretations of the Eiffel Tower, however, these descriptions stand in direct conflict with the rationality supposed by the positivists, principally Viollet-le-Duc, for whom the cathedral was the embodiment of all things methodical, ordered, and precise. In the nineteenth century, this dilemma was politically endowed. Positivists appropriated the cathedral's structural rationale to evidence its inherently secular nature and to claim cathedrals as nationalist symbols. Nineteenth-century architect and theorist Ludovic Vitet specifically cited the construction of the cathedral, in *Monographie de l'église Notre-Dame de Noyon*, as the ideological battleground from which "a new art, secular and urban, emerged victorious," a battle of reason against authority.[20]

However contradictory these claims to cathedrals' secularity might seem, they are supported by the public function they have served since the thirteenth century. Over this period, they provided a venue for government meetings and social gatherings, as well as the liturgical functions of the Catholic Church. Vauchez noted that Michelet called the cathedral the "house of the people." Hugo's novel thus depicts the life of the cathedral quite accurately. The cathedral *was* a literal asylum, but not only in the most dramatic of circumstances. It housed markedly prosaic and diverse urban activities; its cloisters provided dwelling for the homeless and the unemployed as well as places for study for altar boys and university students.

Hugo's assignment of corporeal features to the cathedral is underscored historically in the role of the Gothic cathedral as a precursor to the Renaissance ideal. Not only is the figure of the body inscribed in the plan, but it appears within circular geometries in many of the ornamental features from stained glass to tympaneum structures.[21] In cathedrals, the figural body coincided with the shelter of the literal bodies of its congregation. If their abstract representation was of the Corpus Christi, their functional embodiment was as a maternal protectorate.[22] As in the Eiffel Tower, the institution's ability to accommodate multiple "programs" was complemented by a physical description. The wealth of experience available within the vast structural tracery endowed these buildings with a capacity to shelter diverse domains. The maternal body emerged as a monumental skeletal carcass, available for occupation by all.

64

2.10 Notre Dame, view from transcept tribune. Illustrated in Jean Bony, *French Gothic Architecture of the 12th and 13th Centuries* (Berkeley: University of California Press, 1983, 144). Courtesy Mary Bony.

In the tower and the cathedral, the bond between a monument and its public was similarly conflicted. If Hugo's account underscored the implicit presence of the monarchy in Notre Dame, the tower certainly shares this ambivalence in its relation to the state. During the Occupation, for example, the tower's elevators were cleverly sabotaged; the tower became a popular symbol of the Resistance. Yet to this day, its top houses the radio apparatus enabling surveillance of the public by the paramilitary police, the gendarmerie.

The tower's relationship to the general public is also complicated by its original complicity in compelling modern consumption; the 1889 exposition was intended primarily as a display for newly manufactured products available to the general public. The political import of this manipulation is not as straightforward as might be presumed, and is illuminated by Benjamin's ideas in *Passagen-Werk*. For Benjamin, the bourgeois world of capitalist fin-de-siècle Paris was entranced in a dream state, compelled by consumption of luxury goods that had been accelerated by industrialized mass production. Benjamin's exhaustive quest was for materials or artifacts within existing material culture that would produce, either from their associations with previously held value structures or from their radical disjunctions with the current age, a revelatory effect, an awakening to social realities.

Theorizing that the appearance of such physicality, such as that in the Eiffel Tower, would produce an effect powerful enough to "ventilate" bourgeois attitudes, Benjamin sought to break the historical continuum of domination of the underclass. He wrote in "Paris, Capital of the Nineteenth Century":

> Corresponding in the collective consciousness to the forms of the new means of production, which at first were still dominated by the old (Marx), are images in which the new is intermingled with the old. These images are wishful fantasies, and in them the collective seeks both to preserve and to transfigure the inchoateness of the social product and the social system of production.[23]

An ultimate contradiction in Benjamin's thinking appears. He believed domination of the underclasses was reified by the linearity of technological progress. Yet, at the same time, he advocated a new expression based in the objectivity of science and technology; this attitude was not unusual at the time and may be found in many writings of his contemporary, Emile Zola. Yet Benjamin was aware that

2.11 Eiffel Tower, looking up.

technological expressionism was responsible for its own form of mysticism and euphoria, which for him would ultimately indicate totalitarianism rather than democracy.

The tower's physicality was certainly powerful enough to disturb metonymic associations between sociocultural orders of power and industrial production, as Benjamin theorized. Yet the mystifying effect wrought by the expression of advanced technology remains inescapable in the tower's reading. Benjamin himself realized that the effect of transparent glass and iron construction was inevitably mystifying; in the end, his call for a potent material expression allied with the *volumetric transparency* of Le Corbusier and Gropius, manifested through the "objective" surface of the white wall.[24] Built at the tremendous scales of the urban monument, the exaggerated presence of technology, or technological expressionism, was a reification of whatever power structure seemed to be at hand.

At the time of the tower's construction, the prevalent power was Republican, an anomaly in a Europe still dominated by monarchies. The tower's political symbolism was indeed of a republican government, inspiring detractors to condemn it as antireligious, a "secular insult to the Eternal," and "a cathedral of sedition, the daughter of the Revolution, the basilica of syndicalism, the column of Riot."[25] The language of this nineteenth-century critic emphasized how scientific progress, represented by the structure, was perceived not only as a challenge to all orders of traditional social life but also as a direct substitute for religious systems of belief. Zola, in his novel *Paris,* written in 1896, was unwavering on this point: "Leaning upon modern Science, clear Latin reason sweeps away the ancient Semitic conception of the Bible."[26] The tower, rather than the book, threatened to kill the cathedral.

These revolutionary aspirations were consistent with the tower's specific role as a commemoration of the centennial of the French Revolution. "Coating the tower with iridescent paint caused it to scintillate in the sunlight and to emanate a rosy glow in its gas and electrically lit nocturnal illumination, making more explicit the analogy between the man-made, manufactured structure and the concept of society as a product of mutual interest among individually minded people."[27] The tower was indeed intended to dematerialize, not simply into a romantic atmospheric state, but into a collective hallucination at once symbolizing and microcosmically simulating a democratic liberal society.

Eiffel proposed that the organization of construction be based on a working model representing the ideals of the Third Republic (as extended from the French Revolution) in cultivating a society composed of an extended community of egalitarian producers. Using new systems of legalized unions, construction wages throughout were set through negotiations and independent cooperative contracts. New construction techniques were taught and shared between hundreds of contractors and subcontractors employed throughout France.

On the part of the Third Republic, this novel organization was intended to signify the rewards of labor and allow the French people vicarious involvement in a symbolic community-building process. According to Edouard Lockroy, then Minister of Commerce, Public Education, and Fine Arts, even individual plates and rivets were meant to symbolize an assemblage of individuals; both the work of the tower's laborers as well as that of the larger society.[28] Assigning sociopolitical significance to the process of the monument's construction had yet another source, found in the nineteenth century's interpretations of the Gothic cathedral. Vitet's text notes that since the tradesmen involved in cathedral construction were dominated by fraternal orders of freemasonry, cathedrals came to signify the birthplaces of freethinking.

The tower's overt technological character was intended to complement the exposition's themes. Aside from the prominent display of military technologies, most exhibits were dedicated to new domestic technologies, particularly in the Galerie des Machines at the opposite end of the Champ de Mars. Against a background of disharmonious social change reflecting anxieties provoked by new technologies, the exposition was intended to alleviate the trauma by educating the general public. The symbol of the tower was not only to promote new products, but also to benevolently ground unsettling technological changes wrought in daily life. It is debatable, of course, whether the many symbolic programs associated with the tower's construction could compete with the ensuing rampage of twentieth-century consumerism. Critiques of the series of Parisian expositions continue to this day to expose their role in heralding and playing an active part in encouraging a consumerist society.[29]

The tower's many descriptions are fraught by contradiction: It is an inert monumental obelisk housing intimate carnivals. It is a single finite landmark composed of a series of infinitely fractured spaces. It is an object seen in the landscape serving to view and resituate the landscape. It is a symbol of egalitarian democracy that simultaneously is an instrument to promote capitalist consumption. Finally, it is a technological feat that anesthetizes with the force of a phantasmagoric dream, while simultaneously celebrating the casual, spontaneous event. It is this ultimate resistance to static definition, this fluid vacillation in readings and meanings, that finally gives the term "transparency" resonance for the glass monuments of a later day.

Of all the many possible tangencies that might explain this idea of transparency, it is Gilles Deleuze who most aptly captured the concept. For Deleuze, such a condition is not one of general state, but one of edge. His concept of surface, based metaphorically on the mirror in Lewis Carroll's *Through the Looking Glass,* is a boundary made up of events, a line in a state of pure, *unlimited becoming:* "In Plato, however, this something is never hidden, driven back, pushed deeply into the depth of the body, or drowned in the ocean. Everything now returns to the surface, This is the result of the Stoic operation: the unlimited returns. Becoming mad, becoming unlimited is no longer a ground which rumbles. It climbs to the surface of things and become impassive."[30] For Deleuze, the surface of Carroll's *Looking Glass* represented a state of paradox of infinite identities where "wild discourse slides over language": the line between sense and nonsense.

If in Barthes's metaphor the Eiffel Tower represented such a paradoxical line in space, in Deleuze's terminology the entire building is transformed into surface. As the monumental frame both physically houses plural domains and provokes wildly incongruous types of activities, so the symbolism and physical readings of the tower vacillate between contradictory extremes. For Deleuze, this state of indeterminacy was both transformative and productive, both celebratory and insane. For him the art of such surface was humor.

SURFACE PLAY: THE POMPIDOU CENTER

The powerful elation bared in the Eiffel Tower's latent sense of indeterminacy might have ended here in this text as pure speculation. Ninety years later across the Seine in the Marais, however, the identical mélange of traits was played out again, and consciously amplified, by the young Piano and Rogers.

As was the tower, the building was a product of its times. Besides those larger urban initiatives of Pompidou discussed above, the conception for Center was entrenched in a scheme to rehabilitate a slum area of the Marais known as Plateau Beaubourg, which was previously dominated by the old food markets of Les Halles, the traditional center of Parisian gastronomic culture. Since improved

2.12 Renzo Piano and Richard Rogers, Pompidou Center, 1977, from Rue du Renard.

methods of distribution motivated the de Gaulle administration to relocate the markets to suburban Rungis in the 1960s, there was no longer any reason to keep the glass and iron Baltard buildings much beloved by the general public. Located at the base of Rue St. Denis, the buildings had come to signify, at least for the government, a deteriorating hub for prostitution and tuberculosis, an eyesore since the 1930s. Predictably, it was these very characteristics of marginal urban space that endeared the marketplace area to the Situationists, who devoted several of their "psychogeographic" maps to documenting the area, "correctly identifying a gap in the Parisian spectacle."[31]

By the late 1960s and early 1970s, emotions swirling around the proposed demolition and renovation to the area had grown to a loud and vociferous debate on the merits of the conservation. At the center of this public dispute was recognition that the modernist urbanist agenda was exactly complicit with the government's efforts: modernism's devaluation of traditional urban forms and its zeal to make the city hygienic conformed to the government's agenda to rid the city of its unsightly past. All argument, it seems, was for naught. In August 1971, when most Parisians were out of the city on vacation, Pompidou had the Baltard buildings razed, an event in the city's urban history that still provokes anger among the general public.

It was into this charged setting that the Centre du Plateau de Beaubourg, as it was originally named, was conceived. While the hole left by the Baltard demolition was to be (literally) filled by a vast underground complex—an RER station and a regrettably styled shopping center by Vasconi, Pencréac'h, and others—the Pompidou Center would provide the cultural panacea that would assuage the wounds of Les Halles and, of course, simultaneously provide a legacy for the president. In the spirit of the 1960s and 1970s, Pompidou conceived the building as a happening, a heterogeneous, late-night, multicultural center housing badly needed facilities, particularly a modern art museum and a public library. Also in the spirit of the era, Pompidou launched a completely open competition, an egalitarian gesture to young unproved architects internationally.

Out of 681 entries, Piano and Rogers, collaborating with consulting structural engineers Ove Arup, was chosen. In keeping with the spirit of the competition, their original concept relied on reinventing the practice of programming for the building.[32] In the entry brief, Piano and Rogers stressed inclusion within the institution of nonprogrammed areas, emphasizing their potential to provoke activity outside the confines of the institution and therefore to break open the notion of the cultural institution. An interesting parallel arises with respect to "program" of the Eiffel Tower. As Barthes noted, both scientists and general public continuously reinvented the tower, originally without function, for different uses. Piano and Rogers had essentially the same aspiration for the Pompidou Center. By both over-programming its uses and under-programming spaces in between, the cultural center would be used in many unpredictable layers.

The plaza elevation of the competition entry was notably dominated by images of people as well as information systems dispersed onto the architectural elements, a reference to Oscar Nietschke's 1932–1935 *Maison de la Publicité*. "The center is a public event; thus the greater the public involvement, the greater the success."[33] Implicit in the emphatic concept of event in the initial proposal was a proposition that activity itself constituted a viable description of form equivalent to the physical building and its spaces. A concept for which the architects were indebted to Archigram, it also anticipated ideas much more recently theorized by Bernard Tschumi.[34] In Piano and Rogers's thinking, however, event would become more than a dramatic embodiment of the building, either as public happening or dynamic system of programming. For them, the concept of event was tied to a notion of the physical building in a permanent state of incompletion, an idea that became the basis for their redefinition of transparency.

As the seminal idea behind the design of the building's structure and space, perpetual change echoed the openness of the programmatic intentions. This was manifested in the competition proposal by the deployment of movement systems for people (throughout the building) and cars (on subterranean levels), and by material and structural systems capable of literal movement, or at least easy replacement. Again, a corollary can be drawn to those same traits in the Eiffel Tower, although in this case, actual movements overwhelmed more subtle virtual ones. Piano and Rogers originally intended that enormous floors plates be repositionable, allowing the building to be as flexible in section as it was in plan. The idea had many connections back to Archigram, whose proposals were riddled with such visionary devices, and whose writings proposed reconstituting buildings fundamentally as movement, together with survival, crowd, and situation, among others.[35]

The political ideology of a building as a transformable device was given impetus by Jean Prouvé's *Maison du Peuple* of 1935 in suburban Clichy, another

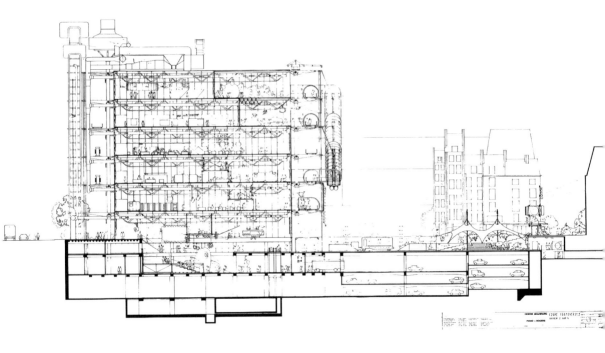

2.13 Centre Georges Pompidou. Section from original competition entry. Courtesy Renzo Piano Building Workshop and Richard Rogers Partnership.

building in which open planning was translated into literal mechanisms capable of changing spatial configurations.[36] Within a matter of minutes, Prouvé's building could be transfigured from open market to meeting hall to cinema by repositioning floor and wall panels and a large segment of sliding roof. Commissioned by Socialist Mayor Monsieur Auffray, the building's capacity to transform was associated, as in the Pompidou Center, with an iconoclastic social mission. Said Prouvé in 1981, "Long before 'Beaubourg,' the Maison du Peuple sought to provide an everyday cultural and communication venue for local people, a free forum for our epoch."[37] Serendipitously, it was he who chaired the jury in the awarding of the commission for the Pompidou Center.

Although the repositionable floor plates included in the original competition proposal were later abandoned to reduce costs, the underlying concept was retained in the flexible exhibition spaces. The building would be conceived as an empty box, an enormous cage responding to the perceived necessity for flexible space. Peter Rice, then project engineer from Ove Arup's office, wrote, "It was a large loose-fit frame where anything could happen. An information machine."[38] Only 60 percent of its internal volume would be filled with programmed spaces, allowing for redispersal of space as desired. The remainder, particularly the ground-floor spaces and terrace levels above, would be left completely open to public appropriation. To support their conceptual diagram, Piano and Rogers pushed all structure and mechanical systems to the exterior. At this scale, such externalization did more than liberate the floor span; it consciously made reference to Notre Dame, located just a few blocks south along the Rue du Renard, across the Seine.

Glass and iron had long been regarded as emblematic constructional materials of modernity. Not only were they associated with the practices of engineering made heroic by modernist rhetoric, but through their capacity to give direct visual access to the constituents of building, centuries of tradition of symbolic representation—of building structure by ornamental language—had been overthrown. In German architectural theories concerned with tectonics, glass and iron were topics of central debates, especially between extremes represented by Gottfried Semper and Carl Bötticher, which situated true spiritual expression between the direct language of the new materiality and traditional symbolic architecture.[39] Glass and iron, according to Giedion, were also to become in the modernist era the "constituent materials" of flexible space. In 1928, he wrote of their contribution to

2.14 Pompidou Center, view toward Notre Dame.

demands of Parisian department stores for "Greatest possible freedom for circulation, clear layout, Greatest possible influx of light."[40]

In their choice of steel construction fifty years later, the Beaubourg's architects reiterated both ontological and typological revolutions. At substantial additional cost and potential political estrangement, the architects and engineers pushed forward the use of steel in a French industrial culture that was dominated by concrete and masonry.[41] For them it was specifically prefabricated steel and glass that accommodated not only pragmatic demands, but also the material sensibility with which they sought to endow their building: "Let's think of ideas that will give the design the same *esprit* of the Eiffel Tower and the Gare de Lyon."[42] The choice of steel as the primary building system did more, however, than fulfill Piano and Rogers's desire for spirit. An intricate system of steel construction fused together the spatial and tectonic morphologies of Notre Dame—a unitary volume with externalized structure—with the complexities of the fractured surface and spaces of the Eiffel Tower.

Piano, Rogers, and Rice imagined a steel technology that belonged neither to the nineteenth century nor to conventional industrial construction of the 1970s. Instead, they planned to use the most advanced type of custom steel production available, which they had observed in Frei Otto's large-scale steel castings used in a Munich stadium. This choice was not made, however, for the pure sake of promoting advanced technology. Peter Rice wrote that mass-produced standardized elements of rolled and extruded steel sections available commercially left no room for personal expression by the architects and engineers. Standard systems of steel would also be overly familiar and connote conventional industrial construction to the general public. Neither would they contribute to the building's attempt to disturb typical expectations of cultural institutions; in this "popular palace of culture," said Rice, only highly customized cast steel would provide the necessary component of shock to undermine notions of elitist culture.

If base steel construction was implicitly characterized by direct communication, as theorized in the nineteenth century by Bötticher, in the twentieth century, through the strange and alien presence of cast steel, this directness was given a dadaist inflection. In this respect, this aspect of the construction could not have been more different from that of the Eiffel Tower, which represented in the type of stock cast members a seamless choice of an industrial material from within its own technical milieu, without the deliberate and conscious inflection of architects. Piano, Rogers, and Rice fully intended that normative expectations for steel

2.15 Pompidou Center, southern flank.

construction be disturbed and unnerved, precisely the type of disturbance to a mnemonic order advocated by Walter Benjamin.

Definite structural and industrial challenges had to be resolved using this provocative system. Testing standards derived from advanced British engineering research in fracture mechanics had to be translated first into French and then into German, where fabricators had been contracted. This was not merely a matter of technical language; it revealed differences in the standards of industrial production across national boundaries. The process of translation did not go smoothly. During final production, many of the main steel members failed at half their anticipated load because of a critical miscommunication.

Although heat-treating the members eventually rectified the problem, this was not attempted until the German fabricators had assurance from German university engineers that the problem could not be attributed to the original British design. The cast material in the columns was also weak under tensile stress. This was eventually overcome by changing the metallurgical properties of the material during casting, centrifugally spinning the columns, and then subjecting them to a highly controlled cooling process. Alhough the tensile properties of the cast steel improved, on-site welding was precluded, especially at connections between members in tension: joints had to be assembled mechanically. Ironically, this constraint meant that the same steel structure, originally intended as the most flexible component, was to be the only irreplaceable system in the building. All the others, particularly the mechanical and electrical systems, could be replaced as technologies advanced over time.

"All members of the team had movement in mind: it goes with change."[43] This sentiment was most inventively realized in the primary structural systems. After several design iterations, the components were finally cast steel columns with enormous stainless steel Warren-truss girders spanning the full width of the building (approximately 44.8 m between column lines). The girders were composed of tubular sectioned members; with the hollow columns, these formed a system through which water was circulated for fire protection throughout the building. To reduce the bending moment in the trusses, the team designed a cantilevered rocker-arm beam—a *gerberette* (named after nineteenth-century Swiss bridge engineer Heinrich Gerber)—along both of the building's long flanks facing the plaza and the street. This beam would transfer the architectural dead load two ways; partially at an interior column line, and partially into tensile force along the

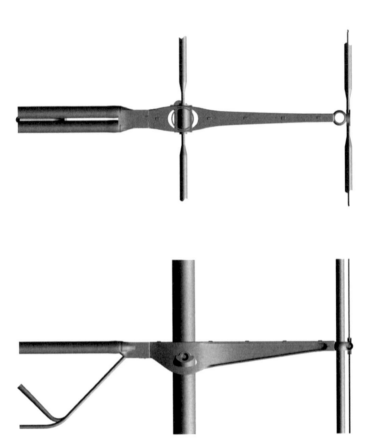

2.16 Pompidou Center, gerberette. (Drawing: Robert Trempe, Jr.)

2.17 Pompidou Center, circulation around gerberettes.

two faces of the building's long flanks. High-tensile steel vertical members at the building's perimeters pulled the ends of the gerberette down, transmitting the load into the ground, not onto the building's foundation.

In the cantilever zone along the building's flanks, the dynamic interchange of structural forces coincides with full activation of the building's physical and social lives through both programmed and unprogrammed means. All the dynamic systems—mechanical, electrical, and water circulation—are along the Rue du Renard flank. Located along the plaza flank are all the elements of public circulation, moving visitors and the general public among various facilities: galleries, a public library, bookshops, a cinémathèque, and public terraces and restaurants at the uppermost level.

Like the Eiffel Tower, movement of users inside the enormous structure constitutes the primary architectural experience; here Benjamin's sense of kinetic engagement achieves hyperbole as spatial sequences; indeed the building becomes composed entirely of literal movement. The visitor ascends to the building's top level in a deliberately slow escalator. Crossing the horizontal datum of five-story Parisian rooftops, it provides a view of the city's fabric and landmarks and harkens back to transgressing the horizontal datum at the first level of the Eiffel Tower. The original competition entry specified no entry fees for the escalator as well as the open ground floor, making both entirely accessible to the French public and tourist alike. The city's diverse social fabric would be pulled in from the open plaza upward along the vertical face of the building, and finally rewarded with the prize of Parisian urban space in the heavenly realm above the rooftops.

Beaubourg, like the Eiffel Tower, makes the city visible. Indeed, the original competition jury anticipated not only the overwhelming public success of the building but a physical description that approaches that of many of Mitterrand's Grands Projets: "But one does not know many buildings resembling this one: not a tower or a skyscraper, but seen from afar, an immense screen, and closer, a mirror offering a constantly changing play of images and reflections."[44] However prophetic, this quotation is not altogether accurate. The Pompidou Center does not represent the city through the reflection of a mirror: Rather than an abstraction of its image, the constituents of the city actually make up the façade. Like in the Eiffel Tower, as the building is filled by the public, it is the citizenry of Paris—indeed the world—who prominently configure the building's surface.

2.18 Pompidou Center, at heaven's gate: the top of the escalator.

Despite motivations of the primary structure and the systems by issues of circulation and flexibility, according to Peter Rice, the essence of the design was consistent articulated assembly at all scales of the building. If the presence of cast steel disturbed a sense of conventional materiality, the assembled systems assuaged the agitated by clearly exposing the constructional techniques to view. "Making the joint the essence of the solution expressed concisely the spirit we wanted to convey . . . Often it is the expressiveness of the jointing which humanizes the structures and gives them their friendly feel."[45] Throughout the building pieces were separated by mechanical assemblage, which, at all points of connection, kept each method of attachment discernable to the most uninformed eye. Piano, Rogers, and Rice agreed that an element of didacticism contributed to their idea of transparency; the rule of intelligibility governed the design at all levels. The color-coding of the technical systems on the exterior is only one of the most obvious manifestations of this intention. According to the architects, transparency would enlighten, amuse, and even comfort the general public.[46]

Within the transparent surface of the Pompidou Center, humor became a guiding motivation. The outlandish scale of its individual elements and the near absurdity of their obvious methods of assembly subdue the mystification latent in the Eiffel Tower's incomprehensible scale and sense of technological advancement. Humor pervades at more subtle scales of the building as well, particularly in details of the secondary glass and steel enclosure. Here Piano and Rogers used a pair of symmetrical steel channels bolted together through their long flanks as the basic system for the exterior glass mullions. The configuration accommodated a number of elements and accessories fabricated specially with a flange to be inserted and bolted between two supporting angles. While the angles were used extensively for attaching functional elements—lateral struts, radiant heating elements, and electric conduits—Piano and Rogers also invented a full range of customized accessories for the most mundane of everyday needs.

Particularly incongruous in the enormous structure are moments when such elements—ashtrays and conventional light switches—emerge as witty retorts to the building's maze of infrastructures, challenges to those who imagine high technology be taken too seriously. (Noteworthy is the public's apparent appreciation of these objects, which were for the most part stolen very early on.) In 1965, Reyner Banham wrote of Archigram's motivations: "It's all done for the giggle."[47] At the Pompidou Center laughter is taken seriously; it is the constituent factor that allows the public to engage the building, at the same level as the architectural critic, and

2.19 Pompidou Center, radiant heating at glass storefront support.

2.20 Pompidou Center, ashtray at glass storefront support.

joins to create, with intelligibility and literal embodiment, Piano and Rogers's notion of transparency.

Many of the observations and speculations in the discussion of the Eiffel Tower apply to the Pompidou Center. It is both a landmark in the cityscape as well as a complex of internal spaces. Its basic geometry as a rectangular box signals an inert form, but this inertia is undermined by its constituent systems, as building technologies, circulation zones, and structures of programming are motivated toward temporality, spontaneity, and kineticism. Its physical manifestation as a monumental structural cage open to all types of occupations is at once a technological invention and a challenge to conventional institutional and political orders.

If the commonplace event was to provide the final embodiment of the Eiffel Tower, provoking such events was the active and deliberate motivation of Pompidou Center's architects. Despite the building's tremendous physicality—its mythic reverie—in the end this trait would be subsumed by the crowds it would attract. The sense of qualified interiority in the Eiffel Tower has disintegrated entirely in the Pompidou Center. As the building becomes progressively more exterior, it might be regarded either as having no void space at all or as a replete void—replete surface—a building composed entirely of event. To reinvoke Deleuze, "the unlimited returns. . . . It climbs to the surface of things and becomes impassive."[48] This notion of event, literal as well as metaphoric, idealizes the qualities of unassignability, openness to interpretation, and permanently incomplete status, each designated by Piano and Rogers not as conditions of event, but as intrinsic conditions of transparency.[49]

In the postrevolution euphoria of the 1970s, many central concepts of the Situationists were indebted to Marxist philosopher Henri Lefebvre. Shortly after May 1968, Lefebvre examined alienation in quotidian modern life in the face of invisible yet determinant powers controlling every aspect of that life. Lefebvre, an admitted utopianist, proposed that the key to countering such disempowerment lay in the constitution of daily life itself.[50] He saw in aspects such as sexual love, innocent play, and the communal festival the opportunity to reinvest contemporary life with a sense of style based not in fashion but in the constituent "prose and poetry" of life. The folk festival would play a central role in his thinking. An unrequited Marxist revolution, it would provide the means of overcoming the deadening social effects produced by ubiquitous control. This idealized community festival would be based entirely in spontaneous, unprovoked events of urban life.

2.21 Pompidou Center, circulation zone.

It would arise seamlessly from everyday practices, idealized to engender a transcendent reinvestment of the everyday with long exiled poetic dimension. The festival was key to countering the larger forces of alienation, overpowering even the force of the spectacle itself.

Piano and Rogers quelled the potential of technological expressionism to associate with systems of power by their relentless imposition of a humorous didacticism. Since its opening in 1979, the Pompidou has admitted five times the projected number of visitors. The city's social context has apparently not only accepted the building but has become obsessed with it and its plaza. Given the continuing disdain of academic architectural opinion, this success is a function of neither intellectual nor aesthetic appreciation, but instead derives from the potential of Piano and Rogers's technological expressionism to attract the masses and the potency of their sense of monumental transparency to generate the festival.

The public has responded unabashedly to the building's invitation by occupying in masses all its spaces and crevices. This festival is not the folk event of the village nostalgically envisioned by Lefebvre, but is reconstituted in the city, consciously indulging in forms of contemporary life that might have been rejected by the Situationists but embraced by Archigram: advertising, commercial media, technology, and tourism. It is also noteworthy that Piano and Rogers intended that advertising systems for the façade portray messages with social content—protests against the Vietnam War, for example—in a gesture that the Situationists might have labeled as their own *détournement,* an appropriation and redeployment of a mainstream cultural element. Frequented by tourists and students, pickpockets and intellectuals, the building and its plaza became the truly communal festival of the contemporary city that Lefebvre had only theorized as belonging to a past era. Since the Pompidou Center's final reference was outward toward Paris, that festival was effectively imparted to the city.

Paris was an unequivocal recipient of the gesture. In their programming of the center, Piano and Rogers complexly interwove many of the building's elements, seen and unseen, into the city's urban fabric. While the western open plaza provides for dynamic interactions within the highly dense fabric, the eastern edge of the building respectfully aligns itself along the building line at the Rue du Renard to support traditional urban street making. Underneath the building, Piano and Rogers designed a large subterranean traffic system, significantly restructuring passage and parking within this part of the city, another gesture to the concept of flux. The parking facilities are not limited to museum goers, but provide a service to surrounding areas.

Sadler noted, "Profoundly divorced from the radical local initiative implied by the situationist urbanism, Beaubourg seemed to be one more piece of territory lost in the battle for urban space."[51] Given the number of devices that stage the building and its plaza as one of many incidents along different routes through the city, this statement cannot represent more than a cursory examination of the building's constituent elements. If understood as a piece of infrastructure, the building's monolithic nature, and therefore its status as a spectacle, disintegrates. As the Center is implicated in the general activity of the city, in Michel de Certeau's terms, it becomes a practiced urban space.

By comparison, the Eiffel Tower is relatively isolated from the surrounding fifteenth arrondissement by the Champ de Mars. And whereas different forms of Parisian practices situate the tower within urban life, notably the tradition of the Champ de Mars as both promenade and parade route, the structure is outside the life of the central city. Consequently, most contemporary Parisians encounter it infrequently; a visit to the tower is a deliberate destination rather than a chance encounter. This affirms its current status as a primarily tourist destination. By contrast, the powerful effect of free access (which cannot be underestimated) and urban relationships in the Pompidou Center keep it safe from such a dim prospect.

The Pompidou Center's unabated consummation by the general public has also, unfortunately, resulted in severe physical disintegration. In January 1998 it was closed for extensive and badly needed renovations to remedy climatization systems, fluid distribution, escalators, and elevators. Renovation was completed in January 2000. It removed all administrative functions outside the building proper and added and redispersed general gallery space. Colors on the exterior elements were refurbished with advanced paint technologies. The entire ground floor was reconstructed, designed by Atelier Renzo Piano in Paris, to accommodate several elements at a new mezzanine level—a *café littéraire*, a multimedia reference area for the center's activities and collections—and a new centrally located entry and information area. The library was consolidated and is now reached not by exterior escalators but from new circulation on the ground floor.

The renovation was the active state of change anticipated by the designers at its conception. The Piano office claimed that all programming and material decisions in the renovation were thoroughly analyzed to continue, or at least carefully

2.22 Pompidou Center, plaza façade under renovation, 1999. (Photo: Andrea Kahn)

augment, the original design goals, from conceptual ambitions to material sensibility.[52] But various exceptions instituted by the museum, and often at odds with Piano's recommendations, are noteworthy. By segregating circulation to the library, students and scholars no longer mix with tourists and museum patrons. At points where the glass escalator runs adjacent to circulation terraces off the library (formerly circulation spines off the escalator), this separation is distressing; glass doors between them are shackled. Moreover, scholars are no longer allowed incidental views of the museum's temporary installations, which used to be provided from the single spine of the escalator. Idealism and conceptual clarity have given way to pragmatic demands that threaten to nullify the building's ideological mission.

Most serious is the museum administration's intention to seal the escalator and roof terraces, and require a substantial museum entry fee. This decision was made in a blatant attempt to control and sanitize the occupation of the ground floor and plaza, which had been seen as unsavory in their increasing attraction to marginal social elements. The irony of gesture is a replay of the 1971 "cleansing" of the Beaubourg Plateau, replete with demolition of the Baltard marketplace. According to Situationists, filth and other signs of abjection were evidence of spontaneity.[53] The fall of the Pompidou into a degenerate state is final evidence that the expressive language of Archigram was perhaps not as complicit to the manipulative spectacle as Situationists might have first imagined: in its state of degeneracy, appropriation of the Pompidou Center was perhaps complete. Predictably, official culture could not sanction such transgression of behavioral orthodoxy in an official setting. Piano and Rogers (especially Rogers) protested vigorously the intended fee as diametrically opposed to the original intention of the building. The fee threatened ultimately to sever the building's relationship with the general public, ultimately castrating the building's redefinition of the transparent urban monument.

Guy Debord and the Situationists proclaimed that at some point in its development, architectural modernism had abandoned its revolutionary fervor. In stripping expression down to white rationalist boxes, epitomized by Le Corbusier's early work, the Situationists accused modern architecture as having become complicit with conservative agendas. The ultimate danger, they maintained, was suppression of common person's desire. Universal expressionism would inter, rather than liberate, the individual. The Situationist dream of Bacchanalian revolt was in the end motivated by a social transformation empowering individual expression.

Roland Barthes's observations on the Eiffel Tower lend the individual expression-ism of the Situationists' dream a collective attribute in noting the inspiration of a "mass societal imagination." Giedion concurred; the demand on a modern monument to provide a "fuller life of community" would be answered by great spectacles capable of fascinating people: Collective emotional events.[54] Benjamin also spoke of utopias of the collective where fantasies arise in unofficial forms of popular culture and where industrial artifacts trigger Proustian memories to reenchant the social world.

With his idea of "irresistible plurality," Gianni Vattimo characterized an idealized postmodern transparent society in similar terms, as one where differences and dialects are liberated: "Nihilistic philosophers such as Nietzsche and Heidegger (but also pragmatists like Dewey and Wittgenstein), in demonstrating that being does not necessarily coincide with what is stable, fixed and permanent, but has instead to do with event, with consensus, dialogue and interpretation, are trying to show us how to take the experience of oscillation in the post-modern world as an opportunity of a new way of being (finally, perhaps) human."[55] In the Eiffel Tower and the Pompidou Center, a conventional notion of transparency was redefined. Enormous, open-ended structures rebounding with implausible technologies and fantastically construed systems of materials impell resistance to describing the structures in any closed set of defining terms. This new sense of transparency is constituted reciprocally with the presence of the *event;* it is this relationship that ultimately approaches Vattimo's position. The celebration that erupted through these two structures signals a new and different sense of monumentality.

Michel de Certeau characterized the French upheavals of the 1960s as having been prompted by loss of faith in traditional values and institutions and mentioned architectural monuments commemorating the grandeur of the past. In his 1974 *Culture in the Plural,* he wrote of the crisis as based in the disbelief in traditional signifiers and fundamental collective references: "The very spirit that animated those representations now abandons them." According to de Certeau's terms, the moment of cultural optimism of the 1970s can be attributed to rebirth of credibility, transference of authority from conventional institutions to populist forms of contemporary culture.[56] The conception and building of the Pompidou Center occurred in this dynamic era of collective cultural beliefs. However short-lived that moment was, incitement of the Pompidou to collective imagination continued unabated (until the very recent unfortunate alterations), establishing a significant legacy in the redefinition of monumentality. This monumentality resides squarely within Benjamin and Lefebvre's fantasies and imaginations of the everyday artifact, the everyday festival. An unexpected form of human activation emerges, egalitarian in its obsession to occupy, to indulge, and to participate. Given the rhetorical claims of the Mitterrand projects to engender a libertarian form of accessibility through transparency, at once symbolic and literal, the Eiffel Tower and the Pompidou Center are ultimate criteria against which to gauge the successes of contemporary attempts.

✿ Cultural Projections: The Institutions of Jean Nouvel

You can just see a little peep of the passage in Looking-glass House, if you leave the door of our drawing-room wide open: and it's very like our own passage as far as you can see, only you know it may be quite different on beyond.

—Lewis Carroll, *Through the Looking Glass*

AFTER THE DEATH OF POMPIDOU in 1974, Valéry Giscard d'Estaing, the new president, immediately halted many of the building projects that were not as far along in construction as the Pompidou Center. After the frenzy of building in the Pompidou era, under the supervision of Giscard d'Estaing and his prime minister, Jacques Chirac, the capital was relatively quiet. Perhaps too quiet, for France the mid-1970s was a period of economic stagnation attributed primarily to the oil crises of 1974 and 1979. Unemployment skyrocketed to 11 percent. However many real reforms Giscard d'Estaing enacted during this period in education, women's issues, and voting age requirements, his administration did not confront the economic recession crippling the nation. Palpable discontent provided the impetus for the ascension of the Socialist party to the presidency in 1981, after a thirty-four-year period of political disempowerment.

When Mitterrand, *l'éternal perdant* of French politics, defeated Giscard d'Estaing in two extremely close ballots in 1981, the national mood was giddy. Celebrations broke out across the country. Immediately Mitterrand embarked on massive programs for reforms that followed his election slogan to *changer la vie.* In the first few months of his presidency he instituted an expansionary fiscal policy whose measures included substantial expenditures on social welfare, a plan to redistribute wealth through changes to the taxation system, and a large program of nationalization of private companies, particularly those affecting transportation and industry. Like Pompidou, Mitterrand embarked on an even more massive building program for Paris, a program that was of course to be known as the Grands Projets.

The celebrations that accompanied Mitterrand's elections and the announcement of his economic programs began to wane after only five months. Mitterrand's visions for a vibrant Socialist economy were undercut as unpredicted changes in the world economy hindered his proposals from reversing the recession. Continuing financial woes provoked Mitterrand to impose austerity measures on those programs he had just instituted. Stymied in his vision for economic reform, he was, however, undaunted in pursuing his vision to change the physical character of the capital: symbolic measures were to be instituted if real economic change could not be. Four projects were focused upon immediately: completion of the two museums initiated by Giscard d'Estaing, the Cité des Sciences et de l'Industrie and the Musée d'Orsay; the renovation of the Grand Louvre (though Pei's project was not made public until years later); and the Institut du Monde Arabe, a cultural institution that had been under consideration since 1974 but had hit a quagmire in negotiations over the site. This last project is known, whether accurately or not, as Mitterrand's first Grand Projet.

Completed in 1987, the architecture of the Institut du Monde Arabe was significantly different from that ten years earlier at the Pompidou. Although this multiprogrammed cultural center was dubbed *un petit Beaubourg,* the Institut never had the Pompidou's aspirations to court Parisian culture on a grand scale. This first of Mitterrand's public buildings was, for better or worse, never intended as a true spectacle, only a relatively modest addition to many second-tier cultural institutions already existing in the city. Similar to the Pompidou Center, however, was the predominance of glass construction and technological expression, although vastly different in conception and execution. Yet the architect, Jean Nouvel, had very little ambition for his glass construction to attain a state of transparency, either in physical fact or in political metaphor. Indeed, if he was motivated by any physical quality for his glass façades, it was for the provocative traits of translucency rather than transparency. This distinction encompasses far more than the visibility afforded by the glass plane; it reaches into the most fundamental tenets of transparency as they have been discussed thus far.

To understand this paradigmatic shift as it appears in Nouvel's two cultural institutions in Paris, we must return to the legacies left by the modern movement, especially to Mies van der Rohe, who unquestionably brought transparency to a culmination in modern architecture. In his work, transparency of glass coincided with transparency of construction to form its central heroic dimension: the disrobement of traditional building revealed construction as the primary element generating space and form. According to Mies, a poetic capitulation to the demands of construction endowed architecture with transcendence equal only to nature.[1] It is thus no mere coincidence that his oeuvre is pervaded with an insistent use of glass as a literally transparent medium—a frame to the nature his work was to equal.

Yet any cursory examination, particularly of his early, canonical small structures—Barcelona Pavilion, Farnsworth House—reveals that despite his rhetorical statements on the preeminence of technology, the quest for horizontally expanding space often subsumed the truthful expression of the buildings' structure. In these steel-framed houses he consistently dropped a false ceiling to avoid the spatial inflection of a modular cell in the boundary of the overhead plane.[2] He also did not allow a logic of construction to interfere with the elegance of many of his composite steel details, often perversely orchestrated in their assemblage to hide unsightly welds or cloaked (without hesitation) by veneers from paint to chromed shields. Suspect too is the ideal of transparency of glass in Mies's work.

Indeed, as Quetglas and many others observed, Mies was not only aware but indeed relished with unabashed aestheticism the physical impossibility of absolute transparency of glass.[3] Recent revisionist readings of his work focused on instabilities arising from his manipulation of the reflective properties of glass rather than its idealized transparency. These interpretations are quickly legitimized in the glass skyscraper project of 1922, where the curvilinear ribboned façade distorts reflections of the surrounding urban context.[4] Similarly in the Plate-Glass Hall of the Werkbund exhibition *The Dwelling* of 1927 with Lilly Reich, where Mies's manipulated intersections and geometries of different orthogonal planes to produce a space that approached the two-dimensional abstraction of a van Doesburg painting.

The qualifications to the traditional understanding of Mies's work correspond to recent developments in architectural discourse that attempted to theorize translucent or "light" construction, among which works Nouvel's are prominently included.[5] Here not only are the optical characteristics of glass redefined, but so is the central modernist principle of transparency. In translucent construction, instead of a miraculous continuity between exterior and interior, separation is typically acknowledged outright. Using subtle manipulations of visual perception, ambiguity between the two realms is often the primary field of inquiry. Accompanying the interruption of space flowing across the exterior boundary is a disturbance to the revelation of the building's spaces and its physical structure at its

3.1 Mies van der Rohe, winter garden, Tugendhat House, 1930. Illustrated in Daniela Hammer-Tugendhat and Wolf Tegethoff, *Mies van der Rohe: The Tugendhat* (New York: Springer Verlag Wien, 90.) Courtesy Springer Verlag Wien, Vienna.

exterior face. Terence Riley characterized this separation as a veil constituted by an imposed delay in apprehension between viewer and space beyond—a "triggered subjectivity."

In his writings on the recent appearance of Parisian glass architecture, Anthony Vidler made a crucial and instructive distinction between two types of translucency.[6] The first, he said, employs deliberate manipulation of the reflection found on glass or polished surfaces, and represents not a paradigmatic opposite to modernist transparency, but rather its intrinsic other. As an unavoidable physical feature of glass, reflection interrupts the essential function of transparent construction to reveal. Vidler's second definition of translucency is situated in a postmodern, critical mode. Here the building is conceived as an enigmatic volume, luminous in its use of light played against many types of translucent materials. The quest for transparency is abandoned outright; from its inception this type of work embraces that which is entirely impenetrable, entirely illegible, entirely inaccessible. Rather than the intrinsic companion to modernist transparency, its dark twin, this sense of translucency is its "complex critique."

Subjugation of modernist transparency by reflection is illustrated most precisely, as Quetglas, Hayes, and others contended, in Mies's Barcelona Pavilion. The precedent for Vidler's second sense of transparency, at least in its physical description, is much closer to the Grands Projets in Pierre Chareau's Maison de Verre in the sixth arrondissement. Vidler wrote of OMA's Bibliothèque Nationale façade (figure 5.2) as if it were that of the Maison de Verre: "an external surface that is, to all intents and purposes, nothing more than a two-dimensional simulacrum of interior space." Yet, the Maison de Verre never had as its ideological mission either the illegibility of the interior or the rationale disciplining the spatial and constructional order of the house. The emphasis of the house on making evident the craft involved in its production tells us as much; in many ways the house might be understood as a manifesto of construction rather than a negation. If the Barcelona Pavilion is a transparent building rendered translucent by lack of honesty in its construction, the Maison de Verre might be viewed equally as a translucent building rendered transparent by the same means. The ebullient display of construction as a primary motivating factor in its design disqualifies Chareau and Dalbet's house from Vidler's second description of transparency. A self-conscious statement associating the illegibility of constituent orders with material translucency, a calculated subversion of Enlightenment principles, would happen much later, although in very close vicinity to the Maison de Verre, in the contemporary work of Nouvel.

3.2 Mies van der Rohe, German pavilion, Barcelona, Spain, 1928–1929. Photograph courtesy Mies van der Rohe Archive, Museum of Modern Art, New York.

3.3 Pierre Chareau and Bijvoet, Maison de Verre, 1931. (Photo: Franck Eustache) © Archipress.

Vidler noted that his two states of translucency instill similar degrees of anxiety. Both suspend the legacy of Enlightenment reason—supposition of clear knowledge—into either uncertainty and ambiguity or outright disbelief. Of the two, spaces of reflection, according to Vidler, represent the most directly fraught by psychological anxiety, associated with the estrangement proposed by Lacan and Freud as belonging to the domain of the mirror. In its manipulation of the familiar, Vidler suggested that reflection renders the image within it, and any space in its vicinity, inherently uncanny. Implicit in his second state of translucency, however, is an equally disturbing psychological prospect articulated not by Vidler but by literary critic Jean Starobinski in his writings on the concept of the veil in Montaigne's Poppea. He noted that latent in the fascination with the hidden and the obscure is the fatalistic draw of disappointment: "Having responded too impetuously to the veiled seductress, our gaze hurtles beyond the possessable body and is captured in the void and consumed in the night. . . . Her lovers do not die for her; they die for the promises she does not keep."[7] Incumbent on the quest for vaguery are frustration and unrequited desire; complete accessibility is inherently denied as part of its most basic definition.

Given Mitterrand's emphasis in the Grands Projets, denial of the Institut du Monde Arabe and the Fondation Cartier to endorse complete accessibility offers an inherent critique of the concept, adding a complex degree of qualification to the buildings' relationship with the public. Both buildings, predominantly steel and glass constructions, might be characterized as translucent in exactly the two ways set forth by Vidler: the Fondation Cartier thoroughly examines the consequence of reflection; the Institut du Monde Arabe manifests distinctly his description of luminous vaguery. Each different mode of translucency also establishes a particular relationship to the city in terms of its incorporation of the image of the city, but also in the experiential engagement of the city within the spatial episodes of the buildings. These relationships, interweaving the actual and the simulated city, have a tangible effect on the buildings' accessibility in establishing continuous or discontinuous conditions with the urban domain, and therefore the general public.

Although wide visitation of the Fondation Cartier attests to its status as a cultural landmark, it is not a Grand Projet. It is not even a true public institution, as it was conceived and is still owned by the private Cartier jewelry corporation, Cartier Monde S.A. Because of this important fact, I have decided to forego chronology and delay examination of the Institut du Monde Arabe (completed in 1987) until a discussion of the later building, the Fondation Cartier (completed in

1993), evolves an operative set of terms and issues of translucency. In this way, the Institut's definition of translucency might be more fully understood in its completely public venue, with the full brunt of its political encumbrances.

In the very nature of the two buildings' steel frame and glass construction, Nouvel provides an illustration of Vidler's postcritical mode of translucency. Neither the structure, nor the constructional process, nor the programmatic differentiation plays a dominant role in configuring the buildings and their systems. In both structures the traditional association of glass with advanced technology is overturned by the architect's profound indifference to any particularly technical aspect of the skin or glass itself. Nouvel is markedly disdainful of the idealism of modernist revelation, the notion of "form as constructed truth," an approach he says reappeared in the British High-Tech movement of the late 1980s and 1990s.

Instead, Nouvel embraces the technologies of images, especially as they appear in the two-dimensional iconography of late twentieth-century contemporary commercial culture. He elaborates: "In cultural terms, architecture has become petrified, but for me it is essentially a means of producing images and is thus influenced by all other forms of image production, past and contemporaneous. . . . As Peter Cook used to say, nowadays it's more important to look at the packaging of a hamburger than the architecture of the Parthenon."[8] Liberally using analogies of microprocessors, Nouvel says contemporary technological systems, although increasingly sophisticated, are also increasingly compact and simple to use. Although these advanced technologies far exceed relatively sluggish advancements in building construction, they are analogous in one fundamental respect: complete expression of operations and functions is, if not impossible, certainly irrelevant.[9]

Yet the technical machinations involved in the construction of his luminous masses are essential in understanding the motivations as well as execution of his work. In his use of curtain wall construction in the Institut du Monde Arabe, Nouvel made use of the same properties that characterize the Maison de Verre: both buildings are luminous volumes by virtue of a glass plane that floats outside of the buildings proper. The Maison de Verre's glass façade lenses were grouped into four-by-six unit standardized panels framed within a secondary steel system and located well outside the primary steel frame and the intermediate concrete second floor. These panels, manufactured by the legendary St. Gobain Vitrage Company of suburban Courbevoie (as was the glass in both Nouvel buildings), indicate that

3.4 Jean Nouvel, Galeries Lafayette, Berlin, 1991. Espace et stratégie communication. Courtesy
Architectures Jean Nouvel.

façade system is closer to glass curtain wall construction than masonry. This is more than a simple distinction.

As in the Nouvel buildings, the translucent surface of the Chareau façade is monolithic from the first floor up, encasing all interior spaces and structural divisions, providing little distinguishing articulation. Representing the particular ability of a curtain wall to float outside the systems of the house without incurring loss of integrity of structural representation, the glass exterior walls at both the Maison de Verre and the later Nouvel buildings neither register nor represent the internal order of the buildings' interior on their exterior surfaces.

In the 1920s, Chareau's façade challenged all prevailing philosophies by rendering glass enigmatic. In the 1990s this quality was fitting of an era that long ago discarded authentic representation of a constructional order paramount. Most important, Nouvel takes the particular representational freedom of the curtain wall one step farther. By embedding complex imagery within the curtain wall in both the Institut du Monde Arabe and the Fondation Cartier, he mobilized a relatively conventional building system as the predominant agent for cultural representation. If the last chapter was dedicated to understanding the precedent of the exaggerated frame, this chapter proposes an examination of the curtain wall sheathing of the building in establishing particular cultural resonance of its own.

Materiality itself, says Nouvel, is an all-important facet in the latent meanings of his buildings. "What characterizes changes in architecture," he states, "is its matter."[10] This challenge to "matter" calls into question architecture's traditional desire for permanence and duration. Evocation of fragility, nothingness, illusion, a sense of change, are his proposals for signifiers accurate to a contemporary condition. "If it is loved," says Nouvel with deliberate iconoclasm, "it will last."[11] In an attempt to trigger emotive fascination, material becomes the primary expressive medium in his work, principally the material of glass.

The glass translucent skins in his buildings are read as oscillating boundaries: between material and immaterial, material and concept, and material as mute constructed fact versus incorporated image. Nouvel would have us believe that at the same moment—or even *line*—of dynamic fluctuation in the reading of his surfaces, the autonomy of architecture vacillates as a distinct discipline. Just as his buildings disappear into their context, so does architecture evaporate into the high art of philosophy and the low art of commercial imagery.

THE RELATIONAL SURFACE: THE FONDATION CARTIER

In the Fondation Cartier Nouvel reiterates a theme explored in several previous buildings, composing a series of episodic spaces embodying different degrees and themes of transparency. A regional headquarters for the Cartier, for whom Nouvel previously completed several projects outside of Paris, the building contains offices, meeting spaces, and a substantial amount of underground parking. These spaces, however, are completely subsumed, in the perception of the general public at least, by the presence on the ground floor and basement level of the prominent Fondation Cartier, an experimental arts organization whose temporary exhibition and installation spaces are open to the public.

The building's functional program, however, is far less important in the composition of the building than the intricate layering of space, surface, and reflection confronting its immediate context, the Boulevard Raspail, a tree-lined Haussmann artery in Montparnasse. Mandated by neighborhood organizations to be placed at the exact footprint of the former building, Nouvel's building replaced a traditional French hotel housing the American Center (simultaneously relocated to a new building designed by American architect Frank Gehry in the Bercy area). The neighborhood also mandated provision of a generous garden to retain the same qualities of the landscape surrounding the first building.

Nouvel characterizes his typical approach to site as "hypercontextualization," a radical interpretation of existing conditions that produces a building ordered by observations usually relegated to secondary status. (A first-order contextual condition might be, for example, a typological order or a material similarity to an existing setting.) The Cartier provides an apt example of this hypercontextualization. In more than simple compliance with neighborhood's mandates, Nouvel's first gesture was to design his building as two enormous glass and steel planes set back from but oriented toward the street. These planes extended laterally beyond the interior space, held tenuously in between at the exact spot of the former hotel footprint.

Another large free-standing steel and glass screen is placed in front of the building directly adjacent to the sidewalk. In the space between the free-standing plane and the building, Nouvel plants a stand of trees to complement an existing historically landmarked cypress planted by Chateaubriand. These trees are in conjunction with trees planted along the Boulevard Raspail and those in the garden around the entire building, designed by contemporary artist Lothar Baumgarten.

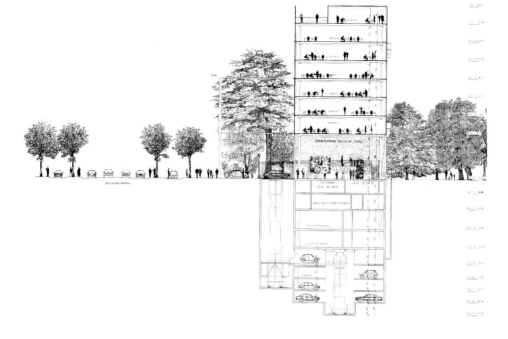

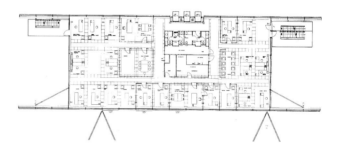

3.5 Jean Nouvel, upper floor plan and section, Fondation Cartier, 1991. Courtesy Architectures Jean Nouvel.

3.6 Fondation Cartier, as seen from Boulevard Raspail.

The effects of the large glass screens are reminiscent of the reflective effects observed in the Barcelona Pavilion. Indeed, Nouvel's primary conception behind the series of enormous glass planes was as a set of parallel reflective planes manipulating the imagery of the Boulevard Raspail, a highly trafficked artery connecting the Place Denfert Rochereau to the Saint Germain area in the sixth arrondissement. By melding the exterior planes and screens of the building with the image of the contemporary city as it is read through and reflected against the glass, Nouvel proposes not a simple reflection but a fractured registration of the actions of the city. He named his use of reflection "environmental design," implying that through reflection he devised a mechanism to reengage the contemporary city actively in its controlled and uncontrolled states: a morphology of static material and moving imagery. This statement decries, with ideological vigor, the inability of conventional static building to convey meaning in a contemporary culture dominated by the production of images.

Whereas the glass screens' placement and scale are the primary vehicles through which the building mirrors and registers urban space, it is the nuance of their configuration and detail that makes their effect profound. Visible behind all the glass surfaces, the screens' structural frames, for example, propel the illusion of reflectivity by generating a visual overlay of different geometric markings. The primary frame is reduced to an abstract grid; that grid is subsequently manipulated against the reflective surfaces of the building. To incorporate the interior structural grid with the reading of the exterior grid, Nouvel chose, at considerable expense, to expose the steel frame throughout the building, deciding to fireproof the columns with an intumescent coating rather than encasing them. The structure of the building is put at the service of desired illusionary effects. This occurs even to the extent of weakening its structural capacity. Nouvel refused to introduce diagonal members to brace the structure laterally because they would intrude into the visual abstraction of the orthogonal grids; however, in 1997 the building was closed when it was noticed that it was deforming considerably in the wind. Diagonal structural bracing members were added shortly thereafter on the ground floor.

Nouvel also employed several other devices in the screens' surfaces to make it difficult to distinguish separate planes of glass, especially when viewed in the oblique light of morning or dusk. At the boulevard, the free-standing screen alternately frames glass and open space. As the trees on the boulevard are reflected in the glass, their reflections are confused with trees actually seen behind the open spaces, and then with those seen through the interior of the building to the garden

3.7 Fondation Cartier, glass façade screens.

beyond. These ambiguities make the natural landscape an integral component in the building's order of illusions against the contemporary city.

The detailing of the screens' surfaces further augments Nouvel's network of misreadings. Registration of the volume of interior space onto its enclosing glass planes occurs, for example, only by the discrete appearance of surface-mounted rolling blinds. All of Nouvel's other details, especially those of mullions in the enclosing planes, increase the confusion between exterior and interior spaces. The mullions of the two exterior building planes, for example, are detailed identically across the façade, whether they actually provide enclosure for interior spaces or whether they are located beyond to the extent of providing unnecessary weather-proofing between exterior spaces (figure 3.7). The interior spaces behind the enclosing glass planes are thus read as only as a slight change in reflectivity and density of light behind the glass; their presence is physically articulated only by the subtle presence of the blinds. [12]

Treatment of the mullions at the free-standing boulevard plane also con-founds its reading against the building interface plane. Nouvel and his associate Didier Brault designed all of the mullions in the different screens with the same vertical and horizontal dimensions, despite differences in their actual construc-tion. At the interface with the building interior, for example, the insulated glass panels are attached to the mullion system with structural silicon, which provides both structural attachment as well as weatherproofing. At the free-standing plane, the single monolithic panes are held by mechanical attachments to the mullion system with joints left completely open (figure 3.8). Nevertheless, the two systems have the same dimensions in elevation; this consistency generates a secondary grid that adds another layer of geometric abstraction to that generated by the primary structure.

The confusion between exterior surfaces is granted its final attenuation by a flush condition of glass to mullion found throughout all of the glass screens. This not only further confuses the two different types of planes (building interface planes vs. free-standing planes) but also increases the reflectivity of all of the sur-faces, providing another layer of ambiguity and possible multiple readings of the surfaces, their reflections, and the spaces in and in front of them.

Nouvel was equally attendant to the effect of details on the interior spaces behind the glass. In bracing the rather unremarkable aluminum curtain wall sys-tem to the concrete floor slabs, he and Brault used vertical stiffeners of transpar-ent glass, normal to the plane of the wall, across the entire interior face of the

3.8 Fondation Cartier, detail of glass façade screens.

3.9 Fondation Cartier. Upper floor office interior. (Photo: Archipress) © Archipress/ADAGP.

enclosing façades. In the office spaces on the upper floors, these glass stiffeners align flush with translucent glass partitions. The glass partitions and exterior curtain walls thus provide a continuous glass wrapper around each office space. At the transparent stiffeners, a continuous slot of space is created just behind the façade; when standing in the offices at the exterior glass, one has a few centimeters to look across the breadth of the entire building. This gesture detaches the exterior glass plane from the interior spaces, heightening the two-dimensionality of the façade as it is read from both inside and outside the building.

The particular details not only reinforce but also generate the sense of the building's dissipation into its context. If Nouvel's mission for the Cartier was that it vanish in favor of heightened awareness of the surroundings of the boulevard and the city, this would be accomplished only by the excruciatingly exact nuance of its outermost skin. In the surfaces at the Cartier, a precise paradox is proposed: a material construction engendered by a desire to read actions and events ostensibly outside of its own physical boundaries, whose success would be measured by the effects produced by its very specific configuration. By the precision of its material orders, the fixed object is elevated to generate zones of occurrence outside its finite boundaries. Rather than the programmatic inscription of event embraced by Bernard Tschumi, Rem Koolhaas, and others, in the Fondation Cartier Nouvel insisted that material, or matter, might be called upon to record the city as filmic experience. Material thus enfolds and subsumes the incorporation of event.

Matter is not generated from a set of internal principles; that is, structural logic or constructional integrity, marking a critical distinction from the modernist technological rhetoric exemplified by Mies. Rather, the material definition of the project embodies the conceptual demands of the larger project first, while answering to practicalities fluidly within the design process. This is consistent with much of Nouvel's thinking: as the metaphor of advanced technology is wedded to complexities of modern industrialized construction, material and structural systems neither warrant nor demand internally construed systems of authentification.

As Nouvel's conception for the Fondation Cartier invokes reflection as the primary motivation of the building, his version of translucency makes hyperbole of Miesian precedent, exaggerating Quetglas's reading of the Barcelona Pavilion's "evacuated interior" and joining it to the urban registration found in Mies's glass skyscraper project. The Cartier, however, lacks all of the Barcelona Pavilion's classical suggestion. Rather than an abstract idealization, Nouvel's conception is that of a vibrant collage of material, subject, and urban surround that quintessentially embraces timeliness. It is quite clear from the architect's writings that he poses the dynamic dimension of the Fondation Cartier as an unsettling of the traditional notion of the architectural object as a static and stable entity: "A building has no meaning and cannot be read except through movement, through a series of carefully pre-established sequences."[13]

However iconoclastic this concept might seem, it might also be interpreted as representing nothing more than a summoning of Baroque ideas of mobility, metamorphosis, and active theatricality as they were instigated against the Renaissance ideals of Platonic harmony and immutability. The Baroque period was, of course, also renowned for its deployment of mirrors and their distortive effects within architectural spaces, an appetite that found its zenith in Louis XIV's Hall of Mirrors at Versailles. Yet the Fondation Cartier is hardly a mere atavistic restatement of Baroque architectural principles. The primary operation of the screens is not to *represent* motion at a frozen moment, as in the plastic relief of a Baroque wall or a half-emergent Baroque sculpture, but to *effect* a literal, cinematic capture of surrounding events.

By reducing his building to a vaporous coating of images gliding over the thinnest possible layer of material, Nouvel provides a physical rendition of concepts of surface and event found again most explicitly in Deleuze's writings on surface: "Yet, what is more intimate or essential to bodies than events such as growing, becoming smaller, or being cut? What do the Stoics mean when they contrast the thickness of bodies with these incorporeal events which would only play on a surface, like a mist over the prairie (even less than a mist, since a mist is after all a body)?"[14] Here surface evolved as an arena of constant and radical shift in scale and event, less material than a line in time and space where the incorporeal assumed substance, a boundary in a pure state of becoming. For Nouvel, Deleuze's mist is an exact conceptualization of the capacity of the building's surface to be rendered relational.

The Cartier's affiliation with the Baroque, however, might very well still be drawn. By pulling the screens well outside the containment of the building, the building essentially becomes an enormous mirroring device, recalling the catoptric devices, *cabinets de glace* and *cabinets lambrissés,* that so compelled the seventeenth-century French aristocracy. Sabine Melchior-Bonnet noted that the stature of patrician residences of this era was enhanced by the presence of enormous mirrors. These gathering halls functioned as social mechanisms, providing dazzling, light-filled panoramas of the social world, a "spectacle of life," where manners cultivated outside the public eye were artlessly displayed as "natural grace."[15] In the halls of Louis XIV, such spectacles of light and clarity were accompanied by "fearsome visibility," eradicating the potential for keeping secrets from the king—or from each other. Of note, Melchior-Bonnet also called such mirrored surfaces relational.

Nouvel's mirrored surfaces similarly constitute theatrical arenas, but their placement in contemporary social spaces raises issues drawn most closely from recent spheres of public art. However repeatedly Nouvel makes reference to American minimalist artists Carl Andre and Donald Judd as influences in his work, his conjuring of the explicitly theatrical dimensions of the mirror in open spaces suggests that he is more closely affiliated with the environmental conceptualist Dan Graham, to whom it is instructive to draw a parallel. Graham's work of the last twenty years shares many similarities with the Cartier: by positioning reflective glass constructions in settings both inside and outside the confines of the museum, Graham questions the particular setting as well as codified relationships among artist, viewer, and art object. In much of his work, simple three-dimensional geometric structures, built of all degrees of transparent and reflective glass, are placed as pavilions in open landscapes or urban situations. As one approaches, there is typically an overlay of the reflected image of the viewer against the surrounding condition as well against other viewers close by. Because of the different types of glass registering against different geometric configurations, the overlay is often complexly orchestrated to multiply and distort the position of the viewer and the viewed against an unfolding space of reflected landscape.

Graham's Alteration of a Suburban House of 1978 (unbuilt) is an explicit testament that these distorted relationships are intended to question not simply the physical composition of the setting but also the latent social institutions present within them. The artist offers a typical suburban American house that has had its exterior wall replaced by a transparent plane of glass. Halfway into the depth of the house, he positions a mirror slicing through the interior. Approaching the house, the viewer's image is trapped within the space of the conventional house as well as its surroundings, a street of conventional, repetitive suburban ranch houses. The viewer's individual identity is thus juxtaposed against a radically disturbed sense of suburban normalcy, which Graham offers as a commentary on the homogenization of the American landscape rendered by commercially motivated real estate ventures.

Such a specific critical posture in the Fondation Cartier does not exist; the projection of the city's fabric across the breadth of the façade is rather more like that of a Baroque mirror, a guileless display of the city in motion. The consequences of Nouvel's imposition of reflected surfaces in an urban domain, however, are quite similar to Graham's: relationships between visiting subjects and the reflection of the urban domain behind them are distorted; the disjunction provokes the visitor to question the original context. Vidler observed that the appearance of translucency is coincident to that of the urban theater, and the intrigues of that theatre are predominantly psychoanalytical. Drawing an analogy to a central Lacanian concept—that the formation of the social "I" at the onset of the infant's language is exactly coincident to its recognition, in the mirror, of its own body as intact and coherent—Vidler wrote, "Here [on Koolhaas's library] two-dimensional physiognomy, the representation of the 'face,' is transformed into the three-dimensional space of subjectivity, place for the staging of social activity. That is the plane of the mirror becomes the space of a theater. . . ."[16] The Cartier realizes this theatrical prophesy more precisely than the Koolhaas project would have, since it uses the concept of reflective mirroring of glass rather than luminous translucency. Yet the problematic implications of this theatrical space revolve around the mechanisms latent in the mirror itself.

If Nouvel's building indeed generates creation of a theater in the city, we might imagine the subject(s)—citizens of the city—partaking of the city as dramatic performance, but one to be viewed only from a distance. For as these same subjects approach the building, they also approach their own image. The moment of confronting their self-image would be simultaneous to the confrontation with the image of the city behind, invoking the Narcissian impossibility of attaining access to either one. Hypothetically, the subject vanishes into the anonymous space of the represented city. Urban space is rendered the uncanny space of the mirror— the space of Carroll's Alice and Cocteau's Orpheus—a space perversely different and disjunctive to that of normative existence. However poised the reflective building is to represent the city in its dynamic complexity, it ultimately results in rendering urban space inaccessible. The subject is left outside of either a personal or a collective realm, wrought with eternal frustration. The potential of the mirror to compel approach, to tantalize the subject ever closer yet to self-destruct at the very moment of final engagement, mandates that distance—literal and metaphorical—always be maintained to keep the fantasy of the city alive.

3.10 Fondation Cartier, ground floor gallery space.

3.11 Fondation Cartier, detail of glass façade screens and ground.

This hypothetical implosion between the city, its subjects, and its representation does not actually occur in the specific configuration of the building. An unexpected release occurs at the ground floor entry, the exact moment at which the intimate reflection of the individual would seem to confront the public reflection of the city. Rather than being dominated by reflected image, the space is overwhelmed instead by the presence of the garden. In a significant display of the detail's discursive power, it is through the nuance of the material manifestation that the dramatic inversion of the event of the mirror occurs.

To complement the interweaving of exterior space in between the freestanding screens and flanks of the building, Nouvel designed the enormous screens to descend directly into the wildflowers of Baumgarten's landscape without distinguishing any of the elements that meet the ground (figure 3.11). In contrast to the other glass on the rest of the exterior screens, Nouvel omitted the low-emissivity coating in the glass above, optimizing its transparency and diminishing its reflectivity.[17] He made these panes fully operable; all around the ground floor space (the exhibition gallery,) twenty-two-foot-high glass sliding panels are provided to open the space completely to the garden in temperate weather (figure 3.12).

Finally, and most important, there is profound relaxation in the degree of finish of all surfaces and material intersections at the ground floor. Here the Fondation's programmatic requirement for flexibility of its temporary installations gave Nouvel leave to radically alter the sensibility of the building's materials, which he did in accordance with the proximity of the ground floor space to the garden. The concrete floors at ground level are left unfinished, with a simple protective coating, in contrast to the stainless steel and plush carpeting of the typical offices above. A galvanized metal threshold grate matching the gray of the concrete floor is provided under the operable door. Detailed to be flush with the concrete floor and the gravel surface outside, this threshold provides minimal interruption to the flow of surface, space, and material between interior and exterior. At the dropped ceiling, the grid for the acoustical tile system is unfilled, leaving light systems and rough construction fully exposed; again in high contrast to the highly finished offices on the upper floors. When the doors are opened, the joint at the head reveals the concrete beam and the rough insulation just under the polished glass spandrel panels.

As the levels of finish relax, the haptic and spatial systems of the interior become seamless with the garden outside. The effect is profound: if on approaching

3.12 Fondation Cartier, ground floor gallery sliding door.

the mirror the image of the city is rendered inaccessible and frustrating, on entering the interior of the building the subject is resituated and resuscitated by the dis-
covery of the garden. Nouvel repositioned the garden as the simultaneous *other* to
the city; as for Carroll, the garden is the fantasy on the opposite side of the mirror's surface.

Nouvel's command of material and space at this particular moment was
tinged with a certain irony. Although the spatiality of the garden is substantial, the
Cartier corporate offices hover overhead. Inaccessible to the public and heavily
guarded by layers of security, the main body of the building remains silent, even
sinister, cloaked in sheaves of translucency above. Inside the intimately dimen-
sioned offices and circulation corridors is a decidedly oppressive maze of reflection
and light effects. Here, the darker side of transparency emerges, particularly its
potential to encourage imposed control. It is rumored that all the workers' personal artifacts must subscribe to aesthetic guidelines, since they are often fully visible from the exterior.

Happily for the building's occupants, its visitors, and the city at large, Cartier
Monde S.A. is a largely more benevolent than ominous corporate organization.
Acquired in the early 1980s by magnate Johann Rupert, it is one part of a consor-
tium of so-called glamour goods—Dunhill, Piaget, Baume and Mercier, and the
like. Rupert's leadership seems to have allowed independent and creative thinking
from within, retaining the legacy of Cartier to continue as an artistic as well as
commercial endeavor.[18] The presence of the Fondation provides Paris with a
much-needed and invigorated venue for contemporary art.

The only negative connotation of the institution was in association with the
Fondation's director, Alain-Dominique Perrin, *enfant terrible du luxe.* It was he
who insisted on commissioning Nouvel as an experimental French architect; however, in several articles from the popular press, the wealthy director was derided as
introducing American concepts of marketing to French gallery culture, at odds
particularly with local artists' groups in Montparnasse.[19] The association with
dreaded American consumerism is multilayered. Perrin's personal collection is
reported as predominantly filled with American contemporary art, particularly
Basquiat and Warhol; that the site itself was a former American bastion cannot
seem to be shaken from public memory. Nevertheless, given the attendance and
favorable press coverage of cultural events at the Cartier, these qualifications are
minor; the Fondation, both architecturally and institutionally, is largely heralded
as a brilliant success.

3.13 Fondation Cartier, exterior, looking up.

As Nouvel's office corroborated, Cartier Monde and Perrin proved an "ideal client," allowing the architect much independent artistic license.[20] Yet, this statement indicates the final dilemma in evaluating the issues of urban translucency instituted by the Fondation Cartier, especially when compared with expansive notions of public accessibility posed by the Grands Projets. However publicly oriented its many programs and architectural devices, the building remains a private institution, representing a relatively simple relationship among client, institution, public, and architect. As such, its aspiration to reflect the city, to vanish into a representation of the city—indeed to *become* the city—can never be adequately fulfilled.

CULTURAL INTERFACE: THE INSTITUT DU MONDE ARABE

A far more complex cultural and politically charged condition is found in Nouvel's Institut du Monde Arabe (IMA). Conceived in 1974 as a central mission in the formation of a league of twenty Arab countries in the same year, the building was to be an educational institute, with its mission "to develop and deepen in France the study, the familiarity, and the comprehension of the Arab world, its language, and its culture." The league of Arab nations and the French government jointly funded the building. This odd circumstance is reflected in the Institut's purpose, which was neither to glorify the French state nor to be a French institution. Its motivation was to represent a foreign culture in both its traditional and transformed states in a modern Western European context.

In the 1970s, this agenda represented an attempt to open a culture perceived and resented by the West as hermetic and even somewhat sinister. This antipathy was no doubt prompted in Western Europe and the Americas by the energy crises contrived by OPEC (Organization of Petroleum-Exporting Countries), whose members included many of the founding countries of the IMA. Paris was ambivalent toward this representation of Arabic culture from the outset. The original site, a thirteen-square-kilometer parcel on the Boulevard Grenelle in the fifteenth arrondissement long promised for this purpose, was blocked by the city for a variety of reasons, most of which seemed generated deliberately to stall the project. The choice of a new site and the project's funding by the French government remained in a quagmire until the election of Mitterrand as president in 1981.

Mitterrand's involvement with Arab culture reflected the checkered past of French relations with northern Africa. In the early 1950s, Mitterrand had been a strong advocate for maintaining France's African colonies, primarily to counter the loss of French power and prestige after World War II, which had seen the country's prominence slip decidedly below that of the United States and the Soviet Union. This was in conflict with the prevailing international trend for most imperialistic powers to begin to decolonize. During this time, Mitterrand even proposed a role for himself as the head of a single large ministry with sole jurisdiction over all the African colonies, a proposal that was rejected by then French president Mendès France. Characteristically paternalistic, Mitterrand's intentions were based on a concept of degreed interdependence, which although allowing various forms of independent governance in the different countries, exported French education and cultural forms in a markedly imperialistic manner. After France's concession of independence to Tunisia and its sub-Saharan African colonies—a blow to Mitterrand—his idealized vision for a Franco-African entity was centered on Algeria, which turned into a political debacle during the brutal war for Algerian independence in the late 1950s. When de Gaulle granted Algeria independence in 1962, Mitterrand's long-held vision for a cultural synthesis with Africa seemed lost; that is, until the symbolic reunion proposed by the IMA. For Mitterrand, the melding of the two cultures was a life-long personal pursuit.[21] For France, the official representation of Arab culture in its capital was to assuage the negative undertones of its past sociopolitical experience, a tangled set of relationships manifested in the present day by continuing ethnic hostility toward immigrants from former colonies.

The Institut's board was finally given a choice of new sites and decided on the prominent location across from Notre Dame at the heavily trafficked intersection between Pont de Sully, Quais de la Tournelle and Saint Bernard, Boulevard Saint Germain, and Rue des Fossés Saint-Bernard. Adding to this complexity, the site was cornered between university buildings of the vast Jussieu campus. The commission for the building was decided by competition in 1981. The final list of functions and spaces in the completed building remained fairly consistent with the program for the competition: a 2.5-million-square-meter library, a 4-million-square-meter museum of art and culture with extra temporary exhibition space, and 1.5-million-square-meters of offices, meeting rooms, and general administration. In addition it had several other elements—an auditorium, a cafeteria, a lobby, museum stores, and 3.75 million square meters of underground parking.

Six prominent French architects were invited to participate in the competition: Henri Ciriani, Edith Girard, Christian de Portzamparc, Yves Lion, Roland

3.14 Jean Nouvel, Institut du Monde Arabe, 1987.

Castro, Gilles Perraudin, and Nouvel. Their final entries differed primarily in the disposition of elements of building mass and open space to the corner intersection. Entries by Ciriani, Girard, and Portzamparc placed an open entry court at the curving corner and pushed the building against the rear edges of the site. In contrast, Lion, Castro, and Perraudin placed solid building masses to flank the street corner, providing internal open space within. Nouvel's winning entry was distinguished by lining the quai edge with a building mass of the same depth as the adjacent Faculté des Humanités, thereby "rationalizing" the existing line of university building flanking the quai. This mass was oriented toward neither the Seine nor the intersection of the streets, but south to a large open plaza facing the Faculté des Sciences, a building long pilloried as a vestige of unchecked modernist impulses. One long slot of space laterally bisected the mass, providing a secondary entry for staff and important visitors, but most important, serving as a point of cultural orientation, the slot originated in Nouvel's interpretation of a closed Arabic court and terminated in a view to Notre Dame.

Nouvel's distinctive massing strategy was matched by a conceptual intention without parallel in the other competitors' entries. Interviews with Nouvel at the time of the competition quote his primary concept for the building as a "screen," a diaphanous, mutable boundary. This idea of screen was doubly loaded: metaphorically, a flexible boundary between the expression of Arabic space within a modern Western setting; and urbanistically, the boundary condition presented by the site's position between coherent nineteenth-century fabric to the north and west and the ragged composition of modernist university buildings to the south and east.[22] This seminal concept of screen was related to that of the Fondation Cartier: in both buildings Nouvel's conception was intrinsically technological, having less to do with the limits of volume than the means of transmission, an interface. In the IMA, however, unlike at the Cartier, this concept was conflicted due to Nouvel's desire to simulate Arabic space: *Notre projet devrait avoir une grande intériorité.* The model for this translucency returned not to Mies van der Rohe, but to Pierre Chareau; not to a reflective translucency of exteriority, but to the luminous, exotic interior translucency based on romantic postcolonial constructs.

The first impression of the completed building emphasizes this distinction. In contrast to the Cartier, the building is perceived as volumetric masses as well as suspended planes. By stretching the horizontal proportions of the glass and mullion systems across each enormous façade and changing the composition of the

3.15 Institut du Monde Arabe, southern moucharabieh façade.

details at each face, Nouvel reduced the building to a collection of huge, distinct planes delicately negotiated at each corner condition. As these planes join together they form masses with opacity at once definite and tenuous, what Nouvel described as a "fabulous solidity" that gives little suggestion of the contained interior. The absence of the primary structural frame is significant on all of the curtain-walled façades—another point of distinction from the Cartier and another intrinsic parallel to the Maison de Verre. Nouvel employed a grid ubiquitously to clothe and abstract the IMA building, and it is composed of the interplay between the mullion and the face of the glass. The hidden primary structural frame, buried within the body of the building, is rendered less an ordering principle than a prosaic necessity.

These relationships were more than a manipulation of glass and its volumetric properties; they also provided Nouvel with instruments to realize his building's original conceptualization. Nouvel used the curtain wall as the primary element in which to embed iconographic and phenomenal references, serving both to interpret Arabic space and negotiate complex site conditions. On the south face, the mobile sunshading diaphragms, an interpretation of Arabic *moucharabiehs,* illustrate the architect's operation of linking the Arab to the Western world, the historical to the modern, and the utilitarian to the representational.[23] As in the Cartier, the mullion system on this face is based on conventional metal and glass glazing, but customized to form thick double panels to house the mechanical diaphragms within: technological gadgetry in a vitrine.

By minimizing the presence of the mullions and burying the diaphragms behind a flush, insulated glass exterior plane, the flank of the building gains formidable massivity through the scale and number of modular repetitions veiled under the glass, especially when viewed from the plaza facing the Faculté des Sciences. More significant, this detail also cloaks a direct view of the diaphragms behind the planarity and reflections of the sheer glass plane, a gesture revealing Nouvel's subtle choreography in the apprehension of various elements. By delaying the complete revelation of the diaphragms' technological nature—their Western attribute—the first impressions of the surface are dominated by the reflectivity of glass and the intensity of patterning and geometric articulation, a reference to traditional Arabic decoration. The technological character is always more than present, however, tantalizing the curious visitor to understand its mechanical gadgetry.

Through the complexity of this reading, a collapse of two distinct iconographic references, Nouvel suggested an oscillation between the representation of

3.16 Institut du Monde Arabe, looking up, southern façade.

the two cultures, an interpretive technique he repeated throughout the building. In his article "(De)Forming Self and Other: Toward an Ethic of Distance," John Biln asserted that the constant reverberations between the two cultural interpretations initiate an inquiry into cultural self-identity that is the basis for the building's profoundly ethical dimension, despite the inevitable dominance of a Western reading by virtue of the Institut's setting.[24] If the event of the Cartier is understood as evaporation of the building in favor of a representation of the city, the event of the IMA is creation of a third cultural condition, formed by the continuous and often volatile juxtaposition of Arabic and Western cultures through different devices throughout the building.

Canonical modernism presented the constructional module as the final manifestation of universalism and objectivity. By sheltering the moucharabiehs in the building's highly regulated, repetitive modular system, Nouvel iconoclastically embedded a cultural referent in modernism's sacred precinct, putting to rest any presumptions of objectivity. The other façades, especially the north one facing the Seine, evolve additional relationships between constructional and iconographic systems. Nouvel provided a seemingly deliberate series of essays around the building's faces, both in the possibilities of highly particularized curtain wall construction and the potential of these assemblies to challenge normative representational modes.

In contrast to the south façade, for example, mullions on the north façade—all horizontal—protrude substantially from the exterior glass surface (figure 3.17). A system of small steel horizontal braces behind the façade transfers both gravitational dead loads and horizontal live loads to the primary concrete columns, eliminating the need for vertical curtain wall framing (figure 3.19). To emphasize the horizontality and scale of this river façade, Nouvel designed it to have digitized images of the city laminated as a layer of silk-screened enameled ink within the insulated glass panes. In the interior spaces beyond, it is impossible to elude the image of the city (figures 3.18 and 3.23). This device has particularly significance in the gallery spaces, where the image of modern Paris infiltrates directly into the reading of traditional Arabic cultural artifacts.[25]

Within the building's laterally bisecting "slot," two more curtain wall systems are encountered, both variants of systems found on respectively opposing prominent façades. The southern flank of the slot repeats the same glazed aluminum system as the southern plaza façade, yet without mechanical diaphragms. The twinning of these systems is revealed at the western façade, where Nouvel pulled

3.17 Institut du Monde Arabe, looking up, northern Quai Saint Bernard façade.

3.18 Institut du Monde Arabe, museum interior (behind northern façade).

3.19 Institut du Monde Arabe, detail inside northern façade.

all support systems for the glazing outside the exterior enclosure: the columnar structure, the lateral framing, and the two parallel curtain wall systems, which have edges that protrude beyond the columns (figure 3.21).

The western façade, in contrast, is deliberately transparent, even didactic; Nouvel revealed not only the structure but the fact that only a thin layer of glass constitutes the building's "massivity". Similar are the two curtain wall systems cladding the northern element (facing the Seine), which meet at an exaggerated angular point (figure 3.20). The thinness of all the façades is revealed at the joints between them, as if to proclaim their insubstantiality as material constructions, enormous screens made as light and thin as possible in the purer service of transmitting images.

Inside, the building's spatial whole is episodically apportioned into various programmatic components. Sectionally interwoven in the southern mass is the library, a portion of museum spaces, administrative offices, entrance lobby, and other ancillary functions—museum stores, and café on the top floor. None of these functions, each of different dimension and spatial character, is articulated on the monolithic façades. By veiling the building's primary structure Nouvel proceeded with blatant indifference to the heterogeneous condition within, another gesture dismissive of functional transparency, and another iconoclastic stab at modernist legacy.

In the spaces behind the southern façade, the subtlety of the mechanical presence on the exterior is completely reversed. The interiors are overwhelmed by the technological presence of highly wrought moucharabiehs in the strong southern light. The exaggeration of technological gadgetry continues throughout the interior. It becomes uncomfortably omnipresent, particularly in the lobby and vertical circulation shaft at the center of the building, as the mechanical workings of the transparent elevator shafts meld into the background of the solar diaphragm wall. This effect is augmented by interior surfaces—highly polished floors, glass walls, and striated ceilings—that reflect and refract the patterns of light and shadow cast by the diaphragm units. Nouvel's treatment of the surfaces bounding his interior spaces do not suggest the placid containment of Arabic interiors, where boundaries always remain coherent. Rather, these boundaries are characterized by shifts and dissolution, resulting in a disorienting effect similar to descriptions of Taut's original Glass Pavilion, "with a glass surface to his right, left, and underfoot, overhead, the novice visitor advanced blindly, without direction, among translucent, illuminated, and dematerialized effects."[26]

3.20 Institut du Monde Arabe, looking up, at building slot.

138

3.21 Institut du Monde Arabe, detail behind moucharabieh façade.

3.22 Institut du Monde Arabe, interior, at elevator hall.

3.23 Institut du Monde Arabe, museum interior.

As in the Cartier, however, Nouvel provided a moment of exact psychological release, here not from entrapment of the mirror, but from disorientation of refracted surfaces, reflected light, and omnipresent geometric technological imagery. At the top floor, the visitor exits from the elevator and crosses a bridge above the slot, traveling adjacent to the Arabic court, the patio. The four interior walls of the square courtyard are lined with an open screen of small, thin, square alabaster tiles. In contrast to the majority of the building's components, which are complex assemblages of machinelike customized members, here Nouvel reverted entirely to a simply crafted system of insubstantial metal clip connections (figure 3.25).

As in the Fondation Cartier, the presence of simple material and simple craft is humanizing. The placidity of the court relieves the tension of a path otherwise unrelenting in its vertiginous disorientation. The pivotal role of the court in the building's sequence of psychological engagements is denoted by its location along the path of travel in the building, but Nouvel also made particularly evident the contribution of materials and details: "The patio, protected from view, around which one turns and at which point one is *lightened* upon crossing the inner surface of very fine opalescent marble, is the key to the organization of the entire building" (my emphasis).[27]

This statement makes evident that Nouvel was acutely aware of psychological effects wrought by all of his spaces and indeed choreographed them deliberately, risking the claustrophobia of the hermetic interior of the spaces below in order to provide release at the top floor. And the space does indeed open at this point, dramatically to the expansive roof terrace above, and then, perhaps most important of all, to the view of Paris beyond. As a therapeutic gesture, the visitor is resituated in the context of the city.

And since the path is truly a public space (all of these spaces are accessible without admission charge), this conciliatory gesture is significant. The roof terrace serves as a *point-de-rendez-vous* for anyone in the city, whether associated with the cultural foundation below or not. The building repositions the subject within the city, while at the same time the city (as in the Cartier) is also represented. As hinted at by the silk-screened images on its northern façade, through its experiential structure the IMA multiplies and overlays the image of Paris into the building, deploying fragments of views to provoke visitors to reconstruct the iconography of Paris for themselves.

3.24 Institut du Monde Arabe, courtyard detail.

3.25 Institut du Monde Arabe, courtyard detail.

3.26 Institut du Monde Arabe, terrace, looking west toward Notre Dame.

Both of these projects use the city as a final frame of reference. They alternatively represent or qualify the city, and by so doing, reposition the subject within its domain. The two buildings constitute filters, which to different degrees and through different devices make the city legible. In the IMA, as the visitor exits onto the terrace, the building's position within the network of axial relationships, and its correspondence to other monuments lifted above Paris' five-story datum, is made fully evident. In the Cartier, it is the ubiquitous vernacular city, consisting of fabric, traffic, pedestrians, trees, and sky, that is both reflected and reflected upon. Thus both buildings further develop different aspects of the Haussmannian precedent. Rising above the city fray along a major arterial intersection, the IMA is poised as a conventional monument within the landscape of Paris ancien refigured by Haussmann. Operating within the instability of its central metaphor—a screen—however, its separation and distinction from the city fabric oscillate tenuously. As discussed in chapter 1, the Fondation Cartier exaggerates this condition, reinstating emphatically Haussmann's transformation of the monument from the static object into the dynamic vernacular fabric flanking the boulevard.

At pivotal locations in both buildings, the effects of material surfaces provoke the dramatic sense of event. At IMA's court, the choice and detailing of alabaster tiles give the patio its profound placidity at exactly the moment that the city is encountered. At the Cartier, it is relaxation of the level of finish that reunites the garden to the concept of the mirrored surface. Nouvel's command of manipulation of surface is evidenced in much of his work, which is characterized by consistent experimentations in the effect of different material surfaces. In Hôtel Saint-James in Bordeaux, he cloaked entirely a set of vernacular buildings shapes in core-ten steel grating: walls, roofs, and windows.

In very recent work, Nouvel continued his experimentations in translucent glass, from glass masonry in the Maison Cognacq-Jay to skyscraper proposals employing serigraphed images on glass. The architect is arguably at the forefront internationally of raising profound questions about the constitution of translucency. Rather than simply serving to render space or form poetic, however, certainly in the two Paris buildings, his use of material is conceptual in motivation and theatrical in execution. Nouvel distances his work from a heroism based in technological determination and is decidedly postmodern in this respect. He uses material to communicate, to provide a critique of a present, contemporary condition. By instrumentalizing the building's constituent material systems to operate within a conceptual order, his use of glass opens a new dimension of criticality in the history of transparency and translucency.

What remains at issue in the Institut du Monde Arabe, however, is its original mission in disseminating Arabic culture. Certainly its radical interpretations of material and space leave open the question of culture; this strategic open-endedness in reading the two systems of cultural reference grants the building its credibility in accomplishing its original goal of opening Arabic culture to a Western audience. Yet the building has also been roundly criticized at various points in the years since its completion for its inability to succeed in more prosaic functions. These criticisms, found mostly in popular journals, are based primarily on operational shortcomings, and they are relevant when examining if the building has indeed succeeded in its mission to make Arabic culture accessible to the public.[28]

The economic burden imposed by maintaining Nouvel's radical departures from conventional assembly systems was substantial; for this reason, building maintenance has been a key issue in the critiques of the project. Maintenance problems were, however, as much a result of international socioeconomic changes as a factor of the design. In the late 1970s, as the IMA was being conceived, OPEC was hegemonous in establishing and controlling oil prices worldwide, and imposed several severe price increases primarily in retaliation for Western support of the Yom Kippur War of 1973.

By the early 1980s, however, at the beginning of the building's active design phase, international socioeconomic circumstances were changing rapidly. As fuel efficiency measures (developed in response to the energy shortages) gained worldwide popularity, demand for oil decreased substantially. As revenues declined, OPEC members began to increase productivity to counter losses. This proved disastrous in the long-term effect on oil prices, and on the economic health of smaller oil-producing countries in particular.

Commitment from the League of Arab Nations to support maintenance of the IMA decreased proportionately. Areas of the building were left long untended, particularly the bifurcating slot, giving the building an air of abandonment. Many of the glass façades were not regularly cleaned; for a period of time the moucharabiehs were inoperative because of maintenance expense. When Chirac replaced the previous director, Mitterrand appointee Edgard Pisani, with Camille Cabana in 1995, it was hoped that renewed negotiations with Arab diplomats would be successful; this was largely disproved. In a hopeful sign, recently the photoelectric cells, which previously controlled the shuttering mechanisms, were replaced with computerized monitoring systems. At this writing maintenance has markedly improved in general, but perception of the institute suffered because of its earlier lack; it was labeled five years after its opening *éléphant blanc,* or just the "Titanic."[29]

At the core of its financial woes is the ambivalence of the institution's ethnic identity. Although Nouvel may have been successful in mixing two cultural expressions, confusion in the institution's ultimate sponsor is evidenced by unwillingness of both parties to accept financial responsibility. Although the Institut has a French director, and the French government sponsors 60 percent of its financial burdens, its visitors are largely Arabs, predominantly scholars working on Arabic research. The events of the Gulf War attest to the institution's perception in Paris as a symbol for the Arabic world; during the war the building was sometimes evacuated five times per day due to bomb threats.

Economic burdens also encroached on the day-to-day functioning of the institution, providing a tangible effect on programs and special events the Institut is able to support financially. This adverse effect is exacerbated by the continuing fractious relationship among Institut members. In the volatile sociopolitical environment of the Middle East and northern Africa, discord has been frequent and unavoidable, related especially to degrees to which different members embraced intolerant forms of Islamic fundamentalism. Frequently, Iraq and Syria were not included in administrative discussions.

This discord is responsible for hampering the institution from mounting controversial exhibits.[30] Subject matter is thus largely restricted to traditional studies, putting the museum at a disadvantage in attracting general visitors, and resulting in perceptions of the IMA as an introverted institution. Representing only "officially sanctioned" culture in a Western intellectual setting of open discourse marginalizes it relative to the city's other significantly timely attractions.

Although Nouvel can certainly not be held accountable for changing international economic and cultural circumstances, his primary concept of interiorization is questionable in light of them. This is reflected most strongly in problems relating to the original siting of the building. At the awarding of the competition, Nouvel received universal accolades from academic peers for his clever placement of the building's masses along the quai. This cleverness in volumetric disposition, however, did not answer to the building's first conceptual challenge, which demanded an urban oscillation—a screen perhaps—between two cultures equal to that of the materials and spatial systems inside. Although successfully oriented to the city at a monumental scale, the building lacks an equivalent success at the pedestrian scale. Because the main entry is indifferent to the typical Parisian prototype—at the quai edge—and is instead located far from the street across a vacuous plaza, the extra journey does not allow for incidental encounters from ordinary passersby.

This last dilemma belongs to the formal transplantation of a Middle Eastern urban prototype without consideration of its cultural or urban context. Orienting a monument's façade toward a large empty plaza is based on Arabic precedent, but in their native settings these plazas are enmeshed within intense, interwoven networks of urban circulation. The great scale of such Arabic plazas grants spectacular release from the narrow, congested passageways that constitute the basic fabric of the cities.[31] Relocated in Haussmann's Paris, adjacent to the expanse of the Seine and the boulevards, the tension of the Arabic plaza against its surrounding small-scale fabric is lost. The ultimate result is simply a plaza too alienating to inhabit, a distance too awkward to traverse. The building proper is encountered only as a deliberate destination. Displaced out of direct public access, Nouvel's invocation of exotic hermeticism remains buried within the building. Pointedly romantic and questionably fraught with postcolonial issues in its construction of a cultural representation from a distanced (and imperialistic) vantage, this internalized exoticism fails aggressively to challenge the situation of Arabic culture within the larger urban domain of Paris.

France in the late twentieth century was beset by ethnic strife, a cultural crisis fueled particularly by the resentment of factions of conservative native French against Arabic immigrants. In an essay entitled "French and Foreigners," Gérard Noiriel contended that the discord is based both in economic strain as well as a more historically rooted xenophobia. He noted that centuries of centralized rule in France established the strongest ethnic and linguistic unification of its type in central Europe. The events of the Revolution buttressed this myth of origin to the extent that it made it impossible for any foreigner to have a place in the country's collective memory. Despite actual history, which statistically establishes France as the leading immigrant host country in the world, Noiriel concluded that officially represented history typically excludes immigration as intrinsic to the country's identity.[32]

Given the apparent tenacity of the French to uphold their own identity and the internal homogeneity of their culture, resistance to external cultures adds an extra burden to the Institut's mission in this moment of cultural crisis. This is particularly timely under the strain granted by the newly resurrected extreme right, whose popular slogan *La France aux Français!* makes the desire for delineation, for separation, and for exclusionary policy painfully evident. The urgency of this strife demands that the representation of Arabic culture be liberated from its internal didacticism and be literally disseminated into its cultural surround. Rather than the romantic representation of the interiority of Arabic culture, societal demands might have been more effectively answered had Nouvel revisited the central agent of the Cartier's exteriority, rather than creating a statement insistently hermetic in aspiration and motivation. Both the city and the Institut du Monde Arabe might have gained much from the degrees of active interface that literal transparency itself would have imposed within the urban domain.

Had I been invisible and powerful like God, I would also have been good and benevolent. . . . Had I possessed the ring of Gyges [supposed to render the wearer invisible], it would have made me independent of men and made them dependent on me. I have often wondered, in my castles in the air, how I would have used this ring.[1]

—Jean-Jacques Rousseau

But in later years I came to understand that the arresting strangeness, the special beauty of these frescoes derived from the great part played in them by symbolism, and the fact that this was represented not as a symbol (for the thought symbolized was nowhere expressed) but as a reality, actually felt or materially handled, added something more precise and more literal to the meaning of the work, something more concrete and more striking to the lesson it imparted.

—Marcel Proust, *Swann's Way*

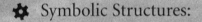 Symbolic Structures:

Details between the Grande and Petite Pyramides

PRESENTING AN UNSTABLE MIXTURE between permanence and ephemerality, rational expression and mystical connotation, spectacle and festival, the Pompidou Center and the Eiffel Tower provide a viable definition of the monument distinct from classical precedent. With the fluidity of their transparent condition, they achieve transcendence from within the everyday and not in distinction to it, dispelling the potentially disempowering effect of their spectacular dimension. Although the question of the everyday continued in the Fondation Cartier's representation of the urban domain, these themes were largely put aside by Nouvel; his two cultural institutions presented deliberately disjunctive relationships between the monument and the urban condition. In the next set of buildings to be examined, it is back to the presumption of a transparent, seamless condition between monument and urban condition to which we return, although on very different terms.

The grouping of projects in this chapter comes from among Mitterrand's most prominent Grands Projets: the Grande and Petite Pyramides du Louvre, designed by I. M. Pei and Partners of New York; the façade at the Cité des Sciences et de l'Industrie at La Villette—the Grandes Serres—by Adrien Fainsilber; and the glass greenhouse structures at the Parc André Citroën by Patrick Berger. Situated in formal, ceremonial relationships in the urban landscapes, typically these buildings are primary crystalline volumes set symmetrically on axes: dignified, nobly inspired, even edifying, they present an intricate array of issues, less those of the spectacle than of the monument, a distinction that calls on an archaic rather than contemporary past.

Built in the decade after the Pompidou Center and two decades after the Revolution of 1968, these buildings signal a return to symbols of authority that the previous era presumed permanently uprooted. Each building is as equally distinguished technologically as the Eiffel Tower and as equally transparent in construction, but the strata of their conceptualization are remarkably different, particularly when compared with the iconoclasm of the Pompidou Center. In reinstituting traditional forms of monumentality, allegiance to state and institution is explicit and unequivocal. Indeed these projects heighten an expression of state, presuming an inert, and even submissive, relationship between the public and its monuments. This is an ironic disjunction between Mitterrand's claims to making elitist institutions accessible and the reifying character chosen to express this intention. In short, this category of transparent buildings signals a retreat into unabashedly classical sensibility. Yet it is in their use of glass, and its associations with absolute transparency, that distinctions to the classical model can be discerned.

Found in formal urban parks, in an enormous system of artificialized nature paralleling the urban order, these projects are also tied to the great Parisian narrative of transformation and rebirth of its landscapes. Both Parc André Citroën and Parc de La Villette are built on land that was reclaimed from industrial uses: the factory for legendary French automobile manufacturer Citroën, and, in the case of the Parc de La Villette, the city's slaughterhouses. This is more than a story of urban reuse; Denis Hollier described the changes at these sites as part of a cyclical ritual purification of deeply rooted places in the city's industrial history.[2] Leisure and science replaced quasi-wasteland, and the general public visits on weekend jaunts without remembering their primordial pasts—"festivals unconscious of sacrificial origins." Even the Musée du Louvre registers such a visceral transformation, since the institution itself, and the public promenade emanating from it, came into modern existence with the beheading of the king.[3]

The buildings discussed in this chapter have another trait in common that profoundly affects their collective presence in the city: each of the architects worked to varying degrees in collaboration with the Irish and British engineering firm of Rice Francis Ritchie (RFR). Certainly RFR's presence is found throughout the Grands Projets; from designing the tensile fabric structure—the *nuage*—under the Grande Arche de La Défense to the steel galeries criss-crossing Bernard Tschumi's Parc de La Villette, RFR's contribution is far more pervasive than that of any of the other Grands Projets architects taken individually. The particular trajectory of the glass projects from the Louvre to the science parks is more specific, however, following mainly the firm's development of glass as a primary structural component. Although glass at the Louvre renovation was not directly involved in this development, the Grande Pyramide, in aspiring to the same sense of idealized transparency, shares common ground, particularly when juxtaposed against its direct progeny, the Petite Pyramide. The glass projects at the science parks and at the Petite Pyramide have identical details in their radically innovative skins, allowing the buildings to emerge across the vast terrain of Paris as closely related events of highly particularized material configurations.

Because of the distinctiveness of details and the question of identity established between them, equally important to understanding RFR's ubiquitous appearance in monumental settings throughout Paris, are their lesser-known works employing the same structural glass, found primarily in commercial settings: the *Grande Nef* (the Great Nave) of the Collines du Nord at La Défense (by Jean-Pierre Buffi); the new entrance to Jean Prouvé's façade at CNIT, also at La Défense; and an atrium space at 50 avenue Montaigne (a collaboration between architects Epstein, Glialman, and Vidal and the American firm of Kohn Pederson Fox). Taken together, RFR buildings in contemporary Paris conflate implications of classical monumentality, material symbolism, nature, and commerce.

In the preface to *Structural Glass,* Rice and Dutton presented a history of glass supporting systems telling of the firm's motivations in approaching not only the design of glass systems, but of its general attitude toward transparency. The use of glass is categorized in different eras and different building types as "one-way" versus "two-way" visibility (between interior and exterior), then a category is created labeled "expressions of surface," a term acknowledging the more recent use of the glazed plane as an entity equal to the framed opening. The text is markedly reductive; for example, Rice and Dutton dismissed light in the Gothic cathedral as "ineffective" because of low quantity of light transmission, ignoring the underlying concept of luminosity in the Middle Ages. Nevertheless, in presenting a concise relationship between glass support systems, the technology of glass production, and the properties of glass, Rice and Dutton made evident the conceptualization guiding RFR's groundbreaking reconfigurations of those relationships. By interpreting the history of glass as a linear sequence of developments in a continuous approach to absolute transparency, RFR proposed that the next logical step in such a sequence would be disappearance of the mullion frame, elevating glass to the primary structural element of the building's skin.

If the second chapter of this book was devoted to unraveling the nature of the primary frame in monumental building, and the third turned its attention to the role of the curtain wall in representing all things cultural, this chapter focuses on the dramatic appropriation of the symbolic function by the material detail. As glazing support systems of the surface gradually disappear with progressive advances in technology, glass makes its debut in determining the expression of the monument in some of the most highly charged settings in contemporary Paris.

MODERNITY, MONUMENTALITY

To appreciate fully the return to a classical monumentality in Paris after the Pompidou Center, it is necessary to revisit the crisis of monumentality in which architecture had been mired since the 1940s. Modern architecture's original complicity with revolutionary political ideologies exiled any desire to be associated with traditional authority, an attitude epitomized in Georges Bataille's writings of the same era: "It is, in fact, obvious that monuments inspire social prudence and often reveal fear. The taking of the Bastille is symbolic this state of things: it is hard to explain this crowd movement other than by the animosity of the people against the monuments that are their real masters."[4]

Late modernism all too keenly recognized the adverse effects of cities rendered without monuments, witnessing the international proliferation of modernist buildings in urban settings. In "Nine Points of Monumentality," a widely read manifesto signed jointly by Sigfried Giedion, Fernand Léger, and Jose Luís Sert, absence of appropriate monumental expression signified dysfunction that was not of the state, but of the collective culture: "Monuments are the expressions of man's highest cultural needs. They have to satisfy the eternal demand of the people for translation of their collective forces into symbols. The most vital monuments are those which express the feelings and thinking of this collective force— the people." In appropriating the monument as an expressive force of the people, modernist polemicists worked to overturn its original function of representing either the state or the divine.

In its quest to reinstitute some sort of monumentality in the city, by the 1940s the architectural establishment became aware of modernism's basic inability to provide the means to do this. Design as a linear fulfillment of functional demands, deeply buried as a central premise in modernist production, was understood even then as having preempted entirely the question of symbolism. Rejection of overt iconographic reference depleted architectural vocabulary of the vehicle to address the domain of content in the public monument. Modernist impoverishment of monumental expression was recognized in the 1940s and was revisited in the late

1970s and early 1980s, serving as a central rhetorical component in the postmodern appropriation of traditional iconographic vocabulary.

In the late 1930s and early 1940s, this dilemma led the architecture of public building in France, as well as other countries, inevitably to regress to a stripped-down form of classicism, typically characterized by abstracted columnar orders and elemental building masses organized symmetrically. It was exemplified in Paris by Auguste Perret's Musée des Travaux Publics and J. C. Dondel's Musée d'Art Moderne at the Trocadero, both completed in 1937.[5] Yet this vocabulary was soon to be burdened, rather dramatically, by the association with Fascist architecture of Italy and Germany. For many years after the collapse of these totalitarian regimes, the expression of monumentality through classical devices was inextricably linked, for the architectural establishment and public alike, to legacies preferably forgotten.[6]

If the Congrès Internationaux d'Architecture Moderne (CIAM) conference in 1952 and a Harvard symposium of 1984 (entitled "Monumentality and the City") can be read as accurate reflections of both eras, both modernists and postmodernists agreed on the fundamental need of democratic societies to develop their own form of monumental expression. According to Giedion, creation of symbols by the people would reveal the conceptions of the current era; monuments constituted artifactual testaments linking different periods of time. Reexamination of monumentality in the late 1940s was provoked not simply by the absence of collective or state expression, but by the need perceived for expression of the sublime in public space. The true monument was regarded as granting a transcendental dimension to the city; an entity separate from the ordinariness of the urban fabric, gracing the city with a contemplative moment. Such an aspiration, however, also underscored the classical origin of the monument as an inspired counterpoint to the vernacular.

After classical vocabulary was discredited as an overt source for any modernist architecture seeking the sublime, few options remained. Scalar exaggeration, one such device open to the modernist monument, had been rendered ineffective in increasingly exaggerated urban skylines.[7] Equally, if the distinction of the modernist monument from the existing fabric was to be accomplished by means of semantic differences, the typical asymmetrical configurations of large abstracted planes and masses of late "functional modernism"—Lescaze and Neutra, for example—were quickly subsumed within cities increasingly made up of vernacular

4.1 Auguste Perret, Musée des Travaux Publics, 1937.

buildings of similar characteristics. Neither scale nor semantic distinction offered viable means by which to confer on modernist monuments a necessary degree of difference to transcend into the sublime.

One last, and timelier, device of the 1940s regarded by modernist critics was the explicit presence of technology. While Giedion's "Nine Points" heralded the use of "modern materials and modern techniques," his advocations for a monumental architecture went beyond constructional means: modern monumentality was to be composed of "mobile elements," of "wind or machinery," of projected artificial light and colors, even of displays of publicity and propaganda. In his essay "The Need for Monumentality," Giedion even claimed that such truly populist spectacles as fireworks or water displays were authentically monumental. The 1948–1949 CIAM conference concurred: if there was to be a modern monumentality, it could be found only in visionary architecture.

Significant examples of technological expressionism used to such ends can be found, particularly in projects such as Tatlin's Monument to the Third International of 1919–1920 and Le Corbusier's Palace of the Soviets of 1931. Giedion, however, admitted only one built work to the pantheon of truly modern monuments: the Eiffel Tower. Certainly, the same manifestation of his list of criteria in the Pompidou Center indicates that it might have been equally distinguished. According to Giedion's definition, the transparent monument, as defined thus far by the Pompidou Center and the Eiffel Tower, is distinctly modern. It is within this polarity of issues between definitions of the transcendent classical versus the visionary modern monument that we must approach later glass projects of Rice Francis Ritchie.

THE GRANDE PYRAMIDE: THE CRYSTALLINE GRAIL

The earliest transparent monument in Paris involving RFR is the façade for the Cité des Sciences et de l'Industrie, completed in 1986, preceding the Grande Pyramide of 1989, the greenhouses at Parc André Citroën of 1993, and the Petite Pyramide du Louvre, also of 1993. The Grande Pyramide du Louvre, however, is unquestionably the most significant building in the city's cultural hierarchy, setting the stage for issues of symbolism and monumentality to be encountered in the other projects. Since RFR was engaged very late in the design process, their actual contribution to the building was limited; the primary structural engineer was actually Nicolet Chartrand Knoll et Associés of Montreal. As such, the authorship for the project resides unchallenged with its architect, I. M. Pei and Partners.

Still using a conventional mullion system for glass support, the structure for the Louvre pyramid is relatively primitive compared with RFR's ultimate technological developments elsewhere in Paris. Yet the Louvre's preeminence within the cultural sphere of Paris opened the way for the use of glass and advanced technology in later prominent public buildings. By explicitly using glass to mark the coming of age of the Louvre into the contemporary moment, Mitterrand and Pei brought glass into a system of symbolism in the country's legacy of material culture.

The Louvre is universally acknowledged in France not simply as the national museum or even the former residence of the king, but as the literal embodiment of the nation's history. Jean-Pierre Babelon, in a critique of the Pei pyramid, noted that the only constant in the Louvre's long history of rebuilding was supersaturation of symbolic content, manifested in ordering and decorative principles throughout the building.[8] Originally built as a fortified castle in 1190 for Phillippe Auguste, through various eras the Louvre gradually became the official royal residence in the growing capital, particularly in the reigns of Charles V in 1365 and François I in 1515. Whereas it functioned as actual dwelling to varying degrees, depending on the caprice of the different monarchs, its most consistent and indelible role was to signify royal presence.

The Louvre became the vehicle through which the king fulfilled his obligations to his subjects to be seen. Its legibility granted palpable form to the monarchy's power, a visual assertion of the king's authority. The presence of the specific monarch was carried through to many decorative embellishments of the building, encrusted throughout with various royal motifs; the east façade sculptures of the Cour Carrée, for example, represent the imperial iconographies of Henri II and Henri IV; the west façade carries the solar symbol for Louis XIV prominently on its entablature.

As the symbol of the king, the Louvre was the focus of considerable upheaval during the Revolution. Yet it was not rendered as superfluous to the nascent democracy as was the monarchy. On the contrary, it was immediately appropriated as a public building during the first stages of the revolt; the act of opening the Louvre to use by the general public signified indelibly the ascent of the new democracy to sovereign governance of the country. Reconstituted as the

4.2 Relief Sculptures, east façade Cour Carrée, the Grand Louvre.

museum for the national collections of art, a national palace for the arts and education, after the Revolution it was institutionalized as the cultural repository of France. Thus it not only overcame the signification of the monarchy, it came and continues to signify all of France. According to Emile Biasini, Mitterrand's minister of public works for the Grands Projets, "The Louvre occupies the subconscious of France."[9]

Equal to its historical significance, the Louvre's termination of the Voie Triomphale reiterated the centrality of its cultural position. At present, the Voie is inscribed as a seemingly infinite line extending westward from the Louvre, through the Arc du Carrousel, down the center of the Tuileries. It proceeds across the focus of the obelisk at the Place de la Concorde to the Avenue des Champs-Elysées, and spirals from there upward through the Arc de Triomphe, culminating as much as a sightline as a thoroughfare down the Avenue Charles de Gaulle through the Arche de La Défense in the misty distance. The wings of the Louvre are infamous for their slight angle off the straight line established by seventeenth-century landscape architect André Le Nôtre; nevertheless, the Louvre renders this geometric impurity insignificant and stands as the climax of the most famous urban axis in the world. All aspects of the building point toward the power of its significance and its powers of signification.

Parties involved in the contemporary renovation, particularly Mitterrand and Pei, understood the circumstances surrounding the Louvre as constituting the most highly charged setting imaginable within which to propose an active change to any building of the ancien régime. According to Emile Biasini, Mitterrand dispensed with the customary competition in the choice of an architect out of unwillingness to put the design at the mercy of the whims of an unpredictable jury. The initial contact between Mitterrand and Pei and months of preliminary research and design were cloaked in absolute secrecy—even from Pei's office—for fear that any amount of publicity would compromise the potential of the project. Even from the beginning of the design process, multiple levels of subterfuge involved in the actual undertaking belied Mitterrand's aspirations for transparency, setting the stage for later accusations of monarchist inclinations.

The fears in fact turned out to be well founded. In a series of highly publicized confrontations among Mitterrand, the French public and press, and various elements of the French government, it became evident that the symbolic mantle of the Louvre would become vulnerable to appropriation by all parties assuming the role of protector of the institution.[10] For the public, intervention of modern architecture into the heart of the old city was painfully reminiscent of earlier fiascos instigated by Pompidou, particularly the hated Tour de Montparnasse and the destruction of the beloved Baltard marketplace at Les Halles.

Academicians also found the sudden imposition of modern architecture within the Louvre complex offensive, not as much for its the contemporary style as for the abrupt departure from the building's diachronic development, an accrual of fragments and layers of architectural styles over the previous 800 years. For other critics as well, the axiality of Pei's placement of the pyramid recalled too closely the defunct style of the Ecole des Beaux Arts, a criticism borne out by Pei's training at MIT. Finally, for the political right the pyramid came to represent the ascent of the socialist left, regarded as "monstrous" by still lingering monarchist sensibilities.[11] The pyramid's architectural challenge to Lefuel's court of Napoleon III was read as an oblique insult to the monarch.[12]

The initial vociferous protest ranged from unanimous rejection by the influential Commission Supérieure des Monuments Historiques to anti-American and blatantly xenophobic personal attacks in the media against Chinese-born Pei. The perceived effect to national identity was particularly slippery. Not only was the contemporary style of the pyramid labeled a sign of "deculturalization" and humiliation of French masters Perrault and Soufflot,[13] so was the shift in the institutional nature of the Louvre from a national museum to a "pseudo-cultural supermarket"—a pandering to the economy of international tourism.[14]

The degree and universality of the clamor underscore the sophistication of the counteroffensive immediately put into place by Mitterrand and Biasini, which was ultimately effective in garnering approval for the project. By mobilizing unanimous support of curators and prominent French cultural figures—composer Pierre Boulez and Claude Pompidou, widow of the conservative former president, key among them—and allaying public fears by building in situ of a full-scale mock-up of the pyramid in steel cables, public opinion began to sway toward support of Pei's design.

For Mitterrand, the eventual victory of the forces behind the renovation was measured by more than physical amelioration of the frayed museum. In the spring of 1986, his political strength wavering and an election looming, he gave orders to speed up construction; if progress on the site proceeded far enough, the project would become irreversible. Mitterrand understood the physical construction of

4.3 The Grande Pyramide to the Voie Triomphale.

the pyramid as one that would "enshrine" his administration.[15] In April of that year, excavation in the Cour Napoléon was complete. In May, Mitterrand's reelection to a second term was secured, indebted in no small measure to the progress of the Louvre. As François Chaslin reported, the president's popularity polls were directly correlated with the public's enthusiasm for the Grands Projets, the Louvre renovation in particular.[16]

This was particularly significant since the election of 1986 was hardly a general victory for the left; the Socialist Party had suffered a devastating defeat in general elections two years before, and the latest election again revealed the country's ambivalence for its leadership. Along with the national emergence of the extreme right party, the Front National, personified by Jean-Marie Le Pen, the election of 1986 promoted Gaullist Jacques Chirac to the post of prime minister, and the country was plunged into an ambiguous two-year period of left-right "cohabitation," in which many of Mitterrand's Socialist initiatives were rolled back. Mitterrand's tenuous hold on the presidency, accomplished by whatever means were available, was significant.[17] As the monarchy had done before him, Mitterrand usurped the identity of the Louvre in an unabashed illustration of political power latent in this most powerful of French architectural symbols.

With the Louvre at its vortex, sociopolitical and historical issues swirling around the project were belied by Pei's dramatically simple concept for the building. Even before the Revolution, occupation of the building had been consistently hybrid. The most recent combination of functions included offices for the national lottery and the Ministry of Finance, rendering circulation through exhibition galleries hopelessly circuitous. The unity and clarity of organization of the entire complex would be finally achieved only by the Pei renovation. By reclaiming all the existing wings of the U-shaped building and taking advantage of the space under the central Cour Napoléon, Pei positioned the pyramid above a vast new underground lobby connecting the different wings.

If reorganization of the building seemed guided by a clever artlessness, the shape of the pyramid too was presented as if arising naturally, without intermediary contrivances, from a set of given circumstances. Pei stated to his French audience that his source of inspiration for pyramidal geometry was the classical geometry of Le Nôtre's garden plans, thus an extension of the Tuileries.[18] More essential to his proposal, however, was the pyramid shape's claim to neutrality. Against the highly charged sculptural façades of the existing Louvre as a pure mathematical form derived from the Great Pyramid of Giza, the pyramid would provide a mute foil. To confirm its unobtrusiveness, Pei also asserted that its geometry would allow for the mass of the building to diminish vertically. By proposing that the pyramid be constructed of glass, he assured his audience that its reduction to neutrality would be absolute.

Despite claims that the geometric derivation of the pyramid was a response to the specific demands of the Louvre, Pei's earlier work confirms a general tendency toward Euclidean geometry as the dominant agent. From the early John F. Kennedy Library in Boston to the more recent Bank of China in Hong Kong, his buildings are consistently distinguished as large polyhedral forms articulated with angular faceting and chamfered surfaces. This motivation is evident even in the details, where prismatic forms are typically synchronized within complex systems of material joinery with their own rigorous geometric order. Abstract geometric systems at the scale of site are layered on the demands of geometry at the scale of the joint. At the Louvre, however, the symmetry of the prominent site mandated that the building not be simply another typically fragmented prism, but a more idealized pyramidal geometry. In his decision to make the legendary shape transparent, issues of geometry in Pei's prisms were pushed into the higher realms of idealization offered by the properties of the crystalline.

In the development of structural and material systems the artlessness in Pei's proposal finally began to give way. As the geometry of crystalline purity began to confront obstacles in the pyramid's actual construction, profoundly important discrepancies emerged between the latent idealization of the Pyramide and everything that seemed to compromise it; discrepancies critical to a larger understanding of the Pyramide's inherent stance on the question of monumentality. At the heart of the issue is the state of autonomy engendered by the abstraction of the pyramid's geometry versus the potential qualifications of all aspects of its embodiment, from systems of construction to experiential dimension and programmatic necessities.

Certainly Pei's first design initiative followed logically from the pyramid's ambitions toward crystalline geometry. Beginning with the largest and clearest possible panels of glass, the diamond geometry represented the most coherent division of the triangular flanks. It is in the constitution of the glass surface itself, however, in which first signs are provided in the gap between the pyramid's ideality and its actuality. After considerable research, St. Gobain Vitrage SA (again instrumental in a Grand Projet's realization) opted to use pure white sand from the quarries of nearby Fontainebleau for the 9.8 by 6.2-foot, double-laminated, diamond-shaped panes.

Building a special furnace to omit the addition of iron oxide typically a part of glass production, St. Gobain obtained a glass product with optical characteristics close to those of lead crystal.[19] At this maximum limit of transparency, the green line was eliminated that would be otherwise visible when the edge of the glass was viewed obliquely at the pyramid's inclined faces. Finally, the glass was transported back and forth to Great Britain, where special facilities polished the surfaces for greatest planarity. These extreme measures to achieve maximum transparency speak not only of the Louvre's preeminence, but also of the appetite of the designers for attaining unprecedented perfection of surface and material.

With such a first impetus toward purity and planarity of surface, every effort was made to minimize the presence of the glazing support systems. Behind the exquisite exterior flush plane, Nicolet Chartrand Knoll conceived the primary structure to provide the largest expanse of unobstructed vision through the panes. This structure, a series of stainless steel bowstring trusses spanning diagonally in two directions across the pyramid's flanks, is placed exactly behind the divisions of the diamond panes, coincident to their geometry. Loads imposed on the glass are transferred directly to the trusses, relieving the mullions of any structural obligation and reducing its dimension to that necessary only to retain the glass units and provide weatherproofing. Since both the bottom and top chords of the trusses intersect at every corner of the diamond geometry, joints were specially designed to accommodate the intersections. In addition, at every intersection of the bottom chords, the joint had to accommodate yet another connection to stainless steel cable tension rings that counteract the outward thrust of pyramidal geometry as well as lateral stresses imposed by the wind.

The contribution of RFR to the project came with the redesign of the bottom chords of the trusses, which were changed from cables to rigid rods for ease of construction.[20] In addition, RFR reconfigured the truss intersection joints as curvilinear nodal elements cast out of stainless steel. Recalling the sculptural plasticity of the Pompidou Center's structural members, the nodes were a reminder that the primary designer in the trio of RFR's membership, Peter Rice, had been responsible for key concepts of the Pompidou while working at Ove

4.4 Grande Pyramide du Louvre, typical panes.

4.5 Grande Pyramide du Louvre, tension rings.

4.6 Grande Pyramide du Louvre, nodal intersections.

4.7 Grande Pyramide du Louvre, flank.

Arup and Partners in London. As at the Eiffel Tower, the design criteria of many of these nodal components included a high factor of adjustability to attain levels of minimal tolerance. While attaching the cabled tension rings to the main bowstring trusses, the nodes were configured to allowed the cable to move freely in response to internal and external changes in pressure. To ensure that the level of exterior glazing finish be (unusually) precise, these same nodes accommodated a screw fitting to hang temporary weights (closely approximating that of the glass) during construction (figure 4.7). The structure was fine-tuned before the expensive glass panels arrived on site; as the panes were installed, the weights were simply unscrewed.

Pei's greatest dissatisfaction with the surface of the pyramid and its intricate assemblage of support was the relatively high level of opacity produced by reflections of the sky on the panes of glass.[21] Despite extreme measures taken to promote its transparency, the geometry of the pyramid imposed an unavoidable condition. Because the determining factor of glass reflectivity is the difference between interior and exterior levels of light, when tilted at an angle, the flanks of the pyramid contrasted the sky, more than the surrounding existing Louvre pavilions, to the lobby interior. Even on overcast days the light of the sky above would be far brighter—the glass would always be highly reflective. Pei's open dismay at the contamination of his crystalline surfaces by reflection is revealing. Inordinate measures taken to heighten the transparency of glass indicated the degree to which he desired to transcend conventional material characteristics. But denial of the natural occurrence of reflection—environmental effects of light on surfaces— indicates a critical discrepancy between the vision for geometric idealization latent in the crystal and its physical manifestation.

This discrepancy is broader in other aspects of the pyramid. By positioning the primary structure to fall precisely behind the edges of the glass panes, the pyramid's transparency worked only when viewed as a frontal elevation. Since the structural systems occupy considerable depth behind the glass surfaces, the purity of the frontal perception is compromised as soon as the viewer departs from distant points along the four symmetrical lines of cardinal vantage emanating from the inclined planes. From any oblique view—which is hypothetically every point of view—the complex hierarchy of component systems dominates perception of the pyramid. This is far from displeasing, as it forms an elegant web of stainless steel components collaged against the textured Louvre pavilions, especially when

4.8 Grande Pyramide du Louvre, structure as collage.

viewed from within. Yet consistent attempts to minimalize and purify all elements of the design to achieve absolute transparency suggest that if it had been possible, the structure itself would have been eliminated.

The long struggle to adapt the pyramid's form to its functional demands finally lays bare the most prominent disparity produced by the ideal of its geometry. As the Louvre's new primary entry, it became necessary to violate one of the pyramid's sides to accommodate passage. Opening the flank structurally was solved by coordinating intervening steel elements into the hierarchical systems of trusses and cables. Under the pyramid at the level of the plaza, a landing had to be provided to allow visitors to descend into the open museum lobby proper below by way of Pei's grand spiral stair and escalator. The landing, configured as a partial corner of the pyramid's geometry in plan, is an awkward intrusion into the pyramidal space. The small area of the landing is also wholly inadequate for the tremendous volume of visitors to the museum each day. (This becomes especially evident in inclement weather when visitors can find no shelter in the Cour Napoléon during their long, bottlenecked wait.) The pyramid's geometric conception is clearly other to its primary function.

As complete as Pei's attention is to the pyramid's geometry, so is indifference to all forms of contingent qualification to its ideal. As environmental reflections, experiential distortions, material limitations, and simple functional demands fall away in importance, the pyramid is revealed as remaining resolutely detached from its worldly situation. All timely considerations dwindle in favor of transcendent geometric perfection. Pei's conception displays a perfect paradox of transparent crystalline construction: theoretically posed as invisible and thus entirely contingent to the view seen beyond, the purity of the geometric abstraction is poised to attain a level of separation from changing or imperfect surroundings.

Thus whereas the pyramid's detractors were outraged by its stylistic modernity, the monument's aspiration was hardly that, at least by the standards of modernity raised by Giedion. Rather, the intentions were to achieve the transcendent sublime of a true classical monument. In superimposing an unrelated order on its site, this form of classicism would not aspire to the precise relationship of the Greek monument to the landscape, but would imply subordination latent in a more imperialistic Roman vein of classicism. Certainly, the proposal early on prompted such critics as Charles Jencks to proclaim the pyramid's harkening to

4.9 Grande Pyramide du Louvre, from reflecting ponds.

the era of Adolf Hitler and Albert Speer; similarly, French critic François Chaslin nicknamed the president "Mitterramsès I."

The dilemma of the Grande Pyramide exists in polarities that have long surrounded the concept of crystal. As historian Joseph Mashek asserted in his discussion of the concept of the crystalline in minimalist sculpture (mentioning Pei specifically), Platonic auspices of the crystal lie in its claims to pure rationality.[22] Whereas the crystal has appeared most prominent in architectural history as a symbol for the "inflexible knowledge" of nature, particularly by Viollet-le-Duc in his superimpositions of diagrams of rhombohedrons of granite crystals, many equivalent dimensions of the crystal are found in blatantly expressionist work. Indeed, a more extended history of the symbology of the crystal, beginning in biblical and medieval periods, provides evidence that it has been used as often, if not more often, for its mystical and even occult evocations.

In her encyclopedic dissertation on the crystal's origin and its use by Paul Scheerbart and Bruno Taut, Rosemarie Bletter traced the architectural use of the crystal in both Jewish and Arabic legends to Solomon's temple.[23] Built entirely of glass floating on a bed of water, the palace was to reveal whether the Queen of Sheba was a woman or a demon by providing a reflection from underneath her skirt. (Hair on her legs was the incriminating sign!) Through this legend, the crystal and its architectural metaphor, the glass palace, assumed the symbolism for Solomon's esoteric wisdom and divine gnosis.

In later history, the symbolism of the crystal remains fundamental to key philosophical and theological concepts of each particular era. In the early thirteenth century, is turned introspective and hermetic. As the precious stone dislodged from God's crown, the crystal assumed the sacred mantle of the Holy Grail: when embedded within an onyx cliff, it emanated a divine light to guide the Knights Templar (Younger Titurel, 1270). This supernatural aspect was made hyperbole by alchemists' transformation of base material into precious stone; the diamond was a symbol of the alchemist's stone, a metaphor for the literal transformation of Christ's body.

For alchemists as well as later Jungian psychologists, the potency of the crystal, and glass by extension, lay in its dynamic polarity between matter and spirit, a "unified opposition" that had the potential to communicate more authentically through mechanisms of paradox rather than rational communication. Bletter contended that to express their fantastic imagery, Scheerbart and Taut used the crystal's historical representation of fluctuation, paradox, and fluidity. For expressionist artists and architects, use of paradoxical form as "irresolute" invited completion of the work by the viewing audience; Bruno Taut's Glass Pavilion was meant, first and foremost, as a chamber to inundate the senses.

The stability of Pei's neoclassical concept of crystalline form at the Grande Pyramide is thus markedly at odds with the alternative crystalline legacy represented by Scheerbart and Taut. Indeed, if any contemporary architects discussed thus far displayed the attributes of the mystical crystal, it would have to be Nouvel, whose concept of glass is similarly underpinned by change and paradox, and whose sense of ambiguous spatial definitions has certain resemblances to those of expressionists Scheerbart and Taut. Nouvel's interior spaces, particularly at the Institut du Monde Arabe, seem closely acquainted with the illusionary light effects described in accounts of Taut's Glass Pavilion. This is hardly coincidental, since Scheerbart, like Nouvel, consciously referred to Arabic literature and architecture in his light-embodied spaces.

Examined through its mystical inheritance, the metaphorical concept of the crystal is, however, most closely congruent with the fluctuation of meaning and symbolic ascription identified as monumental transparency of the Eiffel Tower and the Pompidou Center. As Bletter asserted, dynamic oscillation is at the core of the crystal's symbolic legacy: the final essence of the crystal, accrued through history, is captured most accurately by the radical transformation inherent in the alchemist's stone.[24] Thus both monuments defined thus far as modern—the Pompidou Center and the Eiffel Tower—are essentially, in terms of this argument, crystalline. In contrast, the autonomous classicism of the Grande Pyramide stands in complete distinction, as the symbolic vagueries of the crystal are displaced by the fixity of its elemental and rationalist ascriptions.

If the consequence of the pyramid's classicism is fixed symbolism, the question remains: what is the pyramid symbolic of? Even in the 1940s, assigning monuments the roles of cultural identifiers was fraught with complications. Giedion recognized that lack of cultural consensus undermined the potential for monumental expression: "Monuments are, therefore, possible in periods in which a unifying consciousness and unifying culture exists."[25] Certainly, Pei's intention of the pyramid's neutrality and its benevolence lies primarily in the universality presumed in its elemental geometry.

According to philosopher Ernest Cassirer, the basic pyramid is historically understood not as symbolic, but as *protosymbolic*. Cassirer accorded certain physical symbols the potential to grant spiritual fulfillment across distinct cultural

4.10 Bruno Taut, Glass Pavilion, ceiling.

fields: "... the world of art and myth seem to consist entirely in the particular, sensuously tangible forms that they set before us. Here we have in fact an allembracing medium in which the most diverse cultural forms meet."[26] Hegel expressed similar thoughts. He wrote that pure architecture would transcend meaning and escape any kind of signification: "Symbolic architecture would refer only to itself, would express only itself, would say only what it is."[27] Here we see perhaps the most accurate depiction of the desires motivating both Pei and Mitterrand: to transcend, by virtue of attaining a sublime form, all meaning, all reference, and find purity of elemental expression that would grant a sense of noble placidity to the Louvre, and by extension, to France itself. And yet, as Bataille and others reflected in recent past, it was this very mythical faith represented by the sublime in classical architecture that authorities and dictatorships had traditionally tapped to seduce and enslave a general public.

The technological intonation of the pyramid makes it difficult for the pyramid to silence its cultural context: as we saw in the Eiffel Tower, technological expressionism often comes hand in hand with latent manipulation of the modern spectacle, reifying whatever power structure prevails. Idealized geometry also presents its own dilemmas, stretching from archaic precedent to very recent discourses. Especially important is the pyramid's affinity with minimalist art of the 1960s, with which it shares a faith in geometry as a device for evacuating meaning. Exactly in the same spirit of the Louvre pyramid, the precise rendering of unqualified grids of Sol Lewitt (who worked for Pei as a graphic artist from 1955 to 1956) accorded geometry the guarantor of zero-order neutrality, the final termination in the historical process toward abstraction and away from representational reference. But as artist Peter Halley said even then: "The crisis of geometry is a crisis of the signified. It no longer seems possible to accept geometric form as either transcendental order, detached signifier, or as basic gestalt of visual perception. We are launched into a structuralist search for the veiled signified that the geometric sign may yield."[28] To critic Anna C. Chave, minimalism was ultimately associated with the rhetoric of power.[29]

Despite claims of the Pyramide's complete neutrality, solid evidence, from critical discourses to public reaction, refutes it. Regardless of the symbolic purity of the shape supported by Cassirer, several contemporary commentators immediately noted the implicit association of the Grande Pyramide with the Egyptian obelisk in the Place de la Concorde. As a very real remnant of Napoleonic imperialism, could the association with the obelisk confirm a hidden agenda of

Mitterrand's neocolonialist inclinations? In the hopeless complexities of contemporary referent systems, it seems that no shape, geometry, or technological objectivism can possibly confer neutrality. Given the additional overwhelming interweaving of the Louvre's existing symbolism with the political powers of the ancien régime, it would seem impossible to propose that any addition to the original building could be accomplished without conjuring its own amount of latent symbolization.

In this difficult question, it is finally to the public realm, the ultimate authority, to which we must turn. On July 3, 1988, the Grande Pyramide du Louvre was opened to predictably great international fanfare. Also predictably, Mitterrand immediately seized the symbolic mantle of the site and hosted the international G7 economic summit inside the museum. The opening also coincided that year with another presidential election. Prevailing over Prime Minister Chirac, Mitterrand's victory was largely attributed to the image he had cultivated for himself as a seasoned statesman, which won over the public's perception of Chirac as an impulsive partisan.[30]

Immediately, Mitterrand dissolved the "cohabitation" of the previous two years in both national leadership as well as the National Assembly, and called for new parliamentary elections. He was once again the uncontested leader of France. Throughout these major electoral events in his presidency, the Louvre hovers as a silent conspirator in determining his place in public esteem. At its opening, it seemed that the Grande Pyramide du Louvre would indeed be a legacy appropriated by and attributed entirely to François Mitterrand.

Ultimately, however, the symbol of the Louvre could not be so easily conquered by any specific point of power or political agenda. The strength of the museum as an institution in its own right, as the cultural repository of France and national symbol of the Revolution's democratic victory over the monarchy, has assured that if there is a ultimate symbolism of the Louvre, it points toward nothing but France itself. The public overwhelmingly came to embrace the pyramid. After the opening of the museum, the avalanche of criticism in the popular presses stopped suddenly: "La guerre est finie," noted François Chaslin, observing the reaction of the press.[31]

Le Figaro, which had attacked the pyramid almost daily, celebrated its own anniversary at the Louvre the same month of the museum's opening; the following day its headline proclaimed the pyramid marvelous. The association with Mitterrand simultaneously waned. Even the intellectual media agreed: "How many times has one heard talk of the pharoanic expenses of the former president . . . ?

4.11 Grande Pyramide du Louvre, Cour Napoléon.

The famous pyramid, so decried when unveiled for the first time, has become, to the same extent as the Eiffel Tower, a universal symbol of France—a modern France whose culture has been enhanced."[32]

The Grande Pyramide is subsumed into the Louvre in more than purely symbolic terms. Those very conditions of necessary structure and reflection that thwarted the achievement of a completely autonomous state provided the tangible means through which the pyramid is contextualized within the texture and fabric of the Cour Napoléon. The pyramid is also incorporated in its programmatic and urbanistic context. Together with an equestrian statue placed by Pei at the axial intersection of the Louvre and Voie Triomphale, the pyramid finally negotiated successfully the termination of Le Nôtre's axis.

At a local scale, the renovation afforded new access to the Cour Napoléon by opening and refurbishing the Passage Richelieu (see figure 1.12).[33] The Cour is at last a public space after many years of serving primarily as a private parking lot for finance ministry staff. Finally, the new lobby, despite its shortcomings, successfully reorganized the entire museum to work as a coherent network of galleries and circulation spines.

Despite many conflicts not easily apparent in its simple form and original idea, the Grande Pyramide du Louvre is a success on many symbolic, urban, and programmatic levels. It does not, however, represent the spatial and referential fluidity of the crystalline legacy continued into the latter day by Piano and Rogers. In contrast, its objectivism immobilized its representational capacity. Truly volatile crystalline expressivity, manifested in the minimal presence of glass and advanced steel technology, must be searched for elsewhere.

THE NATURAL ORDER OF GLASS: CITÉ DES SCIENCES ET DE L'INDUSTRIE

In redesigning the cable structures and suggesting fabrication methods for the stainless steel connection nodes at the Grande Pyramide, RFR intervened substantially in the project's final structural and aesthetic refinement. More important, however, the cast steel nodes departed from the pyramid's adherence to a strict method of technological determinism. Using a cast steel member represented a humanistic concept intervening in the pyramid's geometric abstraction. As Peter Rice said of the decision to cast the gerberettes at the Pompidou, "By using this technique, the building does not dominate. It is the details which control the reaction of the public and hence their perception of the scale and warmth of the building. It is a return to the interest and romanticism of Gothic architecture, with its great scale where the trace de la main is still visible."[34]

An inventive materiality, Rice believed, would both enhance the specific intentions of the architect and mitigate the perception of an industrial hegemony that had alienated the general public against modern architecture. By examining the characteristics of specific materials and designing highly particularized systems from them, Rice believed that the systems would convey, subliminally perhaps, their authorship—the creative and benevolent presence of the people who had designed and fabricated these special systems. Rice termed this quality "tactility." It is this quality that distinguished the Grandes Serres at the Cité des Sciences et de l'Industrie, the greenhouses at the Parc André Citroën, and the Petite Pyramide du Louvre, which Rice graced with the tactile dimension of glass.

Although RFR was approached by architect Adrien Fainsilber to work on the façade and internal structure of the Cité des Sciences et de l'Industrie in the early 1980s, the project had been in existence since 1978. Originally planned by President Giscard d'Estaing, it was envisioned as a facility bringing contemporary science to the masses, in the tradition of the Science Museum in London or the Smithsonian Institution's Air and Space Museum in Washington, D.C. The commission was awarded to Fainsilber by competition in 1980 and included the design of both the museum and the surrounding tract for the Parc de La Villette, which was ultimately the focus of a second competition in 1983, won by Bernard Tschumi.

The site and the surrounding land were occupied by a number of preexisting structures. For Fainsilber, the most notable were the foundations for a regional meat-slaughtering and distribution center at the western flank of the site whose construction had been halted when the advent of refrigerated trucking made the facility obsolete. Fainsilber planned the museum as an enormous rectangular structure on these foundations surrounded by a moat of water.

The façade for this box was envisioned as a huge transparent element, broaching a transitional relationship with the park, as well as activating the mission of the museum, which Fainsilber said would assert the "complementarity between science and nature."[35] From the beginning of the design process, this transparent enclosure was conceived almost as a distinct structure; it was even named the *Grandes Serres* (the great greenhouses) after the greenhouse structures at the Paris ancien science museum complex, the Jardin des Plantes in the fifth arrondissement.

4.12 Adrien Fainsilber and RFR, Cité des Sciences et de l'Industrie, 1986.

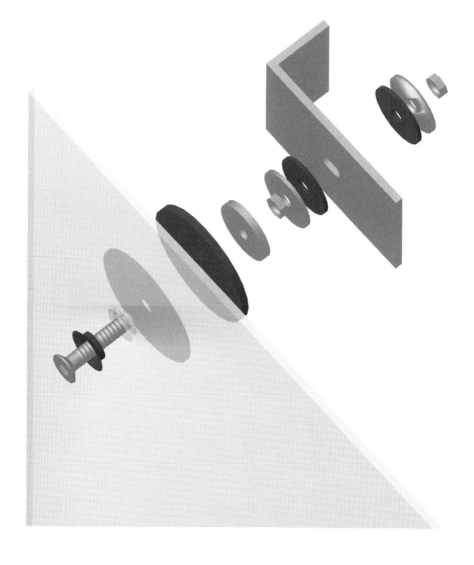

4.13 Pilkington planar system. (Drawing: Marvin Rodriguez and Charles McGloughlin)

As a greenhouse, the purpose of the façade was markedly different from that of all of the glass structures discussed thus far. Rather than serving as a primarily visual device, it would create a "bioclimactic" environment, recovering solar energy and integrating vegetation actively in the museum's interior. Fitted with devices for varying natural ventilation and temperature, the Grandes Serres exposed the workings of a mechanically adjustable glass skin at the scale of an enormous technological spectacle, following the typological and didactic precedent set by Paxton's Crystal Palace. The systems of glass manufacture and support, however, could not have been more different.

The system used by Paxton in the mid–nineteenth century was developed before landmark advancements of glass manufacturing. At the time of the Crystal Palace, molten glass was poured on preheated metal beds and flattened with rollers until the desired thickness was reached, a process relatively unchanged since the seventeenth century. The panes were then submitted to a laborious process of grinding and polishing, giving the surface its measure of transparency.[36]

It was not until 1904 that the Fourcault process was developed; this involved drawing a continuous bead of molten glass through asbestos-covered rollers, substantially reducing the amount of polishing required to produce a transparent finish, and simultaneously increasing the possible size of individual panes.[37] After a number of adjustments to the roller systems, by Libby-Owens and Pittsburgh Plate Glass and other manufacturers, in 1952 the Pilkington Glass Company again transformed the glass-production process. By pouring molten glass across a bed of heavier-density liquid tin and then drawing the precisely cooled glass through an annealing lehr, a box of continuous rollers, the necessity for surface polishing was eliminated altogether. Plate glass was revolutionized as "float glass."[38]

Pilkington was equally innovative in challenging conventional glass support systems. In the Crystal Palace (as in all nineteenth-century industrial buildings) glass was held in place by a continuous lead H-shaped frame around the edges of the panes. Despite numerous developments in the configuration and material constitution of frames, most notably in the development of lighter material support with more efficient environmental separation, the basic concept of a mullioned frame has not changed. Glass is still held in place around its edges in a pocketed frame; the mastic installed between glass and frame accommodates differential movement and provides a thermal and moisture seal. This principle is essentially the same in contemporary systems that employ structural silicon. These systems provide a flush exterior frameless glass surface; on the interior the structural silicon attaches the edge of the pane to a mullioned frame system. Besides the Grande Pyramide, Jean Nouvel and Dominique Perrault's buildings are among the many typically European examples.

Other advances include mechanical technologies that consist of point connections through the pane itself, either bolted or "patch-plated" back to a structural mullion behind the glass. In these systems the weight of the glass is transferred at singular points of support; their limitation is found in stresses that develop around the holes drilled in the glass. As in a conventional frame, these systems do not allow for any sizable movement between the glass and the primary structure. To solve this problem, Pilkington developed a system to accommodate exactly such movement. By installing a flexible washer between a countersunk bolt support and the primary mullion structure, the glass and the bolt move independently, allowing considerable increase in the movement of the pane, either from thermal expansion or deflection caused by laterally imposed loads. Known as the Pilkington planar system, it is commonly available commercially (figure 4.14).[39]

Rice Francis Ritchie went one step farther in dealing with possible movement of the panes in their design for a point-supported system at the Grandes Serres. They began by analyzing the most basic element—the molecular structure of glass. Chemically, glass owes its transparency to the resistance of silicon oxide to molecular bonding after a process of heating to fusion followed by controlled cooling. Like other oxides (boron, germanium, phosphorus, and arsenic) silicon remains amorphous in solid state. Ironically, glass is chemically not actually a crystalline structure; it retains the unstable molecular behavior of liquids.

Glass is notorious for such instability; its lack of ductility (or brittleness) is a measure of its inability to redistribute load under failure and sets low limitations in applying loading stresses onto it. The strengthening process by which glass is tempered takes advantage of this instability. In tempering, a preformed pane is gradually heated to 625° C; air jets then cool its surface rapidly while the center is still viscous. The surface thus retains an amount of compressive stress, burying the potential fracturing tensile stress inside the two exterior planes, very much like a plate of prestressed concrete.[40]

If tensile stresses could be contained within the plane by precisely configuring types of loading, the strength of glass would exceed that of steel. Instead of an inert material, glass could transmit load and be used structurally. Drawing on the concepts of the Pilkington system, RFR embarked on a similar design that would allow the pane a maximum amount of movement, so that neither internally nor externally imposed stresses would ever be taken by the plane. For this point-supported glazing system, RFR designed an assemblage of elements around a head that was allowed to rotate freely on its stem as it passed through the glass. By countersinking this articulated bolt, its axis of movement would correspond with the geometric plane, thus eliminating the potential of the glass to develop bending or twisting stresses. These heads were grouped together in an H-shaped configuration to form the corner joint between four panes (figures 4.14 and 4.15).[41]

While the articulated bolt system dealt with live and lateral loads, for the dead load of the glass, the engineers developed an equally ingenious detail. Grouping four panes into vertical stacks, a special bolt with suspension springs was positioned at the center edge of the top pane (figures 4.16 and 4.17). Four vertical stacks were then grouped together, forming a basic sixteen-pane module that would hang as a unit from a larger primary frame, working together to transmit loads in all directions. As in the Grande Pyramide, RFR used cast stainless steel for the articulated bolts and suspension springs; the other components were designed with fittings manufactured as yacht rigging components.[42]

To transfer the lateral stress from the articulated bolt system to the main structure, RFR devised a three-tiered bracing system. The first tier, glass and its articulated bolt system, was attached to a horizontal cable truss behind—*le raidisseur*—by virtue of compression rods emanating from the stems of the bolts (figure 4.18). Similar in principle to the tension ring cable system at the Grande Pyramide, the cables at this second tier of the structural bracing could pass through the ends of the compression rods, allowing the truss to deform considerably within its horizontal plane when required. The ends of these raidisseurs were clamped to the main framework, transferring lateral loads onto it. This main tubular steel framework, the third and final tier, was developed as a square module accommodating four bays in each direction of the sixteen-pane module. This main framework was one bay deep; behind each horizontal member, was yet another larger cable truss system for lateral bracing (see figure 4.20). The entire structure formed a thick wedge of space attaching to the south-facing façade of the museum.[43]

By allowing for movement instead of actively opposing it, RFR's system is a highly refined reinvention of a principle first seen at the Eiffel Tower. Although it

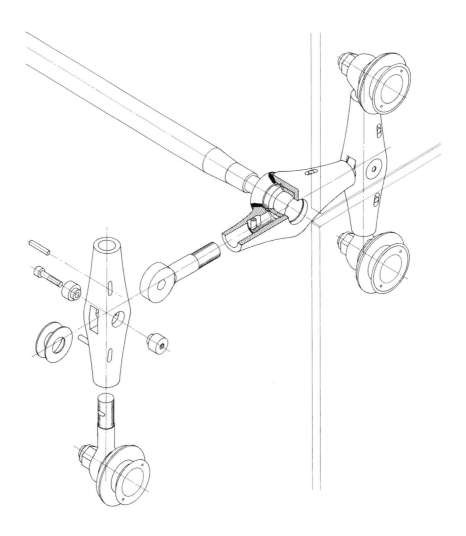

4.14 Cité des Sciences et de l'Industrie, cutaway view articulated bolt. Courtesy Rice Francis Ritchie, Paris.

4.15 Cité des Sciences et de l'Industrie, articulated bolt.

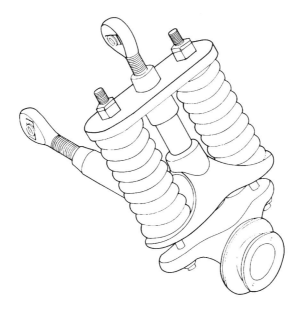

4.16 Cité des Sciences et de l'Industrie, suspension spring support. Courtesy Rice Francis Ritchie, Paris.

(Drawing: Amity Kundu, from original RFR drawing)

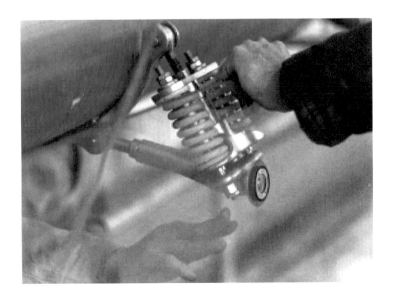

4.17 Cité des Sciences et de l'Industrie, suspension spring support. Illustrated in Dutton and Rice *Structural Glass*. Courtesy Rice Francis Ritchie, Paris.

4.18 Cité des Sciences et de l'Industrie, raidisseurs and primary trusses.

does not allow for wind literally to pass through the structure, it makes a glass skin that is responsive to it, incrementally dissipating horizontal loads through degrees of literal movement in its hierarchical bolting and bracing systems. By eliminating the mullioned frame and using glass as structural support, RFR also substantially reduced the material weight of the support system, thereby also decreasing the weight of the primary tubular structure.

As the dimensions and weight of structure fall away, the visual effect of the space and surfaces of the serres is significant. The façade rises from the water-filled moat below, a sheer, thin glass surface as delicate as that of the water. On the interior, the glass tenuously bounds a space filled with a web of gossamer horizontal tethers, where the diminishment of force is made literally visible. The structural system is far more delicate than that at the Grande Pyramide, achieving a sense of spatial weightlessness attained by the simple manipulation of vector forces in and around the glass plane.

Fainsilber's original competition entry text emphasized his project's relationship not simply to the adjacent Parc de La Villette, but to nature itself. Les Serres were to provide an environmental zone, allowing the park foliage to enter the museum's interior proper, providing both an energy buffer between the south façade and the museum as well as a vehicle to save and store solar energy. As actually built, the climactic systems do fulfill the original goals, although less efficiently than projected. By raising the upper bay above the adjacent museum roof and retrofitting the serres with a louvered natural ventilation system, a zone of natural convection is formed inside the contained volume of air, ensuring an energy zone autonomous to the museum.

The trapped solar energy is stored in the base, recovered at a later date by heat pumps in the museum's main refrigeration and heating systems, saving approximately 3.5 percent of the museum's annual energy needs.[44] The interior space of at least one of the serres also successfully accommodates growth of foliage, and is filled year-round with abundant planting. Through these devices, the serres were intended not only to function climactically, but also to offer a didactic display, furthering the museum's mission to popularize science.

Environmental autonomy, however, came at a price. Spatially and programmatically, the serres are severely qualified by a complete disjunction with the museum proper. With no circulation through them, or at least alongside them, they can be entered only by rising in one lonely elevator from a limited-access interactive children's exhibit on the first floor. Elsewhere, they provide only gratuitous

4.19 Cité des Sciences et de l'Industrie, interior, Grandes Serres.

backdrops of natural daylight for several library spaces, a third-floor café, and other ancillary programmatic elements. Often the museum has even opted to build solid partitions at the serres' edge for its exhibit displays, occluding views of the glassed-in spaces. The museum has retained its own separate internal order; the serres remain as odd appendages.

The distance imposed between the viewers and the serres have consequences larger than simple programmatic and spatial dysfunction. Thwarting active engagement, they are set apart from the viewing public as technological manifestoes, very different from the original design intent. As in the Pompidou Center, Rice intended that the components and apparatus of the structural glass technology be easily apprehended, initiating a didacticism that would establish a playful repartee between the viewing public and the institution. Set at a distance, the intricacy of the structural order and of the climactic systems can never be fully engaged. The remarkable technology is appreciated only aesthetically, only as a spectacular gesture.

This particular expression of technology cannot, however, be equated with the mystification wrought by brutal scale, the realm perhaps of both the Pompidou Center and the Eiffel Tower. When the space tenuously bounded by thin sheets of glass and water inside the one functioning serre is filled with exotic planting, the final effect is similar to Scheerbart's literary fantasies, to which it is instructive again to turn. Through his interest in the crystal as an emblem of mystical change, Scheerbart was led directly to the garden as both metaphor and setting for his glass fantasies. In his novel *The Gray Cloth,* the protagonists, an architect and his wife, journey across the world installing glass gardens in exotic landscapes.[45] With their capacity for literal growth and transformation, the gardens in Scheerbart's novels, were drawn from a long legacy of crystalline gardens found primarily in literary sources; from the king of Toledo's pavilions to the Renaissance garden in Queen Eleutuilda's palace in Francesco Colonna's *Hypnerotomachia Poliphilo,* a "faithful copy of nature in glass and gold," where roofs were covered with creepers and honeysuckle made of gold and precious stones.[46]

Scheerbart's visions tended to combine the crystalline with natural utopian settings; his proposals included glass communities replacing mountaintops and dissolution of cities into smaller crystalline communities dispersed into the landscape. Nature consistently appeared in his writings as transformed into fantastic architectural settings. Indeed, one of his primary themes was transmutation of the natural world through subjective imagery; glass would essentially reveal nature.

Bruno Taut provided the architectural means through which to transform Scheerbart's visions into realities. In their joint publication, *Glass Architecture* (Scheerbart) and *Alpine Glass* (Taut), Taut's contribution included ephemeral drawings of crystalline mountaintops; his accompanying text read as a set of specifications for an architecture meant to intervene directly into nature, "NATURE IS GREAT! . . . It is sentimental to stand idly admiring. LET US CREATE IN HER AND WITH HER AND LET US DECORATE HER! Vorderglärnisch near Glarus in Switzerland. Bare grey rock, rising from the green of the forests. Its haphazard shapes must be smoothed into angular planes. Crystalline shapes of white glass shimmer in their rocky setting. More such crystals in the depth of the forest."[47]

Although esoteric and subjectivist in their reawakening of the mystical symbology of the medieval crystal, Scheerbart and Taut turned introspection back outwards to address society in their visions of crystalline utopias.[48] Through the symbolic origins of the crystal, the fantastic in Scheerbart's architectural visions would instigate collective spiritual transformation. Despite the proliferation of fantastic machines in Scheerbart's imaginative forays, technology is subdued, and indeed conquered, put at the service of humans rather than their domination.

Within the culture of Weimar Republic Germany, these ideas pervaded more than expressionist architecture. As a member of the "Ring" in 1924 with Taut, Mies van der Rohe shared many affinities with the visions of Taut and Scheerbart. All three called for a spiritual renewal of architecture all choosing glass as a medium expressing new values in architecture, and all taking a decided stance on the relationship of technology to architecture, and to human production in general. Yet despite these similarities, the position taken by Mies was informed differently than that of Scheerbart and Taut and developed along very different trajectories.

Mies perceived that the coherence of antiquity and the Middle Ages had been destroyed by technological instrumentalization of the Industrial Revolution.[49] His reform of architecture in capitalist society centered on seizing symbolic control of its technological exploitation of nature, a concept indebted to the teaching of Jesuit theologian Romano Guardini.[50] As Mies confirmed in his IIT lecture "Technology and Architecture," the answer was not less technology, but more.[51] More control of nature, through use of technology that was made spiritual by extreme adherence to its demands, would return freedom and power to the masses as well as to individuals. This reaction informed all of Mies's work, from the details of his material joinery, to his dialectical pairing of structural elements, to his concept of the modern monument.

4.20 Cité des Sciences et de l'Industrie, interior, Grandes Serres.

Mies's union of the technological and the monumental synthesized much of nineteenth-century German architectural theory dominated by the discourse of the tectonic. By raising the expression of construction, especially of steel construction, to a heightened spiritual level, Mies collapsed discussions of such figures as Bötticher, Wolff, Heinzerling, and Lotze, which had long pondered the relationship between objective expression of new technologies and subjective expression of art. As Bötticher had argued, since symbolic ornamentation was not possible in steel construction, artistic value for Mies was shifted to abstract expression of the principles of structure itself, particularly those demanded by the use of the trabeated frame.[52]

For Mies, the frame and its component details became the primary vehicles for spiritualizing architecture, attaining what Kenneth Frampton called the "monumentalization of technique." Evidenced in the mute structure commemorating Karl Liebknecht and Rosa Luxemburg in Berlin of 1926, materials, heightened to a poetic level by a precise attention to construction, attained a sense of the sublime, which in the monument substituted for the traditional symbolism of figurative reference.

Glass for Mies, as for Scheerbart and Taut, was the primary means to negotiate the tenuous relationship to nature. The similarities, however, end here and the disparities in the two positions become radical. Mies's glass panel, held discretely within a trabeated frame derived from the austere classical tradition he inherited from Schinkel and Behrens, controlled the view and simultaneously sealed the interior hermetically from the exterior. Where Mies kept the architectural work in precise opposition to its natural surround, Taut and Scheerbart surrounded the viewer in chaotic compositions of multisensory stimuli. From the Tugendhat House onward in Mies's career, ironically as the amount of glass around the perimeter of the buildings increased, so did the climactic separation between the interior and exterior. Epitomized in the Farnsworth and Resor houses, nature is an element to be viewed, appraised, and contemplated, but never to be physically experienced. Deprived of senses, a person's relationship to nature is ultimately made entirely voyeurist.

Fainsilber's idea to use a transparent element across his museum façade as a way to provide a view of the park landscape is directly indebted to Mies, just as RFR's excrutiatingly exact attention to the demands of structural technology extends Mies's sensibility of the monument. Yet the disjunction between the exterior and interior—architecture and nature—is dispelled as both structural and

4.21 Mies van der Rohe, Resor house, Jackson Hole, Wyoming, 1937–1938 (unbuilt). Interior perspective of living room (view through north glass wall). Courtesy Mies van der Rohe Archive, Museum of Modern Art, New York. Gift of the architect. © 2002 Museum of Modern Art, New York.

4.22 Cité des Sciences et de l'Industrie, view toward the Parc de La Villette.

environmental systems at the Cité became directly responsive to natural inflection. RFR's removal of mullions does more than increase the amount of transparency; it dissolves the discrete frame that formerly controlled the Miesian view, offering a panoramic view.

At the same time, two differently scaled natural systems invade the constituency of the glass enclosure: at a micro scale, in the glass plane force moves through molecules of solid liquid; at a macro scale, as wind presses against the huge thin planes, it is allowed substantially to distort the geometry of the surface. Finally, by incorporating literal elements of simulated nature—natural ventilation, planting, flowing water, and rising mist—the Miesian precedent is overturned. In the serres, as the Miesian frame is removed, the space behind the viewing plane restores the senses. Here, the Miesian mode of classical abstraction is reinvigorated by nature and entwined with the expressionist garden. The concept of the crystal as an abstract rationalization of nature is united with the concept of the crystal representing a mystical, fluid, and natural world.

THE CRYSTAL CRYSTALLIZED: FROM PARC ANDRÉ CITROËN TO THE PETITE PYRAMIDE

The ultimate significance of this union of concepts arises as these exact systems were imposed across Paris in other Grands Projets, forming a network of related monuments in the city's gardens. If the primary mnemonic device for the Grande Pyramide is its pyramidal shape, for these other monuments, it is the distinctive type of glass construction derived from the system at the Cité des Sciences that grants them their particular identity. Detail ascends to the level of monumental, as well as the central symbolic element wedding the Grands Projets to the implications of nature in the city.

First among these is RFR's design for another set of glass greenhouses in the Parc André Citroën (1988–1995). Previously occupied by the Citroën automobile factory, the park site is an enormous, fourteen-hectare swath of land. Like the Parc de La Villette, it is located adjacent to the peripheral highway, *Le Périphérique,* that surrounds Paris. Unique among Parisian parks, the Parc Citroën borders directly on the Seine, although the river is separated from the park proper by regional rail lines at the northern edge. Unlike the Parc de La Villette, the site had no existing structures; one of the most formidable design challenges was dealing with the emptiness of the enormous gently sloping expanse of land. The Parc Citroën also

4.23 Berger, Clément, Viguier, Jodry, Provost, Parc André Citroën, 1988–1995, view looking south to serres monumentales (Berger and RFR).

4.24 Berger and RFR, Parc André Citroën, serres sérielles.

4.25 Parc André Citroën, serre monumentale, the orangerie.

did not have the complex institutional program of the Parc de La Villette; instead it was envisioned entirely as a botanical park, with interior and exterior gardens displaying 30,000 plants imported from all over the world.

Like Parc de La Villette, the design for Parc Citroën was chosen through a competition that was awarded jointly to two separate teams: Parisian architects Patrick Berger and Gilles Clément, with engineers Rice Francis Ritchie, agreed to collaborate with architects Jean-Paul Viguier and Jean-François Jodry and land-scape architect Alain Provost. Together, their first gesture was to place a central axis perpendicular to the Seine. This device was typical of many Parisian esplanades located along the left bank: the Champ de Mars, the Esplanade des Invalides, and the Jardin des Plantes.

Along this north-south axis, a large rectangular expanse of open lawn slopes up at the southern edge to meet two large, identical glass greenhouses, *serres monumentales* (figures 4.23 and 4.25). The *orangerie* and the *serre tempérée* are disposed symmetrically around the axis at the summit of the hill. Between the lawn and the western edge of the Parc Citroën a linear canal is flanked by small stone pavilions, each with a different water feature. Along the eastern edge are seven smaller glass greenhouses, *serres sérielles,* raised above ground level along a connecting walkway (figures 4.24 and 4.27). A cascading water trough emanates from each one, perpendicular to the central lawn below. At the base of these smaller greenhouses are seven enclosed gardens themed along variations of color and environment.

The popular media described the serres monumentales, situated at the crest of the hill, as a latter-day Acropolis, a reference vigorously denied by Patrick Berger, who designed all the glass structures in collaboration with Rice Francis Ritchie. Nevertheless, evidence presented by the buildings' characteristics undercuts Berger's denial of inherent classicism: each rectangular glass serre is raised on a monolithic stone plinth; each is supported along its long sides by a line of paired round columns forming a peristyle. As in a classical entablature, these columns are crowned by a pedimented glass roof resting on a peripheral steel beam. Each roof is broken at its apex by a symmetrical spine running the length of the building to a symmetrical vertical slot, which provides entry from the central lawn.

Berger, in other accounts, frankly described his design as an attempt to combine modernity and antiquity. He referred in these claims specifically to his combinations of materials of vastly different character, particularly in his use of wood to encase the massive double column frame and at the entry doors. These are contrasted to the greenhouses' glass walls, which employ the same RFR mullion-less structural system as the Grandes Serres at La Villette, with however, a few minor variations. The primary structural principle is again based on suspending the glass panes; at the Parc Citroën a full-height sheet of panels drops from the steel entablature. Instead of the entirely horizontal cable truss system employed at La Villette, RFR used vertical trusses attached to the main frame as primary members, forming a two-direction hierarchy. The spring attachment clamps at the top of the glass panes are, however, identical to those at La Villette. The articulated bolt assembly is a star-shaped "monobloc" instead of the H-shape at the museum (see figure 4.29). Since both systems are of the same scale and cast out of the same stainless steel material, these variations are minor. To all but the most observant viewer the details are virtually indistinguishable from those at the earlier museum.

The primary structure for the serres sérielles, is markedly different from that of their larger cousins. In each a single central wood-encased column supports an open rectangular frame stabilized at the perimeter by vertical cables. With the same structural glass system as the serres monumentales, instead of a cable truss system, small horizontal steel beams are placed behind the glass for lateral bracing. Again RFR's system attains a weightlessness unknown to conventional mullion systems, superceding the effect at La Villette. Because both types of greenhouses at Parc André Citroën are free-standing structures, the lightness of the glass systems endows a three-dimensional volume of space, instead of the thick layer appliquéd to the main body of the building at the Cité des Sciences. The flawed conjunction of space and building type in Fainsilber's museum are absent in this singular conception of space, structure, material, and site.

The collaborators' classicism is least successful at the southern end of the park. The main axial view, held spectacularly between the two serres monumentales, frames a nondescript block of contemporary housing that has no discernable relationship to the architecture of the park. Parc Citroën's classical parti denies the prosaic vernacular surrounding, very much like Pei's refusal to admit the contingent reflection of the sky at the flank of his pyramid. Here the mistake is far more immediately perceived, qualifying the park's axis at its most prominent point.

Far from those areas of the park privy to the rise and fall of monumental classicism are Berger's smaller greenhouses, where the ultimate description of the crystalline expressionist garden is invoked. Although also disposed axially,

4.26 Parc André Citroën, serre monumentale, detail.

4.27 Parc André Citroën, serres sérielles.

4.28 Parc André Citroën, serre sérielle, looking up.

4.29 Parc André Citroën, serre sérielle, detail.

perpendicular to the park lawn, these serres sérielles have largely been subsumed into the theme gardens below them. Rather than being confronted and over-whelmed by the symmetricality and formal grandeur of the serres monumentales, the visitor to the eastern edge of the park discovers each small greenhouse as an isolated incident, buried amid the exotic planting of its respective garden. Because paths between the greenhouses navigate through the same thick foliage, other visitors are hidden, making it easy to lose oneself within the network of greenery and crystalline structures. Within this public space surrounded by urban Paris one finds the most intimate and exotic of garden settings.

The smaller scale and direct accessibility of these greenhouses allows the RFR systems to be understood in precisely the *tactile* way that Rice imagined. The size and institutional presence of the serres monumentales, like the serres at La Villette, do not encourage visitors to engage directly with the glass systems. In the small greenhouses, however, the constricted space between the walls and the central column forces visitors to wander within the interstices of the lateral bracing systems. The glass panes can be pushed manually to witness first-hand the system's capacity to accommodate substantial movement. Up close, the scale of the articulated bolt assemblage can be appreciated as close to the human hand. The bolts can be understood as actual mechanisms capable of complex three-dimensional movement. The system is, as Rice articulated, "anthropomorphized."

This is of particular importance in understanding the invocation in these small greenhouses of our newly defined sense of monumental transparency. When the RFR systems are perceived at a distance in the overscaled structures of both parks, their expression remains traditionally monumental, even spectacular, ultimately glamorizing the power of the institution and of the state. In the smaller serres sérielles, a sense of play is invited as the same RFR systems can be engaged as toylike instruments, to the delight of the individual visitor. The serres sérielles are subsumed into the context of their program and into the context of the garden, recalling the transparent occupation established by the seamless relationship between the building and the public at the Pompidou Center.

Scheerbart once fantasized about a system of flora that would grow into houselike structures: *Hausbaupflanzen.* Like glass, these natural building materials would transform light and space, landscape and city, and finally, the collective and the individual soul. Both metaphors were conceived in a similar quest for spiritual reformation and creative enlightenment—"mental flexibility" (Bletter's term).

4.30 Epstein, Glialman, and Vidal with Kohn, Pederson, Fox and RFR, 50 Avenue Montaigne, 1993.

Lacking Scheerbart's grand utopian agenda, nevertheless these little therapeutic moments of play are significant, certainly according to Walter Benjamin, who theorized that it is exactly such moments that harbor potential reenchantment of the social world.

The three Grands Projets discussed thus far—the Louvre pyramid, the Cité des Sciences et de l'Industrie, and the Parc André Citroën—form a significant part of the vast order of formalized nature in Paris. Terminating the Voie Triomphale, the Louvre pyramid completes the Tuileries, the garden axis of Paris ancien; in the two peripheral parks of newer Paris we find prototypes for the futurist urban garden. At both ends of the historical spectrum, glass and stainless steel technologies are emphatically placed into the material culture and symbolism of the garden, an order fundamental to the city.

The highly distinctive RFR glass support systems and their exact repetition in the latter two Grands Projets might have finally fulfilled nineteenth-century German ambition for the monument, where material construction would become equivalent to figurative symbol. Indeed, RFR's structural glass systems might even have transcended mere connotation and become symbols for the Parisian garden, itself a manifestation of the order of nature within the city. Because of their use in an array of other projects, this fascinating possibility in the history of material construction never was realized.

The systems that RFR developed precisely for Fainsilber's museum were repeated, almost identically, not just at the Parc Citroën, but also throughout the city in highly commercial venues. At 50 Avenue Montaigne, a conglomerate of high-fashion boutiques completed in 1993, RFR collaborated with French architects Epstein, Glialman, and Vidal and with the American firm Kohn Pedersen Fox, furnishing the building with a structural glass atrium wall and half-moon glass roof. Here RFR designed a translucent silk-screened glass wall between the atrium and a residential courtyard, employing an articulated bolt system on the outside of the glass (figure 4.31) connecting to a bracing system on the interior. Again, differences in details are minor; the system and its spatial effects are virtually the same as they appeared at La Villette and Parc Citroën.

A year earlier, in 1992, RFR systems were used to embellish a connecting element, the Grande Nef, between blocks of speculative office spaces at the Collines du Nord, by architect Jean-Pierre Buffi, located directly adjacent to the Grande Arche de La Défense. Since the demands were to articulate a primarily interior

4.31 Jean-Pierre Buffi, Collines du Nord, the Grande Nef, 1992.

4.32 RFR, renovation to CNIT, 1989, entry. (Zehrfuss, Camelot, de Mailly and Jean Prouvé, 1958)

4.33 Passage du Havre (architect unknown). Mimicking of structural glass details in a recently renovated arcade.

space, the articulated bolt system and more conventional lateral bracing structure were all placed on the exterior (figure 4.31). The result was again a dramatic interior space weaving through solid stone porticoes, with a continuous, translucent, double-membrane roof above. Next door, however, the success of the RFR systems was not fulfilled to the same extent.

Commissioned in 1991 as part of a renovation and conversion of a 1950s exposition building—the CNIT (Centre National des Industries et des Techniques)—for retail development, RFR was chosen, presumably for their proved design sensitivity, to intervene in the historically land-marked curtain wall by Jean Prouvé. The engineers slipped a central translucent entry element behind Prouvé's large plane of compositely assembled panes; on either side, RFR cantilevered two new large roof structures into the exterior space of the La Défense parvis. In the central entry RFR again employed a structural glass system, but reinvented the lateral bracing components. Here is an interesting twist—vertical cable trusses pass directly through the exterior glass at the point of the articulated bolt assembly (figure 4.32).

The larger project was severely compromised, however, when the developer, Sari Ingénierie, decided to enclose the space beneath the two cantilevers. This was symptomatic of an earlier debasement of the interior, which had once been the largest contained space under a thin-shelled concrete span, designed in the mid-1950s by Bernard Zehrfuss, Robert Camelot, and Jean de Mailly, with engineer Nicolas Esquillan. The 1988 renovation, by architects Michel Andrault and Pierre Parat, severely compromised this space by inserting an awkward, stepped volume of low-quality glass and steel storefront construction. The precision and grace of the RFR intervention was lost completely within this larger context.

It is hardly surprising that the RFR systems were ultimately taken out of the control of engineers and various architects. As a patented system, RFR's structural glazing become a commodity available for purchase and installation in any type of space. It was immediately appropriated by developer culture as a means of endowing commercial space with a fashionable technological flourish. Although engineers were retained along with the system itself, and although nearly all of the projects are successful in terms of both spatial and material character, migration of the RFR glass systems from the most glorified of symbolic overtures to the most base of commercial ventures is significant.

4.34 I. M. Pei and Partners and RFR, the Petite Pyramide du Louvre, 1993.

The historic coupling of glass and nature to commerce adds another dimension to the descent of the tectonic into the commercial. Critic Andrea Kahn wrote that since the great nineteenth-century exposition halls, particularly the Crystal Palace, glass has been the operative feature muddling the distinction between "houses of nature" and "houses of trade." Shopping malls, after all, were created by enclosing streets with glass roofs, most pervasively in the famous network of Parisian arcades. Yet glass, according to Kahn, contributed more than a particular typology of building or street. By uniting the act of shopping and the act of viewing nature, glass in the botanical expositions became an instrument through which simultaneously to "consume nature" and "naturalize consumption."[53]

That the RFR systems coincide with this potential of glass to straddle nature and commerce is evidenced by the most technologically provocative of the engineers' projects in Paris, the Petite Pyramide for the Louvre Carrousel. Again in collaboration with I. M. Pei, RFR was asked to design another structure to light a vast underground connection between the Louvre lobby and new parking and bus-drop facilities under the Tuileries. Pei and RFR chose to repeat the use of a transparent pyramid, placing the structure at the Place du Carrousel, on axis with the original Grande Pyramide and the Voie Triomphale.

Rather than protruding into the space above (a traffic circle connecting the Pont du Carrousel with the Rue de Rivoli), they inverted the pyramid, hanging it like a chandelier into the space below. In contrast to the original pyramid, the Petite Pyramide is not an actual weather enclosure. Covering the lite is a second, completely independent structure, a slightly sloping glass roof that is surrounded by hedges on the street and hidden to traffic. This inversion provides an idealized structural setting to surpass all the benchmarks of the RFR glazing systems across Paris.

The Petite Pyramide takes full advantage of advances in structural glazing made since the Grande Pyramide, while sharing its basic geometric derivation. Each flank of glass is composed of diamond shaped planes, but the mullion frame and the heavy lateral bracing at the larger pyramid have disappeared; indeed there is not even sealant physically connecting the panes. Rather, independent panes hover in space, held within the precise pyramidal geometry by a supporting structure consisting almost entirely of stainless steel cables held in tension by the weight of the suspended glass. This supporting structure is organized in the same three-tiered hierarchy of other RFR glass projects.

4.35 The Petite Pyramide du Louvre, structure.

At the "exterior" surface (actually the concourse interior), are the glass and its articulated bolt system, followed by a system of fine cables connecting the center point of the panes to the primary truss system, the third element in the structural hierarchy. These four trusses hanging from a concrete edge beam above are almost entirely in tension. The only compression members in the entire system are stainless steel rods that act as intermediate chords of the cable trusses. These vertical rods appear to hang miraculously in the interior space of the pyramid, coming together at a virtual cube at its center (figure 4.35).

In designing the inverted pyramid as a device to light an interior space, RFR accepted and exploited the reflective effect inherent in surfaces tilted to the sky, exactly what had so annoyed Pei in the Grande Pyramide. Because sunlight is captured on the discrete planes of the pyramid's interior surfaces, an enormous amount of light is transmitted onto the glass surfaces in the dark underground chamber. Through reflection, the geometry of the pyramid is inscribed in light. At the same time that the structure is reduced to the most minimal of cables, light is rendered into a coherent volume. The effect is dazzling. From a distance, the pyramid reads as a crystalline volume of contained light, suspended tenuously in a dark interior. Seen close up, the space is a maze of wires and layered green lines as the edges of the open panes bask in voluminous light against the sky. Where the effort in the Grande Pyramide was to overcome the nature of material and structure, RFR was all embracing in discovering the rationales contained by the smallest and largest of their structures' components. As a culmination of idealization begun in the Grande Pyramide and carried through all the technological advances of the serres, the Petite Pyramide is a coherent statement about crystalline construction. It unites highly advanced structural glass technologies with idealized geometry, protosymbolic form, and the mystical luminosity of light from the Middle Ages. What results is certainly is the epitome of technology in late twentieth-century glass construction.

Yet where does all this glory unfold and what does this latest pyramid signify? The immediately perceived context of the Petite Pyramide is neither the museum nor the urban location on the Voie Triomphale above, but is essentially a French version of an American shopping mall. The pyramid is read in relation to the luxury chain stores that the Louvre imported from all of France to increase its revenues. Replete with the sunglass boutiques and environmentally correct nature stores so rampant in malls and airports all over the world, the Petite Pyramide is as representative of global economic homogenization as the Grande Pyramide is

4.36 The Petite Pyramide du Louvre.

symbolic of France. If the Grande Pyramide was accused of initiating the decul-
turation of the Louvre, the Petite Pyramide completes it, becoming the cave of Ali
Baba, full of jewels for the consumer.[54] In a French sociopolitical culture currently
torn with strife over this issue, the two pyramids, mirroring each other above and
below the horizon of the Voie Triomphale, create an exquisite expression of the
fragility of France's national identity in the fin-de-siècle era of international economic expansionism.

❈ Neutral Enclosures:

Perrault's Bibliothèque Nationale de France

L' Etat, c'est moi.

—Louis XIV, king of France 1643–1715

IN 1988 FRANÇOIS MITTERRAND embarked on the last of the Grands Pro-jets, the Bibliothèque Nationale de France, whose ambitions to represent all of France would equal that of the Louvre renovation. In July of that year, Mitterrand announced that the new building would house "one of the biggest and most modern libraries in the world," an unabashedly nationalistic effort to grant the French institution a facility to compete with similar libraries internationally, particularly the renowned Library of Congress in the United States. At the same time, Mitterrand an-nounced the anticipated date of completion as 1995. Setting up an im-plausibly accelerated phase of design and construction, this was intended to coincide with his last year as president. As an acknowledged man of letters, Mitterrand clearly intended the Bibliothèque Nationale as a sym-bolism of his presidency. As the culmination of the Grands Projets, it would mark the grand finale of the colossal undertaking to rejuvenate the country's cultural heritage, an undertaking that he clearly planned to be historically attributed entirely to himself.

Certainly, Mitterrand did not contrive the need for a new facility to house the existing collection of the Bibliothèque Nationale. Begun as the royal personal library of the early French kings, the collection of books, manuscripts, maps, prints, and coins had over the centuries severely outgrown its former residence at the Palais Mazarin on the Rue de Richelieu. By government decree in 1793, a copy of every publication—book, journal, or newspaper—was required to be furnished to the national archives. In recent years, this stipulation had been expanded to cover all films and electronically published media in France including videos and even compact discs. By the 1980s, the growth of printed matter alone had accelerated to some 40,000 additional volumes each year, bringing the total collection to 11 million volumes in 1988. It was anticipated that the existing bibliothèque's hundred miles of shelf space on the Rue de Richelieu would be completely filled as of 1995.

As the holdings of the nation, however, the library's public nature was belied by its policy of limited access. Due primarily to the shortage of space in Labrouste's famous reading room of 1868, access was granted only by interview and after evaluation of research, typically restricting entry to the most elite of France's scholars. Indeed, since French university libraries are notoriously underfunded, the public had very little access to any literary or scholarly archive in Paris. At the time of the Bibliothèque Nationale's completion, the city's only truly public access library with any sizable collection was the one at the Pompidou Center, which in the recent past was so overused that there was frequently a two- to three-hour wait at the entrance. It was the inability of the French public to access its own literary heritage that culminated Mitterrand's mission to open the nation's culture, formerly perceived elitist, to the general populace—*le grand public*. In this effort, the original competition brief included provisions for exhibition halls, restaurants, ten cinemas, and even a Turkish bath.

The site chosen for the new library building was a seven-hectare tract on the Seine in the thirteenth arrondissement, previously occupied by train yards and head houses leading south from the Gare d'Austerlitz. The site ran 2.5 kilometers east-west, between train tracks to the south and the river to the north, with an eight-meter drop in between. These difficult conditions had long left the site disconnected from urban life. This situation, however, was poised to change with plans for large-scale development on both banks of the Seine. Directly across the river from the library site, the recently redesigned right bank ZAC Bercy area included a new sports palace (the Palais Omnisport by Pierre Parat, Michel Andrault, and Aydin Guvan of 1983), the new Ministry of Finance (another Grand Projet by Paul Chemetov and Borja Huidobro), and Frank Gehry's American Center (now defunct), all surrounded by new tracts of housing.

On the left bank, plans for development surrounding the library—the ZAC Rive Gauche—similarly included large areas of new housing and supporting institutions to the west and east. Along the southern edge, a new east-west boulevard, the Avenue de France, was to be built over existing train tracks running from Boulevard Masséna to Boulevard Vincent Auriol. To connect the library site to the city at large, Mitterrand planned a footbridge across the Seine, as well as a new

5.1 Site model, Bibliothèque Nationale and Bercy area. (On display during the library's construction, 1997.)

metro line—*la ligne Météor*—leading directly into the heart of the Paris's financial district on the right bank. The new Bibliothèque Nationale would be the center-piece of an enormous revitalization of an entire sector of the city in both the twelfth and thirteenth arrondissements. This urban restructuring dwarfed the program for the library, itself comprising 2 million square meters of usable floor surface.

Unlike the private commission for the Louvre renovation, in 1988 Mitterand announced an international competition for the library, to be reviewed by a jury headed by none other than I. M. Pei.[1] In April 1989, an initial field of 244 com-petitors was narrowed by a first review phase to an eclectic mix of 20 internation-ally renowned semifinalists. The second phase of competition reduced this field to four equally eclectic finalists, whose approaches represented the extremes of the previous twenty. The first finalist, James Stirling, Michael Wilford and Associates, presented an urban-minded experiment displacing more traditional schemes by Alvaro Siza, Ricardo Bofill, and Bernard Huet, who had each proposed modestly restrained L-shaped buildings around large public plazas. In contrast, Stirling's entry disposed several monumentally scaled figural elements, replete with a refer-ence to Etienne-Louis Boullée's visionary Enlightenment library, around a series of landscaped terraces cascading toward the Seine.

The approach of the second finalist, Future Systems Incorporated, a London-based group of architects and engineers headed by Jan Kaplicky, could not have been more different. Two enormous bulbous shells were dropped onto a site ren-dered as a flat, nondescript plaza. Inserted in between the shells was a raised vehic-ular bridge originating across the river and cutting across the entire library site. As it traveled through the interior of the shells, the bridge was intended to give pass-ing city traffic a vicarious glimpse of the central informational display inside. The ordinary passerby would be immersed in a spectacle of electronic systems, herald-ing the new digital order that had been called for in the competition brief as part of the library's reorganization.

Although not one of the finalists, the translucent library of Rem Koolhaas and the Office of Metropolitan Architecture represented a related approach. This entry, a glowing translucent block raised off the ground, was stratified subtly by ramp-ing floor levels. Enmeshed within them was a series of amorphous voids contain-ing special function rooms but also serving as points of orientation to the city outside. With floors organized by the library's reference systems, the bibliothèque generated an architectural order from the electronic reorganization of cataloguing

5.2 Office for Metropolitan Architecture, competition entry, Bibliothèque Nationale, 1989. Courtesy Office for Metropolitan Architecture.

knowledge, one that Koolhaas represented as quintessentially dynamic. Koolhaas proposed that, as critic Marc Bédarida put it, "knowledge is no longer a circum-scribed field but a network of exchanges, flows, and immaterial passages of con-stantly changing fields of information."[2] At the same time, as Koolhaas wedded translucent imagery to his concept of ambiguous exchange, he strongly dismissed revelation as an organizing metaphor that dominated so many of the other entries. Much touted by the academic intelligentsia, Koolhaas's entry was to stand in stark contrast to that of the eventual winner, Dominique Perrault.

The third and fourth finalists, Chaix and Morel and Dominique Perrault, respectively, represented a large category of semifinalists slavish in their use of transparency as a symbol of the opening of the library's resources to the public. In Nicholas Grimshaw's entry, an enormous glass gallery, predictably fashioned in technological garb, spanned the full length of the site facing the Seine. Similarly, Fumihiko Maki oriented a grand central transparent nave toward the river between transparent pavilions. In Hermann Hertzberger's glass village, parallel transparent blocks emerged from under an enormous solid plate of office cubicles, a megastructural roof replete with a bridge suspension structure. In Nouvel's entry, glass tendrils emanated from a long glass gallery along the river and unrav-eled into a park component behind, motivated by his notion that the library was a living organism rather than a closed coffer. Parisian architect Francis Soler divided the entire site into parallel transparent halls, each 130 columnar bays long, with planting interspersed throughout. Against a wide array of complex transparent projects, conceptually and figuratively, Chaix and Morel and Dominique Perrault, offered far simpler proposals.

In Chaix and Morel's scheme, an enormous roof plane covered a simple glass volume containing reading and reference space (figure 5.3). The roof plane, in-scribed underneath with the words of great authors, gave a literal metaphor of the building as an open book. Yet Perrault's project gave full impetus to transparency as the central metaphor of the new institution. If, according to Vidler, Koolhaas's cube of glass was conceived as a frustration of transparency's claim to authentic-ity, Perrault's scheme presented its dialectical opposite.

Four symmetrical, twenty-five-story glass towers rose from a monumental plinth hovering above the river and the bordering quai. Like the Chaix and Morel scheme, the basic symbolism of the L-shaped towers was the open book. Perrault, however, reinforced the metaphor programmatically proposing that the towers function as storage for the stacks. Equally literal was the material transparency of

5.3 Chaix and Morel, competition entry, Bibliothèque Nationale, 1989. Courtesy Atelier d'Architecture Chaix Morel et Associés.

the towers' glass envelopes, which would allow the public to view the gradual yet continual accrual of the library's literary matter. The public would not only be able literally to access the national archives from reorganized public spaces and reference systems, they would also be able to see the library fulfilling its central mission of continual growth. The paradigm of transparency inherited from the Enlightenment was activated literally and metaphorically: as glass revealed the interior function and contents of the building, the image of books was an overt symbol of the exposure of knowledge to the gaze of the public.

Spanning the full dimension of the site (see figure 5.4), the horizontal plinth between the towers was placed level with the uppermost southern edge; its other three sides negotiated the changing site section by a continuous perimeter of descending stairs. At the center of the plinth Perrault placed a sunken garden fully surrounded by subterranean reading and reference areas. In his original entry, a large central opening broke the perimeter stairs under the plinth, allowing for an expansive view of the garden from the quai and providing direct entry from the river's edge. This opening, together with a set of overhead bridges crossing the garden, was abandoned during the development of the project; entry to the library complex was eventually gained by ascending the monolithic perimeter stairs. Once the opening under the plinth was sealed and the view to the garden occluded, the garden was rendered hermetic. A final exotic touch flavored this meditative quality nationalistically: the planting of the garden was simulated from a photograph of the legendary forest at Fontainebleau.

After only two days of deliberation in April 1989, the Pei jury unanimously voted to premeate Perrault's competition entry to final review by President Mitterrand, whose authority it was to choose the winner.[3] Given the extreme disparity in the four finalists' projects and the diversity of a reportedly strong-willed jury, this unanimity was considered highly suspicious by press and public alike, implying that the president had influenced the final decision. The actual degree of this influence remains ambiguous. Certainly Mitterrand's disposition to minimalist forms wrought in glass skins was well known, possibly predisposing the jury to anticipate his preference.

Significant was Mitterrand's original competition brief, which, for a building of this size, complexity, and prominence, was remarkably free of specific functional requirements. Instead, the brief and the ensuing judging of entries were guided implicitly by a series of platitudinous definitions described by Mitterrand: The institution was to express its own exceptional character; it was to be endowed

5.4 Dominique Perrault, competition model, Bibliothèque Nationale, 1989. Courtesy Dominique Perrault Architects/ADAGP.

with an appropriate dimension of monumentality; and it was to combine simultaneously an expression of the sacred with the openness of democracy. One critic wrote that the new library was dually to express the joy of immersion into the written word (*l'expression du bonheur de l'immersion dans le livre*) and the expression of social collectivity.[4] With such timeless aspirations, compared with the other three finalists, Perrault's project was assured as the eventual winner.

Unfortunately, the glory of revealing the books to public view in Perrault's scheme was accompanied by tremendous practical problems, since books, especially rare and archival books, risk disintegration when exposed to ultraviolet rays of sunlight. In the rush to attain symbolism, this one rather obvious hazard was apparently overlooked by all parties involved in the competition entries, from Dominique Perrault to François Mitterrand. Imminent danger to the books gave impetus to a vociferous and emotional international backlash against Perrault's design, equaled only by outrage directed at the perceived insensitivity of the raised plinth to the site's urban potential. Wrote Patrice Higonner in a 1991 issue of the *New York Review of Books*: "The building for the new French National Library that is just about to be constructed in Paris is a threat to French culture. It is hostile to books, hostile to people, hostile to the city of Paris."[5]

This was only one of many highly negative criticisms, many taking the form of personal attacks against the president and the young architect. In an open letter by former head of the Bibliothèque Nationale, Georges Le Rider was joined in his condemnation of the project by 700 international intellectual figures. In response to the petition, on October 9, 1991, mayor Jacques Chirac ordered that all work on the site be stopped. One hour later, however, Jacques Lang, Mitterrand's Minister of Culture, announced that work would indeed proceed; the state had taken control of the site away from the city.

Although this was the most dramatic event, the controversy continued well into later stages of design development. In response to a report by the Conseil Supérieur des Bibliothèques, Mitterrand did finally make some minor concessions, an apparent attempt to placate criticism without changing the fundamental concept and components of the Perrault project. The height of the towers was shrunk by 10 percent (two floors), Mitterrand conceded that 20 percent of the books in the towers would be stored underground, and he approved suggestions for increased ventilation.

Perrault was as obstinately resistant to reconsidering the design as Mitterrand. When criticisms of the effects of storing books under glass were first voiced, he

5.5 Bibliothèque Nationale, book-storage towers.

5.6 Bibliothèque Nationale, shutters, book-storage towers.

countered with a proposal to use a special optical glass developed by NASA that blocked ultraviolet light and heat. This proved, predictably, far too expensive to consider in the floor-to-ceiling dimensions required around the building's enormous envelopes. Perrault's next proposal, to encase the books in a concrete and lead-lined inner sheath inside the glass boxes, was also rejected for its obvious redundancy.

Finally, Perrault offered the option that was partially built: the towers would be fitted with operable wood shutters that could be opened and closed manually during the day. Dear to Perrault apparently was the idea of chance animation; as the shutters would be indiscriminately opened and closed, the patterns on the façade would register the passage of the sun across the building face.[6] Fully opened after dusk, the shutter system would allow at least partial fulfillment of the originally envisioned spectacle at night, particularly from the Seine.

In the version of the towers ultimately built, the possibility of viewing the books was finally thwarted permanently by the lingering threat of potential damage. Half the books were moved to the basement; administrative offices occupied the rest of the towers' floors. Floor-to-ceiling wood-veneer aluminum shutters were installed but they were operable only on administrative floors. Wherever book stacks remained, shutters were fixed in place. Stripped of their original mission to provide a view of books slowly accruing from floor to floor, the glass towers remain odd, unrequited vestiges of the earlier vision, as unfilled physically as they were conceptually.

GLASS, *LE MUR NEUTRALISANT*

Perrault must have been bewildered by the political storm ignited by his romantic concept. Prior to this competition, the thirty-six-year-old architect had been unknown to any public forum. His most significant commission had been a 21,000-square-meter speculative industrial building nearby on the Rue Bruneseau, located adjacent to the same run of rail tracks issuing from the Gare d'Austerlitz. Despite being less than one-tenth the size of the bibliothèque, the Hôtel Industriel Jean-Baptiste Berlier was doubtlessly persuasive in gaining Mitterrand's trust for the larger commission.

Designed as a simple concrete frame encased in a transparent envelope, the hotel anticipated Perrault's intention for the library towers as mute containers, pristine glass volumes activated dynamically by their contents. As a speculative building, the floor plans of the hotel were left deliberately unarticulated, punctuated

5.7 Dominique Perrault, Hôtel Berlier, 1990.

only by nondescript elevator and bathroom core elements. The open spaces were completely flexible, left to the needs of the particular lessee. Similar to the display of books at the bibliothèque, activities of the tenants, together with reflections of the sky, would grant the monolithic glass skin of the commercial building its texture.

The hotel's glass envelope is its most compelling feature. Using an economical system of doubly laminated glass attached with structural silicon to an aluminum frame behind, the surface of the glass is uninterrupted around the entire building, except by minimally inscribed silicon joints. At the corners, base, and upper edge of the building, Perrault made no effort to distinguish the joinery. Especially at the parapet, where he hid the solid roof slab behind the surface of glass, all of the building's edges terminate against the sky.

To shield the interior from sunlight, Perrault developed a *brise-soleil* made of horizontal shelves of galvanized expanded metal mesh, attached mechanically to the mullion-glazing frame behind the glass. The lowest of these shelves allows for hanging round mechanical heating and cooling ducts; the uppermost supports the electrical raceway that provides service link-up into tenant spaces. Veiled behind the sheer plane of glass, the building systems are fully apparent, yet relegated into an elegant subservience within the larger order of glass bays. Read together from outside, the nuanced relationship between building components and glass indicate Perrault's mature command of his building's enclosure. The refinement of details renders the envelope as a delicate continuous wrapper around a thinly etched volume of transparent space.

"If Mies had been practicing today," said Perrault, "he would have designed glass as I do."[7] Perhaps. Like Mies, Perrault's overture to advancing technology is predominantly rhetorical. Neither his library nor his hotel, like Nouvel's Fondation Cartier and Institut du Monde Arabe, exhibits the overt pretense of technological advancement present in several of the other Grands Projets, notably those engineered by RFR. But Perrault maintained that his glass systems are indeed informed by technological advancement, although those relating to production rather than structure. As evidence, he cited his buildings' realization of architectural possibilities of structural silicon and his use of enlarged panes made possible by new manufacturing processes.[8] Like typical Miesian skyscrapers of the 1950s and 1960s (for example, the Seagram, Lakeview, and Wacker Drive) the primary structures of both the library and the hotel are entirely conventional frames;

5.8 Hôtel Berlier, glass curtain wall.

5.9 Hôtel Berlier, brise-soleil behind glass curtain wall.

the architectural intention of these buildings lies predominantly in their glass surfaces.

Both of Perrault's buildings, again like those of Mies, are faced entirely by glass curtain walls composed of floor-to-ceiling panels of one ubiquitous bay dimension (figures. 5.12 and 5.13). Unlike Miesian precedents, Perrault's projects omitted the spandrel panel at the floor junction. Instead, in the library towers, he pulled the dropped ceiling structure inside the boundary of the primary structure, leaving only a thin concrete slab cantilevered to support the curtain wall. As at the Hôtel Berlier, he detailed the library mullion to fall behind the exterior plane of the glass, but here the glass surface is broken by a thin angle, which bands the four edges of each pane and is attached to the mullion using structural silicon (see figure 5.10). On the interior, a continuous, stainless steel vertical fin stiffens the vertical mullion.

The difference between this detail and a Miesian system is again noteworthy. Although 1950s technology would not have allowed Mies to bury his mullion behind the glass, there is every indication that he never would have chosen to do so. Mies not only exposed the mullion in his skyscrapers (figure 5.11), he also articulated each vertical bay division with his infamous appliquéd I-beam. The additional I-beam represents actual structure at only half of the bay divisions; as is well known, at the other half, the I-beams are completely false, located at mere window mullions. Mies was so compelled to endow his glass surface with a sense of structure that he was willing to deny the authentic representation of the actual building structure.

Differences between Perrault and Mies's glass surfaces are quickly apparent. As Kenneth Frampton observed, Mies's detailing results in a subtle balance between corporeality and transparency: "The dichotomy revealed itself most sublimely in his attitude to glass, which he used in such a way as to allow it to change under light from the appearance of a reflective surface to the disappearance of the surface into pure transparency: on the one hand, the apparition of nothing, on the other hand, an evident need for support."[9] The ontological flux of Mies's details seems not to be the goal of Perrault who, like Nouvel, was far more interested in the effects brought about by the registration of temporality in both the transparent and reflective properties of glass.[10]

Through the nuance of details, the library towers are reduced to a set of dematerialized boxes, conceptual containers awaiting embodiment by the presence of actual books as well reflections of the sky: "The same gift of metamorphosis, of transfiguration, seems to have attached itself to the Library; massive as it is with its

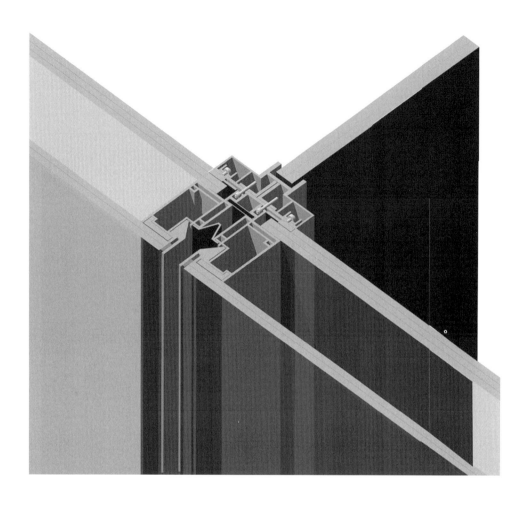

5.10 Dominique Perrault, Bibliothèque Nationale, plan detail, glass curtain wall. (Drawing: Marvin Rodriguez and Charles McGloughlin)

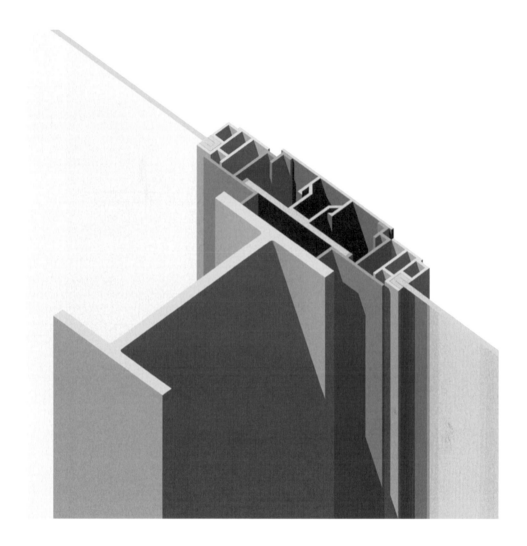

5.11 Mies van der Rohe, Lake Shore Drive Apartments, plan detail, glass curtain wall, 1948–1951. (Drawing:

Marvin Rodriguez and Charles McGloughlin)

5.12 Bibliothèque Nationale, glass curtain wall.

5.13 Lake Shore Drive Apartments, glass curtain wall.

four towers when seen from Paris, it seems to dissolve and blur away as soon as you enter it. From the esplanade, the weight of the architecture is subordinated to the views of the city, and to the sky as it rushes into what we call the building."[11] Rather than using the reflective surface to register the complexity of the urban domain, as Nouvel did, Perrault envisioned the surfaces turned upward, embracing the timelessness of the sky.

The Bibliothèque Nationale's monumental character joined with heightened political sensitivity to prevent Perrault from refining off-the-shelf systems for the glass enclosure, a sensibility that had guided the design of glass at the Hôtel Berlier. Nevertheless, the basic concept of the building enclosure as a system of protective layers behind a glass envelope derived largely from the earlier project. Since floor-to-ceiling wood shutters were set a full meter behind the glass, a thick wedge of air space was created between the exterior and the books, serving as a substantial thermal barrier.

The layering was recreated microcosmically in the insulated glass curtain wall. The 180 × 360-centimeter panes were doubly and triply laminated, on the exterior and interior faces, respectively, held apart by stainless steel mullions buried in an interior air space of 70 millimeters. To reinforce the environmental systems in the building, forced air was provided to cool the space between the panes. Through all the surfaces of the four towers as well as the subterranean garden walls, ten liters of filtered, dehydrated air per hour circulated through flexible tubes in the horizontal mullions. In addition to increased interior climate control, this provided other strengthening measures: formation of condensation within the glass layers was avoided; lateral wind resistance of the façade increased; and the interior was provided with a thick layer of acoustical isolation from the sounds of the city outside.

With this radical system of environmental control, the building provides tantalizing parallels to earlier modernist works; not to those of Mies van der Rohe, but to those of the more locally venerated Le Corbusier. Indeed, located very close by, south of the library and diagonally across the tracks from the Hôtel Berlier, is Le Corbusier's great experiment in the design of a hermetically sealed building, the Cité de Refuge or Salvation Army of 1933. A vanguard for climatologically controlled buildings, the Cité coupled a fully mechanically conditioned interior with a sheer façade designed as a sealed glass wall. Whereas these characteristics are now ubiquitous in contemporary commercial construction, the details and intent of the Cité have an eerie correspondence with Perrault's buildings.

At the Cité, Le Corbusier proposed a curtain wall of insulated glass to sheath a conventional concrete column and slab structure (figure 5.14). Originally, each pane was designed as a composite construction consisting of a thin steel angle box frame holding apart two planes of glass (figure 5.15). As at the bibliothèque, supporting these thick composite panels was a structural mullion system buried at the interior face of the panel, attaching the steel angle frame to the concrete slab behind. Minimizing evidence of structure at the exterior glass surface, Le Corbusier was clearly experimenting with a support system to provide a flush glass façade. The steel angle frame was veiled behind the exterior glass; the mullion system was contained in a deep reveal between the composite panels.

Most relevant to the details of the bibliothèque was Le Corbusier's intention to furnish his glass composite panels with a secondary ventilation system that would force cooled air between all of the panes across the south-facing façade. As in the bibliothèque, small tubes in horizontal mullion frames would accommodate this independent air system. Le Corbusier labeled the two necessary components *exacte respiration,* referring to the ability to control the interior environment completely through mechanical ventilation, and *le mur neutralisant,* describing the window walls' circulating air systems. Implicit in the latter term was the neutralizing capacity of the glass wall to isolate the building from its exterior surroundings.

The failure of Le Corbusier's systems at the Cité de Refuge, never built as originally designed, is legendary. Due to cost reductions, the glass installed across the south façade consisted of only one thin sheet of fixed, inoperable panes. The primary mechanical cooling system for the building was changed to provide merely ventilating air. The separate system intended to cool the glass façade was omitted altogether. Since the building was not simply the institutional headquarters for the Salvation Army, but a rehabilitation center providing housing and facilities for Parisian indigents, the outcome was disastrous.

During the exceptionally warm summer of 1933, doctors for residents of the Cité complained of abnormally high room temperatures. When the circulating systems were shut off at night, lack of circulating air combined with dangerously high levels of carbon dioxide, a particular concern in rooms housing families with young children. In anticipation of battles over glass in the bibliothèque, Le Corbusier was not dissuaded by the objections made by parties he perceived to be overly pragmatic. When ordered by the Seine Préfecture and then by the police to install operable windows in January 1935, he countered with the testimony of his own personally procured experts. No surprise, they supported his claim that the

5.14 Le Corbusier, Cité de Refuge, exterior façade on Rue Cantagrel with originally built glass curtain wall, 1933. (Photo: George Qualls)

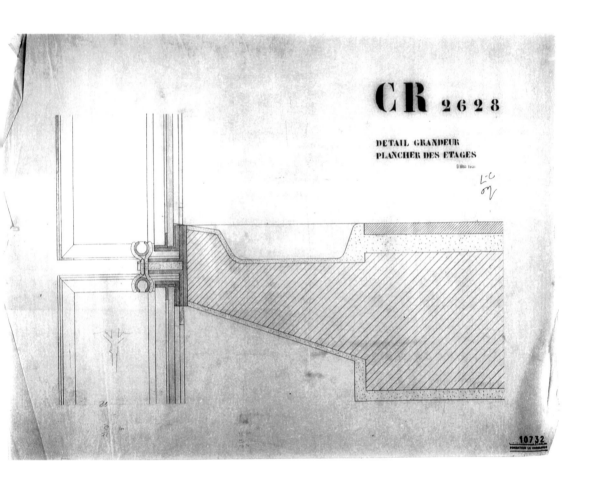

CR 2628

DETAIL GRANDEUR
PLANCHER DES ETAGES

10732

5.15 Cité de Refuge, detail section of glass curtain wall as originally designed, 1929 (unbuilt). Courtesy Fondation Le Corbusier/ADAGP. © FLC.

existing systems were sufficient to warrant altering the curtain wall to provide natural ventilation. [12]

Le Corbusier's tenacity in resisting the simple alterations that would remedy his façade was a clear indication of underlying ideological interests. As Brian Brace Taylor wrote in "Technology, Society, and Social Control," Le Corbusier had two revolutionary goals at the Cité de Refuge. The first was to advance the cause of a rapidly modernizing architecture by challenging contemporary building practices and regulatory codes with newly emerging systems of building. The second was inscribed with far more problematic social mission. Le Corbusier intended the Cité de Refuge as both metaphor of and physical setting for the Salvation Army's reformative methods. These therapies, applied to the individuals housed within, were intended both to train and rehabilitate indigent individuals back into a larger cooperative social whole; they consisted of imposing isolation from the exterior world while simultaneously immersing inmates into "work-aid programs."

On a daily basis, Salvation Army treatment centered on hygienic practices; the individual's maintenance of physical health and personal cleanliness was equated with spiritual cleansing. As Brace Taylor observed, Le Corbusier's sequence of spaces at the ground floor of the building represented a ritualistic choreography through which newly admitted individuals were both physically cleansed and psychologically counseled. As individuals ascended to the private quarters above, they would progressively become more isolated from the exterior world. Finally, sheathed behind the glass wall in their private quarters, they would be able to gaze out to a surrounding world in which they would not be able to participate; that is, until the therapies of the Salvation Army had proved them capable of rejoining a normative sphere of social and economic practices. [13] Le Corbusier's conception of the sealed glass container was as a disciplinary mechanism.

Given these paternalistic leanings, Le Corbusier's zeal to maintain the status quo of his façade against outcries of contemporary critics can be more easily understood. To break the monolithic enclosure would not only deny the building's central metaphor but would endanger rehabilitation of the Cité's indigent population. Taylor concluded his essay by noting the dilemma of an architectural order construed to discipline individuals into a cooperative social whole, especially when standards for appropriate social behavior were imposed, as in the Cité, by a remote upper class in a capitalist society. Taylor drew clear corollaries between the architectural mechanisms of the Cité de Refuge with those observed by Michel Foucault in his study of the historical evolution of disciplinary institutions. As Foucault

5.16 Cité de Refuge, view from dormitory behind original curtain wall. Courtesy Brian Brace Taylor.

(Original photographer unknown)

noted, the disciplinary model—particularly of institutions employing transparency as a device through which to structure behavior—does not contain a benevolent agenda of rehabilitation, but an implicit propensity to discipline transgressive behavior into conformative compliance. [14]

In addition to parallels in their glass enclosures, the systems of entrance and passage in the Bibliothèque Nationale are similar to those at the Cité de Refuge: both are scripted as *promenades architecturales*. Like the sequence of cleansing spaces on the Cité's ground floor, each stage of the library's entrance procession is intended as an incremental removal of the visitor's sense of engagement in the timely domain outside. All visitors first enter the complex by ascending the substantial perimeter wooden steps up to the plaza level from the lower quai edge. Leaving the city behind, the visitor reengages it only moments later from the changed vantage point afforded by the plinth's elevation.

The enormous flat surface, a horizontal datum registering the city's vertical fray, is imbued with atmospheric nautical allusions. Lovingly specifying precisely crafted hardwood decking remembered from an experience on a Boston boardwalk, Perrault scatters maritime elements—stainless steel pontoons, stairways, and guardrails—across its breadth. [15] The city, distantly viewed and acoustically muted from across the vast surface, becomes an oceanic mirage. The nautical allusion is as transportive as it is transformative, much like the Cité de Refuge, whose primary physical metaphor is also that of a ship (derived from Le Corbusier's first commission for the Salvation Army, renovation of the Ile Flottante).

After crossing the plinth, the encounter with the sunken garden at the heart of the complex is significantly delayed until the visitor has almost broached its precipitous edge. A continuous stainless steel brise-soleil around the plinth opening does not shade the glass walls of the reading rooms below as much as it occludes a view of the garden from above. At this point, to enter the library the visitor must travel around the enormous perimeter of the sunken garden to either of the two grand escalators at its extreme ends. After having been made to ascend to the plinth, the visitor is now compelled to descend again to the entry of the building proper. At every level of descent, the datum of the towers above diminishes; this last visible vestige of the exterior world gradually disappears, marking a continuous retreat from the life of the city.

After a short stop on an exterior terrace level (the closest point to actually entering the garden), the visitor encounters the security check and catalogue lobby of the first reading room level. Finally inside, the magnitude of the library's

5.17 Bibliothèque Nationale, the perimeter steps.

5.18 Bibliothèque Nationale, on the plinth.

5.19 Bibliothèque Nationale, view of brise-soleil from below.

resources can be fully appreciated. This upper level, reserved for the general public—*le grand public*—rings the entire garden, one spacious double-height reference and reading room following the next, organized sequentially around thematic material contained within. Yet this is the last point of passage that is open to the general public. Underneath this level is a vaster, triple-height ring of reading and reference rooms, but these spaces admit only the most advanced scholars. As at the former Richelieu site, these scholars have their research topics and credentials screened for access to special collections and archival material. Even the monumental escalator shafts leading into the second research level from the base of the towers are entered by special permission only.

Given the rhetorical idealism of the Bibliothèque Nationale to open the library to the public, their exclusion at this last capacious level is a curious reinstitution of the hierarchy of the Richelieu site, a situation originally necessitated by the library's shortage of space. This vestige of elitist order is reiterated in an auspiciously public setting. At all levels, the walls flanking the sides of the garden use the same glass system employed by Perrault in the towers, yet partially shaded by the trees of the garden, they are transparent rather than reflective. As at the Cité de Refuge, the promenade architecturale for the general public terminates in a glass wall that is heavily inscribed with relationships of accessibility and privilege, here the hierarchies of French academia. As were residents at the Cité, the general public is confined on the level above, peering from behind a glass wall, gazing down on a vast realm that is ultimately unattainable.

In fairness to the bibliothèque, several parts of the site, yet unbuilt at this writing, will reduce the steps in the entry sequence, thereby lessening the problematic manipulations inherent in the promenade. The adjacent Avenue de France envisioned at the onset of the competition remains incomplete. It will run level with the top of the plinth, along the higher elevation at the eastern flank of the site, contiguous to new housing also to be built on top of existing train tracks. Mass transportation will be provided along this avenue, emptying visitors directly onto the plaza. The footbridge, the Passerelle Bercy-Tolbiac, awarded by competition to Feichtinger Architects and Rice Francis Ritchie, shows slow but steady progress through political negotiations; when complete, it will provide even more pedestrian entry directly onto the plinth level.

Large numbers of visitors will be able to access the plinth without being forced to climb the perimeter steps; thus one substantial step in the arduous and

5.20 Bibliothèque Nationale, view from public reading room to entry escalator and scholars' reading level.

redundant passage sequence into the building will be eliminated. Other elements will, however, remain the same. Visitors will still be compelled to circulate around the garden on the huge unprotected plinth before descending to the entry proper. They will still be prevented from entering the garden and reserved reading areas, while being tantalized by views of these spaces. For the sake of evoking certain poetic associations and experiential phenomena, the route through the site simultaneously invokes relationships of privilege.

As a library, the Bibliothèque Nationale will never claim the same degree of specific bodily control as the Cité de Refuge, whose mechanisms were supported by the specific function and ideology of the institution itself. But given the number of individuals the library controls and the heightened symbolism of the institution at national and international levels, the gestures of power implicit in the library are far more influential. As the glass surface in Cité de Refuge represented the solid boundary between private transgression and public social norms, the library's glass surfaces poses an equally precise metaphor of a boundary preventing public's admission to the highest cultural and intellectual strata. The two metaphors are endowed by the personal roles of Le Corbusier and Mitterrand. Implied in the long battles both men undertook to realize their architectural visions against an unwilling public, there is a clear indication in both buildings of personal symbolism imposed from above, a lofty paternalistic attitude toward a perceived lower social stratum.

WITHIN LA VILLE MINIMALISTE

If the bibliothèque's glass curtain wall opens profound implications for the politics of space at an interior building scale, so does it also for the larger relationship of the site to the city. Brace Taylor noted that Le Corbusier claimed in *The Radiant City* that the mur neutralisant was a necessary corollary to his urban utopian proposals. Rayner Banham even contended that the internationalism of Le Corbusier's urban proposals hinged on maintaining an ideal artificial interior temperature of 18°C: conquering and subsuming the local climate was necessary if an international style was to be imposed upon local cultures. Just as the mur neutralisant forced hygienic and aesthetic standards on an interior space, the internationalist city would impose the same hygienic and aesthetic standards on the city at large. As the indigent population of the Cité de Refuge was cleansed and respiritualized by sunlight and mechanically cycled air of the building interior, so the inhabitants of the city were to be morally renewed by the light and open space pouring in from huge boulevards.

If the mur neutralisant represents Le Corbusier's attempts to transform society at the scale of a building element, the macroscopic realization of his ambitious undertaking is manifested in his plan for the City for Three Million of 1929 and his Plan Voisin of 1925. Indeed, when the plans for the Bibliothèque Nationale are overlaid on those of the Plan Voisin (originally proposed on the Right Bank near the Ile de la Cité), there is marked similarity between the scale of building elements and plaza spaces. The configuration of the L-shaped towers is easily recognizable as bifurcated versions of Le Corbusier's cross-shaped figures. The site plan for the bibliothèque offers substantial evidence that it is yet another proposal in a lineage of long discredited mainstream modernist urbanistic ideas. In eradicating local culture and local circumstance, the site was universalized in an operation at once autonomous and imperialistic. The site plan seems perfectly coherent with the political mechanisms that produced it, giving form to the forceful imposition of Mitterrand's plans on the unwilling city.

Fortunately for the library as well as for Paris, taken alone the site plan does not adequately describe the project's experiential dimension, which adds a considerable layer of subtlety in fully understanding the mechanisms embedded in the building's siting. Perrault gives a substantial clue to these intentions. Besides repeatedly acknowledging the influence of canonical architectural modernists, particularly Mies and Louis Kahn, he invokes American minimalist sculptors, especially Donald Judd and Robert Morris. Thus we return to the specter of 1960s minimalism haunting monumental Paris, first encountered at the Grande Pyramide.

Here the salient aspect is not minimalism's presupposed lack of signification or its neutral geometric expression, but rather to the complex relationship in minimalist sculpture between the work and its context. As Rosalind Krauss repeatedly asserted, the premise of minimalist work is not in its ideality but in its contingency; that is, installation of the minimal form in a context does not reify individual sculpture as much as it redefines the setting in which it is placed. Hal Foster wrote, "In short, Minimalist sculpture no longer stands apart, on a pedestal or as pure art, but is repositioned among objects and redefined in terms of place. In this transformation the viewer, refused the safe, sovereign space of formal art, is cast back on the here and now; and rather than scan the surface of a work for its topographic mapping, of the properties of its medium, he or she is prompted to explore the perceptual consequences of a particular intervention in a given site."[16]

Under the auspices of minimalist sculpture, the sequence in which the spaces and elements of the bibliothèque are engaged take on a new light. The fact that Perrault made an attempt to alter the way the city outside was perceived through the mechanism of his horizontal plinth is more than a mere experiential anecdote. It indicates that the Perrault library's relation to its context is hardly the same as its Corbusian precedent, which presumed that the city had been erased. This distinction is enormously significant. It reveals the mechanisms of the library site to be diametrically opposed to the autonomous presumptions of the Plan Voisin, and indicates that minimalist operations of recontextualization are indeed at play, moving the bibliothèque closer in spirit to the Nouvel buildings than might be imagined from a cursory inspection of respective site plans.

The insistent reference to minimalism is also telling in many other respects. The original competition entry included an analysis that articulated the presence of significant urban empty spaces—*les grands vides*—along the Seine. In the drawing, the plinth was integrated among a network of urban spaces that included, among others, the grand esplanades of the Invalides, the Champ de Mars, and the Tuileries, as well as smaller plazas associated with significant buildings (including the plaza at the Pompidou Center). The original concept for his scheme thus comprised not only the transparent towers of books, but more significant (according to Perrault), the garden sunken into the raised plaza at the heart of the complex.

Yet unlike the urban plazas referenced, the bibliothèque's garden space is truer to the extended translation of the French *vide*, which resounds with poetic connotations of pure emptiness: cut off from possibility for actual entry, the garden is rendered literally nonanthropomorphic—lacking human scale as well as simple means of physical access. It is intended to remain significantly and provocatively vacant, a quality imparted to a lesser degree on the plinth itself.

This loss of center is an identifiably Eastern concept, and the configuration of the library's plaza and garden is similar to emblematic Eastern urban spaces, particularly in Japan, where access to a final central space or object is precluded. Rather, the center of often complex configurations of buildings, spaces, and processional routes is supposed to be felt rather than physically accessed or even directly perceived.[17] Instead of a participatory space, the garden was intended as a meditative object. Yet this particular instance of Eastern aestheticism at the Bibliothèque Nationale runs counter to qualities consistently claimed by its supporters.

5.21 Dominique Perrault, "Paris: les Grands Vides Accrochés à la Seine." (Drawing from Bibliothèque
Nationale competition entry, 1989) Courtesy Dominique Perrault Architects/ADAGP

In the face of criticism, Mitterrand contended, "Between the earth and the sky runs the library's esplanade, open to all, a broad public space in which people can meet and mingle, of a kind that is all too rare in the new quarters of modern cities."[18] This introductory quotation to the official library monograph reflects Mitterrand's unwavering belief that the plaza truly was a social space. Yet all evidence points to the contrary; the allusion to the East indicates spatial practices based in solitude and aesthetic meditation. In the translation offered to a meaning-hungry Western audience, the Bibliothèque Nationale runs the risk of encountering, and does indeed eventually confront, the *horror vacui* reserved in the West for both emptiness of meaning and emptiness of spaces.

The vision for the bibliothèque's plaza certainly included human participation. Perrault's vision was definitive in this respect; imagining sparsely dispersed small groups and individuals wandering in a slow meander, the ambiance of the plinth would provoke mental and spiritual contemplation. Indeed, whereas the basic formal gesture of his building did not derive from motion studies (in contrast to other contemporary buildings, particularly Frank Gehry's), he conceived that the movement of visitors against its uniformly gridded surfaces would provide its final activation.[19] Although incorporating people in the original concept of his building's embodiment is humanistically derived, problematic issues arise when considering that his projected occupation of the plinth was considered in visual terms only.

Perrault's particular idea of chance inhabitation also served as the seminal concept for the Hôtel Berlier, where the architect envisioned his glass wall subtly displaying the activities of the industrial tenants. Yet, in a telling anecdote, he was reportedly annoyed with the tenants' tendency to use the expanded steel brise-soleil elements as shelves, since placing storage boxes and industrial supplies too close to the surface of the glass undermines the delicate veiling effect of the glass and enclosure systems.[20] As the tenants' belongings intrude graphically into the ephemeral image of the glass surface, its fragile apparition-like quality is destroyed. Perrault's predisposition is obvious: the conception of his buildings relies a particular image or visual quality that is reified often at the expense of all other factors, pragmatic and conceptual.

This inclination was, after all, at the root of the dilemma sparked by the original concept of the library's towers, where the poetic image of accumulating books superceded the functional demands of the building to provide protection for its precious load. The human figures Perrault imagined on the surface of the plinth

5.22 Bibliothèque Nationale, view across plinth.

start to appear less like human beings and more like fragments of a visual composition. Imagine the consequences: to achieve the poetic virtuosity of his vision, the physical description and activities of the figures would have to be finitely defined. Numbers of people on the plinth would have to be limited; types of activities would have to be restricted.

Taken to a hypothetical extreme, even aesthetic parameters would have to be set to have Perrault's vision fully realized: visitors to the plinth would always be dressed in simple dark clothes to contrast sharply with the building's wood and glass material palette, and they would all walk with the same leisurely contemplative gait. Certainly Perrault never actually proposed regulating the activities or appearances of visitors to the plinth, but it seems appropriate to his vision that library security stands ready to prohibit picnicking or any other overly recreational activity on the great public surface.

More than simple observations on Perrault's privileging of the visual dimension of his work, the finite proscriptions of his visions are complicit with the controlling measures of the building's glass enclosure and its promenade architecturale. As the body's route is proscribed in space, it is taken out of its disordered habitat in the city and subsumed further and further into progressively hermeticized spaces within the thick enclosures of glass. Meanwhile, during its travels, the body is clearly intended to be viewed from both the interior and exterior of the building, appropriated as a silhouette against the glass surface, used opportunistically to grace the composition of a visually controlled space. As the body is abstracted to function as part of a visual composition, it is instrumentalized, subsumed within the tyranny of a finite aesthetic vision.

The effects of Perrault's vision of transparent surfaces are diametrically opposed to those that emerge at the Eiffel Tower and the Pompidou Center. The Pompidou's concept of transparency as a framework open to chance animation, inclusive of both refined and not so refined occupations, was decidedly anti-aesthetic. The bibliothèque, with its extreme aestheticization of transparency, is closed to all but the most specific occupations. We might remember the transparent condition in the Pompidou Center as essentially unstable, constituting an ever-oscillating surface between states of meaning as well as conditions of space, finite and infinite, spectacular and mundane. As a finite aesthetic construct, in contrast, the transparent condition at the Bibliothèque Nationale is fixed, forever closed as a system of meanings as well as a physical state, altered only by timeless reflections of a changing sky.

SURFACE CLASSICISM

Perrault's allegiance to the minimalists is illustrated most profoundly in the most interior portions of his project, on every surface surrounding spaces and every surface coating objects and furnishings. "Because of this demonstrable attack on the idea that [Minimalists] works achieve their meaning by becoming manifestations of a hidden center, Minimalism was read as lodging meaning in the surface of the object, hence its interest in reflective materials, in exploiting the play of natural light,"[21] wrote Rosalind Krauss on and around the topic of Mies van der Rohe. As the visitor enters the library proper on the first reading level, a full range of sensuous surfaces defines every element. A plush red carpet is laid flush with borders of warm wood floors. Above the concierge station is a 6-meter-high soffit of repeated, stainless steel industrial panels, where one panels is occasionally turned backward to give a random textural effect.

Other mass-produced industrial products are used throughout the building, including dozens of different lustrous stainless steel screens, stock items specially manufactured to specifications. Perrault reinvented the screens to finish ceilings and walls; typically they are detailed as fabrics, slightly porous to reveal mechanical systems buried beyond. In the public reading room ceilings, for example, framed panels contain a screen element, their edges "sewed" to the frame with stainless steel cable. In the grand escalator halls descending to scholars' level, the industrial material assumes a monumental character. Here are hung enormous 60-meter vertical panels of roughly woven stainless steel screen, with edges at the sides and bottom left unseamed and unattached, creating literal tapestry wall hangings.

This treatment is similar to the ceilings of the scholars' reading halls, where continuous lengths of stainless steel screen droop slightly above the space, looping over a horizontal tube at the corner, and continuing down vertically against the full height of the wall. Stainless steel screens are also used on smaller elements throughout the library, especially at numerous free-standing lighting and mechanical outlets, where they are rolled to different radii, creating a variety of vertical conduits through which air and electricity pass.

Perrault kept his palette firmly in check. However ubiquitous, these finely crafted stainless steel elements do not overwhelm the spaces with particularly industrial material sensibility. Augmenting the screens are the warm red carpet and the many different exotic woods employed in the interior furnishings and special wall elements. At points actual canvas fabrics are used adjacent to the screens. In conjunction with all these materials, Perrault provided an especially fine,

5.23 Bibliothèque Nationale, interior, at concierge.

5.24 Bibliothèque Nationale, interior, at scholars' entry, escalator hall.

lustrous finish to the enormous concrete portal frames that pass through and structure all the subterranean levels.

As all these materials and finishes come together coherently, Perrault's mastery of the surface conditions endows the interior with a subtle range of material luminosity. This effect is repeated in reference room after reference room, as the architect never seemed to exhaust the possibilities of his different material inventions. Compared with the neutral exterior, the voluptuous interior suggests a hermetic entombment that is quintessentially erotic in its endless evocation of the haptic nature of the surfaces. Displaced from the realm of the city into the aura of the book, the visitor enters the sacrosanct body of the building, which, rather than being transparent, is an entirely opaque, private, and hermetic domain that is closest in spirit to, say, the Maison de Verre.

A further examination into minimalism substantiates this return to the haptic nature of the body. Often called "literalism," minimalism relied on the recognition and simultaneous transcendence of simple, everyday material. By placing everyday objects in a "situation," the disposition of the beholder was called into question as the original context was challenged. In the 1960s, this theatricality provoked critics Michael Fried and Clement Greenberg to assail minimalism as an attack on conventional sculpture, on the presumption of "presence" over the fundamental definitions of high art. As minimalists strove to eliminate the anthropomorphic reference of traditional or late modernist figurative sculpture, it was the body that was reinvigorated; not the image or reference of the ideal body in sculpture, but the body of the moving subject perceiving the work of art.

Perrault's treatment of materials in the Bibliothèque Nationale was clearly inspired by the same transcendent aspirations as the minimalist artists. In his use of stainless steel screens, the material's industrial origin is constantly maintained yet the context changes in a number of different ways: a clever change in function, a severe alteration of scale, or, at the scale of the detail, a consistently imposed planarity across inventive connections to other materials. As on the building exterior, these devices presume the presence of a moving, perceiving subject. Here, the overt control and surveillance in other aspects of the building are considerably qualified.

Within the sequence of vast public reading areas, the visitor is free to wander aimlessly and indulgently. The effect of the materials surrounding spaces is diametrically opposite from that of the exterior. If the exterior of the building sublimates the body by controlling and instrumentalizing it to serve an aesthetic purpose, the interior generously returns the body to its subjective prominence.

5.25 Bibliothèque Nationale, interior detail.

5.26 Bibliothèque Nationale, scholars' lounge. (Photo: Robert Cesar) © Archipress/ADAGP

The body perceives, both mentally and physically. At the same time, Perrault's orchestration of materials provides the body with exalted levels of physical comfort, swaddling it and effusing its haptic and visual senses with provocative surface after provocative surface.

Yet, despite these great triumphs, the dilemma of the larger site issues remains to haunt a final assessment of the library. However successfully the interior works to qualify the library's problematic issues, the institution's scale and prominence in the city unfortunately guarantee that it is the exterior that will dominate the final reading. Even the nuanced sense of contingency toward the city and the sky stands to be overwhelmed by its disposition on the site. In their absolutely symmetrical organization and monumental scale, the building mass and space continue to indicate a classical autonomy more akin to Pei's pyramid than to Nouvel's urban restatements. Certainly, as Rosalind Krauss noted in reference to minimalist Agnes Martin, the presence of contingency does not guarantee that a work be regarded as *subjectively* disposed and therefore beyond classical (objective) parameters.

In "The Grid, the/Cloud/, and the Detail," an essay explicitly challenging contemporary revisionist readings of the Barcelona Pavilion, Krauss described the evolution of classicist sculpture as a series of attempts to overcome the shadow present in the classical relief, the ultimate emblem of contingency. Rather than portraying subjectivity as an external challenge to the objectivity or autonomy conventionally considered dominant in classical production, Krauss contended that the two aspects have always been conjoined. In addition, the grids of Agnes Martin's work, objective in concept and subjective in reception, might be seen as yet another stage of classical production, a contention Martin herself supports.

This final invocation of minimalism reconciles contradictions latent in Perrault's work. The absolute symmetry of the building's configuration is consistent with the pervasive and ubiquitous presence of the grid across all of the surfaces. This grid, less motivated by structure and tactility than a proclivity toward immateriality, is symptomatic of an effort to reach a purely objective mode of expression. To understand Perrault's fundamental distinction one must return to Nouvel's projects. Although a gridded glass surface was equally pervasive in Nouvel's buildings, in neutralizing the building's form, his grids encouraged different cultural representations to emerge as dominant entities. In contrast, Perrault's gridded surface is motivated only toward its own self-reflective, internalized expression, revealing the project's resoundingly classical dimension.

5.27 Bibliothèque Nationale, book-storage towers.

Clearly what appealed to Mitterrand is not the building's attention to contingent activation, but its image of iconic timelessness. Indeed, the classicist impulses of the bibliothèque are implicitly reiterated countless times by Mitterrand himself. "The building of a library for the 21st century has been a response to certain practical necessities. But in addition to answering these necessities it was deemed right that France should make clear, in the form of an exemplary monument, both her sense of the value of her intellectual heritage and her confidence in the future of books and the act of reading."[22] The invocation of timelessness comes, however, at a price. Perrault's exquisite objectivist constructions are so neutral that they cannot be contaminated by popular culture. In this they eliminate all but the smallest sense of collective fantasy afforded by the Pompidou Center or the Eiffel Tower. Despite its transparent glass walls, the library's *surface* has become opaque. The institution can finally connote only elevated culture and only the culture of the state. Even the provocative interior materials and furnishings are tainted, accused in the popular press as expensive seductions employed to overcome the library's controversy.

THE STATE OF THE GLASS STATE

In the nation's rush to reembrace the beloved institution of the Musée du Louvre, the symbolism of the Grande Pyramide shifted from signifying the role of Mitterrand as instigator of the museum's renovation to signifying all of France. The Bibliothèque Nationale was not, however, as fortunate in escaping specific political association. After Mitterrand's death in 1996, the library was renamed for the ex-president and is now known as the Bibliothèque Nationale de France *François Mitterrand*. Certainly, this gesture was undertaken with considerable irony. The financial expenditures and political debate surrounding the library are rumored to have contributed substantially to the demise of Mitterrand's socialist regime in 1993. In addition, since the opening of the library in 1998, the facility has been plagued by tremendous operating problems and maintenance expenses. These are especially associated with computerized systems transporting books across enormous distances from storage towers to reading areas. As the last of the Grands Projets, the Bibliothèque Nationale will doubtlessly taint the greater body of works Mitterrand so ambitiously inaugurated twenty years before. Just as it qualifies the reception and memory of all of the Grands Projets, it also qualifies the specific symbolism of transparency that Mitterrand co-opted to express monumentality in late twentieth-century Paris.

That a leader of state would construe and assign personal symbolism over a national capital might be seen as radically incongruous in a democratically governed country. History, both archaic and recent, provided Mitterrand the authority to do exactly that. De Gaulle's constitution of 1958 empowered the president to allow much large-scale expenditure without the aid or obstruction of legislative procedures; Mitterrand largely determined the allocation of eleven billion francs to produce the Grands Projets. We have seen, at various points in this book, that Mitterrand's claim to singular leadership and control of the Grands Projets sparked a great deal of controversy. Nevertheless, the French public remains conflicted with regard to less-than-democratic guidance of cultural achievements, especially when they pertain to the capital city. "Imagine putting aesthetic choices to a vote in the French Parliament," a critic mused, "Nothing would ever get done. At least from a monarch you get a decision. It is a very positive system in its way. The French are complainers, anarchists, individualists, and so on, but they have an enormous respect for grandeur."[23]

Nowhere is this penchant for a monarch to assume the power of national symbolic expression better illustrated than in the history of monuments in France. In the most vivid example, Louis XIV co-opted the symbology of the sun in the mid-seventeenth century to associate his reign with the presence of divinity. The specific elements of this solar symbolism in his gardens at Versailles are notable with respect to the emergence of transparency: rampant in the garden was Le Nôtre's use of infinite perspectival vistas to align the king's chateau to the diurnal passage of the sun. Deliberate also was Le Nôtre's play on properties of reflection in aquatic pools, a spectacular event complemented inside the chateau in the Hall of Mirrors by Jules Hardouin Mansart and Charles LeBrun.

Allen S. Weiss called this symbolic appropriation of the sun as one of the greatest aesthetic representations of *vanitas* in history.[24] As Louis XIV's chateau was aligned with the sun, so every social space in the palace was controlled by his gaze. The king was rendered the omnipresent God at the center of a great panoptic device. According to Weiss, the moment of Versailles corresponded not simply to the last great gasp of the baroque in the face of encroaching neoclassical tendencies (a typical art historical understanding), but to a much larger paradigmatic philosophical shift: "This conflation of God and king is not merely rhetorical: it is an integral part of the new metaphysical position of the century, where each subjectivity is constituted within a paradoxical condition. The essence of humanity is no longer guaranteed by the powers of a transcendent God, but at the same time this essence transcends the limitations of human reason." Weiss stated that the era of Versailles was distinguished by the separation of the study of aesthetics from theology and science.

Poised against the great philosophical rupture of the seventeenth century, Mitterrand's appropriation of transparency seems radically unfounded, at least without the vantage of 300 years of retrospection. It is noteworthy that no contemporary French political or aesthetic theorist has, at this writing, discussed Mitterrand's use of transparency and his symbolism of accessibility in any substantive way. It is unbelievable that the era of Mitterrand and his monumental imposition on Paris is passing without remark.

This book only begins to probe the significance of the Grands Projets, limiting discussion to the question of specific architectural issues, and curtailing many larger historical and political issues. The question of the projects' symbolism remains equally tumultuous, although perhaps this is to be expected. As post-structural criticism demonstrates, assigning symbolic meaning in a contemporary cultural realm is an infinitely complex, if not entirely futile, exercise. In the wake of this semiological haze, the pointed attempt by Mitterrand to endow transparency with a renewed ideological symbolism remains even more intriguing, if not bewildering. Transparency is hardly the most apt term to describe Mitterrand's interaction with administration and public alike in his tenure as president. As one critic said of the particularly French contradiction in its regard for its leaders, which Mitterrand seemed to embody:

France is a country in which the head of state is appreciated as such, independent of (and often more than) what he does. The test of his mettle is his demonstrated capacity in the realm of pure power. He is expected to undertake, and to succeed in, maneuvers that connoisseurs will appreciate. Even when the head of state is democratically elected on a specific political platform, his talent is judged in terms of his ability to invent strategies, and to create the conditions for surprise attack. This language seems strangely Machiavellian, yet it lingers on a society that for two hundred years has wanted to think only in terms of transparency while valuing nothing so much as mystery in what politicians do; a society that is obsessed with legitimacy in government yet is pleased to imagine governing as the exercise of absolute power independent of any reference other than itself.[25]

Plagued by numerous scandals, from the covert 1985 bombing and cover-up of a Greenpeace ship in a New Zealand harbor, to continuing posthumous accusations of financial improprieties rocking the international press, Mitterrand's rhetoric of transparency seems especially hollow. Neither is the possible larger association of transparency to Socialist ideology particularly convincing, especially in light of the man's political history, which is checkered by ambivalent allegiances and compromised by strategic maneuvers between the right and left in French politics. Mitterrand's early Catholic childhood and university affiliations were with the right; during the occupation and postliberation periods this extended into involvement as a minor player with Marshal Pétain, regarded as a German collaborator, a connection that continues to haunt Mitterrand's ghost.

Mitterrand's final ascension to power in the 1960s and 1970s came out of his mercurial ability to compromise between various fractious platforms within the leftist party, a testament more to his political prowess than to a genuine position supported by the various parties on the left. Even his own Socialist party often considered him an opportunist without authentic ideological conviction. The man's commitment to various socialist programs, however, was in fact constant throughout the larger part of his career. He consistently supported democratic constitutionality and Socialist economic planning, including nationalization as a general right and the obligation of government in the redistribution of wealth. Biographer Baumann-Reynolds explains Mitterrand's personal interpretation of socialism as based essential in a Catholic system of value, finally as paternalistic and sentimental.[26] If the transparency of the Grands Projets comes to be regarded by history as annotating the country's political present, it will most likely emerge under vague paternalistic benevolence that is rooted entirely in the persona and *vanitas* of Mitterrand, rather than to any definitive leftist ideology.

Whereas this symbolism is certainly tainted by Mitterrand's desire to establish a personal legacy, it is hardly endowed with the heroic grandeur of Louis XIV. France at the turn of the twenty-first century is no longer the culturally and traditionally homogeneous state of its 800-year-old legacy. Increasingly, this oldest of European states has had its mythically autonomous traditions challenged. Since World War II its military power has slipped to secondary standing, well behind the United States, Russia, and China. European unification has diminished its economic autonomy and its preciously held agrarian cultural tradition. A huge immigrant population, by far outstripping immigration to the United States on a per capita basis, has diminished its ethnic homogeneity. Since the Liberation in 1944, American youth culture has permeated popular French culture, particularly in language, music, cuisine, films, and fashion. French companies, until recently disdainful of American "brutalist" corporate practices, have begun silently to adopt them.[27]

If we are to draw a conclusion from recent scholarship, the common French perception since the late 1970s and early 1980s is that of a besieged culture in danger of annihilation. In 1984, Pierre Nora, a leading French intellectual, gathered eminent colleagues in a massive undertaking to document elements of French culture deemed universal to the constitution of the French persona, and that were perceived as rapidly disappearing. This seven-volume text, *Les Lieux de Mémoire*, takes as its task the representation of France, all of France, and nothing but France. As the largest intellectual project in the country's recent history, it is in many ways more significant for arriving at an understanding of the symbolism of the Grands Projets than any explicitly stated goal or affiliation with particular political philosophy.

The impetus to gather, and collectively to express, all of French culture and tradition is entirely coincident, after all, with Mitterrand's vision for the Bibliothèque Nationale, and for which Dominique Perrault's original competition entry provided a physical and symbolic manifestation. Indeed, both the bibliothèque and *Lieux de Memoire* illuminate the motivation of all the Grands Projets: to represent French culture at a particularly precarious moment in its history. The Bibliothèque Nationale's aspiration to timelessness should be regarded not as a reiteration of power (as in the era of Louis XIV), but as the permanent marking of a culture in steady decline. Walter Benjamin once changed the nickname of Paris from the "City of Light" to "Looking-Glass City." If history remembers the emergence of fragile transparency in the Grands Projets as having any amount of symbolic coherence, it will be with the pathos of a rich civilization portending its imminent demise.

What then does the appearance of transparency in Paris mean to the history of architecture if not specific symbolism? This book revolves around a metaphor of transparency characterized by fluidity, a tenacious resistance to the assignation of symbolic import, a perfect wedding of conceptual and material attributes of glass. Given the extreme shift in meanings and possible readings instituted by the transparent surfaces of the Grands Projets, transparency's essential fluidity is reiterated each time. As various points in the text have attempted to elucidate, it is exactly this open concept that the Grands Projets prompted as a viable expression for the monument in our time, an expression all the more remarkable for its economy of means. In the thinness of surfaces, between the most nuanced relationships of materials, lies the fragile and enormous potency of glass.

Epilogue: The Discourse of Details

As it evolved in nineteenth-century Germany, embedded in the concept of the tectonic was the unification of architectural symbolism with new materials and construction techniques. Tectonics presented a reconciliation just before the emergence of European modernism between "the objective presumptions of a public technological society and the philosophical aestheticism of private subjectivity."[1] In his book on the origin of modernity within German architectural theory, Mitchell Schwarzer described the discourse of the tectonic as a Vitruvian legacy delving into the movement between essence and its representation. The propensity of the tectonic, or the poetic "techne," was to assume for various German authors a totalizing capacity, subsuming all other factors in the generation of building form.

Of all the nineteenth-century German theorists—Bötticher, Redtenbacher, and Heinzerling among others—it was only Gottfried Semper who broke the model of the primordial structure as ideally derived from its own internal principles and redefined it according to principles of human need. Semper's structure of a supporting framework with hanging carpets was to be distinguished as a shelter; the analogy of building cladding to human clothing was his central concept. This qualification of the ideal, the technical, the technological, with the human was of significant consequence.

Semper's idea of the tectonic was distinguished principally from Kantian philosophy, which held that the "judgement of an aesthetic object should be divorced from social comprehension." Gevork Hartoonian said, "Semper propounds an associative understanding of architecture, in which a building is a fragment of larger reality; it becomes the construction of the conditions of life."[2] For Semper the artifact was subordinate to its embodiment.[3] Semper's theories provide the basic concept and operative definition of the tectonic in this book; namely, that the design of a building's technological systems is incomplete without considering the participation of a human audience at many different levels.

Considered alone, Semper's theories are inadequate in describing the instigation of glass technology in latter twentieth-century public architecture. In glass and steel buildings, especially when considered in the wake of Mies van der Rohe's stripped glass and steel boxes, Semper's concept of structural-symbolic is rendered mute: as the structure is made fully visible, its conventional representational capacity collapses. Semper, in contrast principally to his contemporary theorist Bötticher, subordinated material and structural expression to traditional ornamental orders.

This study on glass in the late twentieth century shares no such historicist leanings; it accepts that the advent of glass and steel construction in the last 200 years has rewritten the largest morphological orders in buildings as well as the underlying concepts of traditional representation. Semper's concept of incompletion is essential nonetheless, providing a new lens through which to examine the most general elements of contemporary glass construction as well as the most specific moments of their details in light of the buildings' situation in social, political, and theoretical realms. In the glass buildings of Mitterrand's Paris, mute construction systems are intended to perform in highly charged politically and socially symbolic realms. This is a far more complicated setting and notion of symbolism than could ever be broached by Semper's irreducible primordial structures and his concept of primitive dwelling.

Of all current architectural theorists, no one has labored so tenaciously as Kenneth Frampton in situating Semper's ideas, particularly that of the structural symbolic, in contemporary orders of production and consumption. In his "Rappel à l'Ordre: The Case for the Tectonic," an essay seminal to his later work, Frampton distinguished three categories of constructional expression—*technological, tectonic,* and *scenographic.*[4] In addressing the contemporary monuments built by Mitterrand all three of these terms might be activated, although simultaneously rather than independently. It becomes evident that each of Frampton's terms taken in isolation is inadequate to describe fully the role construction plays in buildings' expression; exposing the limitation of the terms themselves as well as the overarching issue of legitimizing the physical entity of a building by the authenticity of structural representation alone.

The glass projects of RFR provide a telling example. As products of overt technological determination, generated from a technical question the buildings would thus seem to fall within Frampton's category of technological objects. The buildings, produced through collaboration with various architects, have limited architectural identity; they might be dismissed as naive extensions of highly advanced technologies. Yet RFR's glass support systems are also nuanced explorations in their own right, results of applied efforts of engineers and industries engaging and testing the limits of material, assembly, and structure at a level of analysis and execution comparable to traditional craft.

Although technical feats, they provide evidence of a culture rarely encountered within engineering practice, one highly sensitive to the poetics of ontological expression. RFR also was motivated in designing support systems by a desire to enrich the interiors in which they were employed with a particular spatial quality; these spaces provoke an experiential dimension that Frampton called in later writings "a corporeal imagination." According to much of Frampton's terminology, the RFR works must be accorded dimensions simultaneously technological and tectonic.

With his concept of the tectonic, Frampton challenged the prestige in architectural discourses of the past forty years of both the figurative (from the fine arts) and the semiotic: the building is a "thing" rather than a "sign." Yet in the same RFR buildings, despite attention lavished on the local order of tectonic elements, the immediate iconographic status granted to this form of technological expressionism in Paris catapults these buildings into a dimension equally scenographic. Not scenographic in Frampton's sense (which relies on repression of construction within the local order of the elements of the work), but as it is present in the monument—the emergence of the iconic. As explored in chapter 4, expression of the tectonic in RFR's works is overcome with the propensity of details to accrue raw symbolic power in a contemporary realm of images.

According to Saussurian structuralism, words are symbols that acquire meaning within complex networks of elements and rules. Each element of these languages is subject to inflections of meaning dependent on the context of its utterance: Saussure's notion of *parole*. Saussure's point is that the meaning of words, as attributes of symbolic phonetic sounds, is highly contingent; their symbolism is highly volatile. Details of the RFR structural glazing systems are part of a complex network of building systems, but are also constituent elements in a language of materials that is burdened by exactly those systems of meaning associated with paroles.

The RFR details make Saussure's point of symbolic volatility doubly evident. Most engineering feats are portrayed as objective conceptions; inflexible to any demand beyond those of mathematical measurements, efficiency, and material science; impermeable to the effects of subjective derivation or perception. Yet as with paroles, RFR's structural glazing details are expressions received and understood within subjective domains, connoting a wide array of issues, from the expression of the state (the Grande Pyramide), to an invocation of a more naturally disposed mysticism (serres at Parc de La Villette and Parc André Citroën), to the ultimate propensity of consumerist culture to appropriate both technological and symbolic languages.

Nouvel's institutions also provided an example of detail's capacity to assume a pivotal role in conceptual structures embedded deeply within his buildings' cultural agendas. The detail in the Eiffel Tower was an illustration of its potential to activate rational intelligibility, ultimately counteracting the mysticism inherent in the spectacle. The deliberately humorous didacticism of Piano and Rogers's details generated a sense of genial transparency between the Beaubourg and the public. As later creations of Peter Rice, details in RFR's glass works in Paris extend these issues but also provide a controlled study in the associations and connotation of one particular detail as it is played out in different venues across the city. Too often the role of the detail is relegated, particularly in academic discourses, to performing within vaguely defined haptic systems that function primarily to comfort, enshroud, and even center the body in space. Here we see irrefutable evidence that the detail might also participate in larger conceptual and intellectual orders of buildings and projects. Clearly evident in all of these cases is detail's capacity to order, to connote, to refer, and to signify.

Like all of the Mitterrand projects, the RFR projects present and represent progress, in the iconic power of their pieces and in the image of the buildings as a whole. Their resonance is thus soundly assured—and precariously located—in an economic realm that has long appropriated technological expressionism for its spectacular value. Made indelible through countless popular publications, these technological images directly engage with the world of consumerism, serving as the vehicle through which the city is marketed to global tourism. Tectonic character, at least as Frampton defined it, is complicit, or at least confluent, with iconic and spectacular dimension.

In a recent popular publication on tectonics, critic Sandy Isenstadt coined the term "spectacular tectonic" for the potential interactions between states of politics and construction evidenced in the projects of Paris; identifying the precise encounter between the tectonic and the spectacle not an opposition but an intersection. Drawing on a statement by Guy Debord—"The spectacle is not a collection of images but a social relation among people, mediated by images,"— Isenstadt wrote that architecture is shaped by multiple terminologies. Social values themselves compete for form. As Semper might have agreed, diagrams of structure and construction generated entirely from their internal demands and principles are ill equipped to acknowledge these multiplicities adequately. Rather than renouncing social relationships and concentrating on tectonic issues that are self-referential, construction can be mobilized to explore contemporary social and cultural conditions that are always constituted by a vast array of complex issues.[5]

Isenstadt's remarks are instructive. Not only is a work of architecture ultimately received and qualified by a multivalent social present, but it can also be conceived initially as such, particularly by strategically employing the process of production and its ability to accumulate various cultural conditions. Isenstadt's suggestion that construction can represent a legitimate conceptual order, to be employed in a contemporary realm, suggests that it might be organized to address a number of issues found in many domains, even in different disciplines. This notion is in diametric opposition to recent discussions that proposed a recovery of architecture's potency exclusively through the demands of material and structure with site and type. In these arguments, construction was used as the primary device through which to return architecture to a primordial condition, presumably after the ravages of post-structural analytical modes of conception and production that were instigated outside the discipline. This study of glass architecture in Paris illustrates that for true resonance in a contemporary sphere, the discourse of construction must depart from such essentialist conceptions.

Practices of contemporary construction hardly exist in any state of purity themselves. Radical changes in engineering, the sciences of materials and assemblies, and buildings' dependence on political and financial institutions have wrought tremendous upheavals in the underpinnings of construction.[6] It is significant that Frampton, in *Studies in Tectonic Culture,* mentioned only once, in discussing the work of Norman Foster, the possibility of tectonic expression in any type of newer lightweight, mass-produced construction in favor of stereotomic masses of stone and earthwork. The material preference presents a continuing dilemma in rendering the discourse of the tectonic disjunctive to contemporary practice, whether in the academy or in the profession. Any such discourse must

integrate the vicissitudes inherent in the culture of production itself as complementary to a basic understanding of the process of building as aggregate and
inclusive.

Rather than opposing contemporary culture with consistently arrière-garde
attitudes, creation of a work of tectonic dimension might equally include elements
that are at once timely and able to exist in a world embraced as manifestly irresolute.
For the ameliorative effects proposed by Frampton, the tectonic can—indeed,
must—incorporate rather than exclude the present. Only when acknowledging the
vast range of conditions can construction engage a larger field of contemporary
material culture without either descending into the recent flaccid mimicry of
pseudohistorical iconography or indulging in a hermetically guarded poetic, inaccessible to all but the most privileged.

Notes

PREFACE

1. This book goes to great extremes to qualify this concept; suffice to say that this is the predominant notion associated with glass architecture. See particularly chapters 3 and 4 for lengthy digressions into translucency and crystal symbology.

2. See Jay, *Downcast Eyes,* chapters 1 and 4, and Hollier, *Against Architecture,* pp. 14–19.

3. Weiss, *Mirrors of Infinity,* p. 84.

4. Melchior-Bonnet, p. 108.

5. "The machine gives prismatic opportunity in glass. The machine process can do any kind of glass: thick, thin, colored, textured to order; and cheap; and the machine in the architect's hand can now set it, protect it, and humanize its use completely," from "In the Nature of Materials," in Kaufman and Raeburn, *Frank Lloyd Wright,* p. 226.

6. Vidler, "Transparency."

7. In Riley's introduction to *Light Construction* he refers to Starobinski's speculation on the veil of Montaigne's Poppea in *The Living Eye.* Starobinski repeats his fascination with concepts of transparency, veiling, reflection, and the crystal in *Jean-Jacques Rousseau,* ultimately more pertinent to this study of the Grands Projets.

8. For Moneo, "formless architecture" included both "fragmented deconstructivist operations" and "indifferent neutral containers" with minimalist aspirations. Whereas the reference is specifically to the work of Swiss architects Herzog and de Meuron, clearly many of the French projects fall within this characterization. See Moneo's essay "Recent Architectural Paradigms and a Personal Alternative," p. 74.

9. Krauss, in discussing Mies van der Rohe in "The Grid, the /Cloud/, and the Detail," p. 134.

10. See Marco Frascari, "The Tell-the-Tale Detail."

CHAPTER **1**

1. MacMillan, p. 232.

2. From "They Love It," *The Economist* (May 26, 2001), p. 50.

3. Leading French intellectual Pierre Nora edited a seven-volume collection of essays in 1984 titled *Les Lieux de Mémoire [Realms of Memory: The Construction of the French Past]* that attempted to document the nuance of the French persona, as it was inherited traditionally, in both the celebrated and mundane elements of French life and history. Belief in a collective French sensibility is implicit in the undertaking of such a project. See Tony Judt's critique of this aspect of the work.

4. Ibid.

5. Vidler stated the conundrum more clearly: "Why then transparency in the first place? To make huge cubic masses, monumental forms, urban constructions of vast scale—disappear?" From "Transparency," p. 221.

6. In von Spreckelson's competition entry he wrote: "An open cube/A window on the world/Like a momentary pause on the avenue/Looking to the future." Quoted in Christian Dupavillon and Francis Lacloche, p. 52.

7. Riley, introductory essay in *Light Construction,* p. 29.

8. See the catalogue of the same title edited by Bernard Marrey with Jacques Ferrier.

9. See Melchior-Bonnet, *The Mirror,* pp. 13–62.

10. Giedion, *Building in France,* pp. 120–143.

11. See Silverman, "The 1889 Exposition: The Crisis of Bourgeois Individualism," and Bennett, "The Exhibitionary Complex," in chapter 3 of Dirks, et al., *Culture/Power/History.*

12. Aragon, p. 22.

13. In its permanent exhibition documenting the dynamic condition of contemporary Paris, the Pavillon de l'Arsenal consistently exhibits Haussmann's projects parallel to contemporary work. Equally, in its 1988 exhibition and catalogue, *Paris: La Ville et ses Projets, a City in the Making,* the precedent of Haussmann's Paris was the consistent springboard for most speculations on then unbuilt Mitterrand projects. The catalogue, edited by Jean-Louis Cohen and Bruno Fortier, featured essays by a number of highly regarded French critics and urban historians, many of whom revisited the legacy of the Haussmann to comprehend fully the proposals of Mitterrand. See, for example, Loyer, "Haussmann's Paris," and Babelon, "The Classical Boulevard" in that catalogue. It is also noteworthy that the advent of the

Grands Projets in the 1980s spurned several new significant studies of Haussmann's Grands Travaux. See de Moncan and Mahout, *Le Paris du Baron Haussmann*, and des Cars and Pinon, *Paris-Haussmann*, both of which were published in 1991.

14. See des Cars and Pinon, *Paris-Haussmann*, and Van Zanten's chapter 6, "Haussmann, Baltard, and Municipal Architecture," in *Building Paris*, for a full description of new features added throughout the city.

15. Saalman, p. 16.

16. My thanks to Sarah Bonnemaison for providing this insight, and many others in this section, in her Ph.D. dissertation chapter in *Allegories of Commemoration*, p. 42. Julia Trilling also reported that the Bastille Opéra was conceived to replace Mitterrand's earlier plans for a Socialist World's Fair commemorating the French Revolution, cancelled in a political pas de deux between Mitterrand and Jacques Chirac. Both the fair and the opéra were, Trilling noted, vehicles to "monumentalize Socialism." See her "Paris: Architecture as Politics."

17. See Lowe, "Design Control in France," p. 96. See also his more comprehensive *Modern Architecuture in Historic Cities*.

18. See essays by Jean-Louis Cohen and Alain Grellety Bosviel in Cohen and Fortier, *Paris*. In refocusing city planning attention on the inner city, Andrea Gleininger gives much credit to the "Atelier Parisien d'Urbanisme" (APUR), founded in 1967 as a self-initiated advocacy group but evolving into an official organ of the Paris planning authority. See Gleininger, "Paris—Architecture and Urban Development in the 20th Century," in her *Paris Contemporary Architecture*.

19. This study does not have within its scope or ambitions a recounting of the political machinations among Mitterrand, Chirac, and Giscard d'Estaing in the history of the Grands Projets. These vast programs involved various periods of progress, conflict, abandonment, and expansion. See François Chaslin's "Paris, Capital of the Pharoah's Republic" in Cohen's and Fortier, *Paris*, as well as Winterbourne's short but well-researched account of the effect of several policy decisions, for an introduction to the complicated political history.

20. See Benjamin, "Paris."

21. See Bennett, "The Evolutionary Complex," in Dirks et al., *Culture/Power/History*, p. 128.

22. See Antoine Picon, "L'Echappée royale, de Le Notrê et Perrault à Perronet," in Pinon, ed., *Les Traversées de Paris*, pp. 131–134.

23. See Shelley Rice's discussion in chapter 1 of *Parisian Views*.

24. Ferguson in *Paris as Revolution* argued, through an examination of nineteenth century literature, that in every urban domain and social practice in Paris, "fixity yields to fluctuation." See especially chapter 4 on Haussmann's Paris.

25. Weiss, *Mirrors of Infinity,* p. 69.

26. Bryson, "The Gaze in the Expanded Field," pp. 88–94. See also his *Vision and Painting.*

27. See Shelley Rice's observations in chapter 3 of *Parisian Views.*

28. From Engels, *The Condition of the Working Class in England,* cited by Benjamin in "On Some Motifs in Baudelaire," p. 166.

29. Sadler, p. 91.

30. Benjamin, "On Some Motifs in Baudelaire," p. 169.

31. Jay, *Downcast Eyes,* p. 14.

32. The definition and effects of the *gaze* are numerous and diverse. According to Bryson, in "The Gaze," the basic texts are philosophical and psychoanalytical: Sartre (*Being and Nothingness*), Lacan (*The Four Fundamental Concepts of PsychoAnalysis*), and Rorty (*Mirror of Nature*). Art historians, however, widened the number of different interpretations. In this short passage explicating the effects of the gaze, I have tried to represent a number of salient ideas that are central to an examination of architectural consequences within an explicitly political arena.

33. In Foucault's seminal work, *Discipline and Punish,* he traces the role of visual devices in the development of French disciplinary institutions. Particularly influential in recent architectural discourse addressing vision is "Panopticism" (chapter 3, part 3)

34. I am indebted in this section to Gerhard Auer's "Desiring Gaze and the Ruses of the Veil."

35. Panofsky attributed this development to the Renaissance. From *Perspective as Symbolic Form,* p. 63: "In this way the Renaissance succeeded in mathematically fully rationalizing an image of space which had already earlier been aesthetically unified. This, as we have seen, involved extensive abstraction from the psychophysiological structure of space, and repudiation of the antique authorities."

36. Auer, "The Desiring Gaze," p. 37.

37. From an interview with Mitterrand in Michel Jacques, and Gaëlle Lauriot-dit-Prévost's *Bibliothèque nationale,* p. 8.

38. Paraphrased from a lecture given by Emile Biasini, Minister for Building Projects under Mitterrand, at the University of Pennsylvania in spring 1995. See also Biasini's *Grands Travaux.*

39. The vehicle through which this "democratization" of the art form was to be accomplished was the size and programming of the building. Not only was the new opéra to be twice the size of the Garnier Opéra, but also the (two) main auditoriums were planned to allow a flexible rotation of performances; both measures undertaken to increase the audiences and decrease ticket prices. See Trilling, "Paris" for a full account. This intention to popularize opera caused debates within musical circles about the nature of the art form.

40. See Winterbourne, "Architecture and the Politics." Winterbourne is corroborated in her accounts by innumerable popular press releases accompanying the construction of several of the Grands Projets.

41. See François Chaslin's early (1985) account in *Les Paris de François Mitterrand*.

42. Ibid. Winterbourne stated that funding for regional culture outside of Paris dropped by 50 percent during the building of the Grands Projets.

43. Ibid.

44. Architectural critic Hélène Lipstadt wrote: "The rebalancing of the Parisian development to the east is a literal reorientation of the city's cultural focus. The project of La Villette represents the clearest example of the Socialist attempt to redress, through cultural patronage, the centuries-old Western drift of wealth and its amenities." From "A Paris of the 21st Century," p. 108.

45. Curtis, "Grands Projets," p. 76.

46. Bonnemaison, same as note 15.

47. Starobinski, *Jean-Jacques Rousseau,* p. 21.

48. Sierksma, "The Transparent Authority," p. 3.

49. Simon Schama reported that these invasions, in which rooms would be suddenly filled with ten or more men with sabers, pikes, and guns, did not necessarily elicit revulsion from the public. He quoted Mme. Julien de la Drôme as saying, "I approve of this measure and the surveillance of the People so strongly that I should have liked to have cried 'Bravo! Vive la Nation!'" *Citizens,* p. 626.

50. McMillan, *Twentieth-Century France,* p. 232.

51. See Vidler, "Transparency," p. 217.

52. A general homage to the (in)famous essay of Colin Rowe and my colleague Robert Slutzky, in "Transparency: Literal and Phenomenal," in Rowe, *Mathematics of an Ideal Villa.*

Rowe and Slutzky positioned Le Corbusier's cubist representation of space in his *fenêtres longueurs* against Giedion's early idea in *Space, Time, and Architecture.*

53. "The new spirit which already governs all modern life is opposed to animal spontaneity (lyricism), to the dominion of nature, to complicated hair-styles and elaborate cooking," by van Doesburg and van Eesteren, "Towards collective building," reprinted in Conrads, *Programs and Manifestoes.*

54. A quick view of Martin's *Guide to Modern Architecture in Paris* provides ample evidence of Le Corbusier's thorough infiltration into French vernacular architecture. See especially examples of lesser-known architects in different periods since the 1930s, of which there are far too many to cite definitively: from Louis Faure-Dujarric's Magasin des Trois Quartiers of 1932 to Mario Heymann's housing of 1969 to Gérard Thurnauer's and Hervé Delatouche's housing of 1981 and 1986 (pp. 41 and 166). Le Corbusier's influence extends to more well-known contemporary architects as well: Henri Ciriani, Paul Chemetov, Christian de Portzamparc, and so on.

55. One of the most fascinating, if not frustrating, aspects of engaging the research for this book was the scarcity of intellectual conjecture on what is clearly a profoundly important topic. As Martin Jay contends, the literature on vision in France is widespread; the lack of speculation on Mitterrand's tremendously significant transparent operation on Paris is noteworthy in itself. See Jay's introduction to *Downcast Eyes.*

CHAPTER 2

1. Debord's reiterative aphorisms in *Society of the Spectacle* explores the reduction of all experience to image. Ultimately society is hypnotized, lost in a dream of consumerism: "Where the real world changes into simple images, the simple images become real beings and effective motivations of hypnotic behavior," part 1, no. 18.

2. MacMillan, p. 186.

3. Sadler, p. 65.

4. Baudrillard, *L'Effet Beaubourg,* p. 27: "A vrai dire, le seul contenu de Beaubourg est la masse elle-même, que l'édifice traite comme un convertisseur, comme une chambre noire, ou, en terme d'input-output, exactement comme une raffinerie traite un produit pétrolier ou un flux de matière brute" (author's translation).

5. Cited in Silver, *The Making of Beaubourg,* p. 24. Silver's revisitation of the Beaubourg and its construction described the events of making the building in a far more comprehensive examination than this brief account can ever attempt. To this book and its original research, my description is thoroughly indebted.

6. See Warren Chalk's advocation for new housing in Cook et al., *Archigram,* p. 17.

7. See Sadler's discussion of Situationist concepts of psychogeography and drift, pp. 76–95.

8. The quintessential account of the evolution of iron construction in World Expositions is to be found in Giedion, *Building in France.* See pp. 120–145.

9. Buck-Morss, *The Dialectics,* pp. 81–86.

10. See Joseph Harriss's thorough account of the tower's construction in *The Tallest Tower.*

11. Buck-Morss, *The Dialectics,* p. 74. See also Benjamin's *The Arcades Project.*

12. Barthes, "The Eiffel Tower."

13. From Henri Loyrette's quotation of Louis Aragon in "The Eiffel Tower": "... between her spread iron legs, the unsuspected genitals of a woman," in Nora, *Realms of Memory,* vol. 3, pp. 348–375.

14. Barthes, "The Eiffel Tower," pp. 248–249.

15. See Giedion, *Building in France,* p. 91.

16. Barthes, "The Eiffel Tower," p. 249.

17. See Mark, "Structural Experimentation in High Gothic Architecture," chapter 4 in *Light, Wind, and Structure,* especially pp. 91–105.

18. André Vauchez notes in his essay, "The Cathedral," that had the tower at the Cathedral of Strasbourg been completed, at 466′ it would have been equal to roughly half of the Eiffel Tower's height, in Nora, *Realms of Memory,* vol. 2, pp. 36–68.

19. See Scully, *Architecture,* Chapter 7, "The Gothic Cathedral."

20. Vauchez, "The Cathedral," in Nora, *Realms of Memory,* vol 2, p. 57.

21. Scully, *Architecture,* p. 156.

22. For Georges Bataille the maternality of the cathedral extended to the national domain. As Dennis Hollier wrote on Bataille's early *Notre-Dame de Rheims:* "The cathedral is the symbol of this continuity, embodying it in a mystical radiance bringing together all the history and geography of France to turn it into a vast and glorious resurrected body, a maternal body in glory—intact, removed from life and death because it is sustained by an immortal heart," *Against Architecure,* p. 20.

23. Benjamin, "Paris," p. 148.

24. See Detlef Mertin, "The Enticing and Threatening Face of Prehistory."

25. Henri Loyrette, "The Eiffel Tower," in Nora, *Realms of Memory*, vol. 3, pp. 348–375.

26. Emile Zola, *Paris*, p. 330.

27. Levin, *When the Eiffel Tower Was New*, p. 25. In this catalogue of an exhibition of popular images at the time of the original opening of the Eiffel Tower, Levin traced the symbolic language of the tower and its construction. Her primary source was Edward Lockroy's preface in Emil Monod's *L'Exposition universelle de 1889: Grand ouvrage illustré, historique, encyclopédique, descriptif,* 3 vols., Paris, 1890. My description of the tower's organization of labor structures and their implications is indebted to her account.

28. Levin, *When the Eiffel Tower Was New*, p. 23.

29. See Silverman, "The 1889 Exposition."

30. From Deleuze, *The Logic of Sense*, p. 7. Since it is difficult to paraphrase Deleuze definitively, see chapters 1–4. Deleuze's ideas are particulary apt to the phenomena of line at the Eiffel Tower. Constantin V. Boundas maintains that Deleuze's reading of the Stoics, central to his ideas on surfaces and events, is an ethical one: "To be worthy of what is happening to us, Deleuze concludes, means to will what is always both differentiated and the same in each moment of our lives, to raise the banal and mundane into the remarkable and singular . . .', from Boundas's introduction to *The Deleuze Reader*, p. 9.

31. Sadler, p. 63.

32. See Alan Colquhoun "Critique", in *Centre Pompidou* for accounts of the competition.

33. Cited from a lecture in which Piano and Rogers defended their programming decisions. In Silver, *The Making of Beaubourg*, p. 104.

34. "Within the dramatic sense that pervades much of the [our] work, cinematic devices replace conventional description. Architecture becomes the discourse of events as much as the discourse of spaces." Bernard Tschumi, "Space and Events," reprinted in *Architecture and Disjunction*, p. 149. It is noteworthy that Tschumi was a young architect involved in the Paris student revolution of 1968, and so shares a cultural legacy and generational affinity with Piano and Rogers.

35. From an extract of *Living Arts Magazine*, 2 (June 1963), featuring the 1963 "Living City" exhibition at the London Institute for Contemporary Art. Reprinted in Cook et al., *Archigram*, p. 21.

36. Although Prouvé is typically granted credit for the Maison du Peuple, the design of the building was actually a collaboration among Prouvé, architect Eugène Beaudoin, and engineers Marcel Lods and Vladimir Bodiansky.

37. Quoted in Charlotte Ellis, "Prouvé's People's Palace."

38. From Rice, *An Engineer Imagines,* p. 25.

39. See Mitchell Schwartzer's discussion in chapter 4, "Freedom and Tectonic," in *German Architectural Theory and the Search for Modern Identity,* pp. 167–210.

40. Giedion, *Building in France,* p. 117.

41. Rice noted that steel construction was not common in France in the 1970s. When the steel was put out to bid, French companies tried to stall the building by joining forces and fixing the prices 50 percent over the estimated budget. Eventually the steel was contracted to the German company Krupps who were able to guarantee on-budget delivery of the pieces, an outcome that was of course not welcomed by French industry. See discussion by Rice in *An Engineer Imagines,* chapter 1.

42. Silver, *The Making of Beaubourg,* p. 30. Silver quoted, albeit loosely, engineers Rice and Happold with this statement. Much of my account of the building's structural and mechanical systems are indebted to Silver's description.

43. Silver, *The Making of Beaubourg,* p. 31.

44. Cited from the jury report of the Ministries of National Education and Cultural Affairs, in Silver, *The Making of Beaubourg,* p. 45.

45. Rice, *An Engineer Imagines,* p. 26.

46. My gratitude to Giorgio Bianchi, project architect for the renovation of the Pompidou Center, for expressing this freely in an interview, June 1998.

47. Cook et al. *Archigram,* p. 5.

48. See footnote 29 in this chapter.

49. Again, from comments provided by Giorgio Bianchi.

50. Lefebvre wrote, "Only when considering the life of the working classes—and by redeeming and extolling their creative ability—did it become clear that there was a power concealed in everyday life's apparent banality, a depth beyond its triviality, something extraordinary in its very ordinariness." See *Everyday Life in the Modern World,* pp. 1–67.

51. Sadler, p. 65.

52. From my conversation with Giorgio Bianchi, June 1998.

53. Sadler, p. 32.

54. Giedion wrote, "Everyone is susceptible to symbols. Our period is no exception. But those who govern must know that spectacles, which will lead people back to a neglected community life, must be re-incorporated back into civic centers, those very centers which our mechanized civilization has always regarded as non-essential," in "The Need for a New Monumentality," p. 61.

55. Vattimo, Gianni. *The Transparent Society*, p. 11.

56. de Certeau, "The Revolution of the Believable," *Culture in the Plural*, p. 8.

CHAPTER 3

1. See the argument put forward by Richard Pommer.

2. See Rowe, pp. 139–158.

3. Quetglas, "Fear of Glass."

4. Hays provides a thorough analysis of the Friedrichstrasse glass skyscraper project in "Critical Architecture." A number of the "revisionist writings" mentioned may be found in Mertins, ed., *The Presence of Mies*. Also seminal is Evans, "Mies van der Rohe."

5. A reference to the exhibition and publication mentioned in chapter 1, MoMA's 1995 "Light Construction," curated by Terence Riley.

6. See Vidler, "Translucency," pp. 216–225.

7. Starobinski, *The Living Eye*, p. 2.

8. Béret, Chantal, interview with Nouvel, p. 28.

9. From a lecture given by Nouvel at the Royal Academy of Arts in London on June 13, 1998.

10. Ibid.

11. Ibid.

12. Where the glass planes bounded interior space, Nouvel used a low-emissivity (low-E) glass, which no doubt contributes to the difference in color and reflectivity. The primary factor, however, that distinguishes the interior from exterior glass on the façade still occurs as a result of the light differential across the surface as it crosses in front of interior space.

13. Published in excerpts from an interview between Jean Nouvel and Gilles de Bure in Blaswick et al., eds., p. 26.

14. Deleuze, "Second Series of Paradoxes of Surface Effects," in *Logic of Sense*, p. 5.

15. Melchior-Bonnet, p. 141.

16. Vidler, p. 223. Vidler's references is to Lacan's "The Mirror Stage as the Formation of the Function of the 'I,'" published in Lacan's *Ecrits*.

17. According to project architect Didier Brault, had low-iron, or "white glass," been commercially available at the time, it would have been used in this location. Nouvel intended the glass on the ground floor be as transparent as possible, in distinction to that on the upper floors.

18. Note recent museum exhibits of Cartier jewelry in both New York at the Metropolitan Museum in 1997, and in Paris in 1990 at the Petit Palais (closely preceding the opening of the foundation). Rupert's leadership is examined in *Forbes* (April 2, 1990) and *Economist* (January 18, 1997).

19. From two articles in *Le Monde* (May 9, 1994): "Initiatives: Pourquoi se regrouper?" and "Culture Architecture Le Nouveau Siège de la Fondation Cartier à Paris: Nouvel en Sandwich."

20. My thanks to Didier Brault and Brigitte Metra at Nouvel's office in Paris for providing this information.

21. See discussion by Baumann-Reynolds, chapters. 3, 4, and 5.

22. Much of the information about the competition and its entries was taken from an interview between Patrice Goulet and Jean Nouvel, in Goulet, "I. M.A.: Le Concours pour l'Institut du Monde Arabe, Paris."

23. These statements are paraphrased from similar texts in a number of architectural journals, most notably Levene and Márquez Cecilia's *El Croquis 65/66*, Patrice Goulet's essay "Institut du Monde Arabe," and in Olivier Boissière's dossier on the building in *L'Architecture d'aujourd'hui*.

24. Using Derridean criticism, John Biln analyzed the Institut: "It disrupts self-privilege and opens a space for doubt that can be filled only with some mobile re-conception of the self-other relationship. This can only be accomplished in, through, and as a de-stabilization of those self-conceptions founded upon reflected 'images' of the other," p. 36.

25. Ibid., p. 32.

26. Quetglas, "Fear of Glass," p. 141. Rosemarie Bletter, in her Columbia dissertation, "Bruno Taut and Paul Scheerbart's Vision," suggested that Scheerbart may have been much influenced by the jewellike light, surfaces, and ornamentation of traditional Arabic spaces, particularly in the interior of the Alhambra. See extended discussion in chapter 4, this book. See also Bletter's, "Paul Scheerbart's Architectural Fantasies."

27. "Le patio protégé des regards, autour duquel on tournera et sur lequel on s'éclairera à travers des parois de marbre très fines et légèrement opalescentes, est la clé de toute l'organisation du bâtiment" (author's translation), Goulet, "I. M.A.," p. 86.

28. See "Critique: Culture Clash," *Progressive Architecture* (Sept. 1995), pp. 62–67.

29. Quoted from "La Vitrine du Monde Arabe," *Le Monde* (Feb. 23, 1993).

30. Ibid.

31. For example, see Herdeg's analysis of urban spaces in Iran and Turkistan.

32. See Noiriel, "French and Foreigners," p. 144.

CHAPTER **4**

1. Quoted by Starobinski in *Jean-Jacques Rousseau,* p. 255. Originally from Rousseau's Rêveries, Sixth Walk, *Oeuvres complètes,* I:1057, pp. 101–102. Paris: Pléiade, 1959.

2. See the introduction, "Bloody Sunday," in Hollier, pp. ix–xxiii.

3. Ibid.

4. Bataille, "Architecture," in *Oeuvres complètes,* vol 9:171. Cited by Hollier in *Against Architecture,* p. 47.

5. See Frampton's "Architecture and the State: Ideology and Representation," part II, chapter 24, *Modern Architecture: A Critical History.*

6. As Elizabeth Mock (then director of the architecture department at the Museum of Modern Art) stated in "Built in the USA," modern architecture, in its democratic aspirations, certainly had no use for such contaminated imagery: "A totalitarian nation demands buildings which will express the omnipotence of the State and the complete subordination of the individual. When modern architecture tries to express these things, it ceases to be modern, for modern architecture has its roots in the concept of democracy," p. 85.

7. Christiane C. and George R. Collins's, "Monumentality," pp. 15–35.

8. Jean-Pierre Babelon, "The Louvre: Royal Residence and Temple of the Arts," in Nora, *Realms of Memory,* vol. 2, pp. 253–292. For a more thorough account of the Louvre's decorative development, see Bautier.

9. Biasini, officially Mitterrand's President of the "Etablissement Public du Grand Louvre," previously served under André Malraux, de Gaulle's Minister of Culture. Quoted in Wiseman, p. 235.

10. Between January 1984 and spring of 1985, renovation of the Louvre was featured on the front pages of French newspapers almost daily, especially in *Le Figaro,* which featured criticism of the Pei pyramid nearly every two days.

11. Historian Jean-Paul Aron rejected the electoral victory of the left as a "monstrosity . . . against the laws of nature." Wiseman, p. 251.

12. Bruno Foucart, in *Quotidien de Paris* (January 26, 1984), cited by Chaslin in "Grand Louvre, Prisme Changeant de l'Opinion," p. 8

13. "La décadence de l'art français a-t-elle été jugée si profonde qu'aucun architecte de notre nation ne possédait les qualités requises pour présider aux agrandissements du Louvre? Quelle humiliation pour le pays des bâtisseurs de cathédrales, des Perrault, des Soufflot. . . ." *Le Figaro* (May 14, 1985), cited by Chaslin, "Grand Louvre," p. 8.

14. See André Fermigier's editorial in *Le Monde* (February 24, 1986), cited by Chaslin, "Grand Louvre," p. 8. Chaslin also reported that when confronted with the perceived affront to cherished French neoclassicism, Pei responded that this period in French architecture had descended into eclectic pastiche, a statement that only inflamed the debate in the French press.

15. Wiseman, p. 251.

16. Chaslin, in "Grand Louvre," noted that in January 1985, one year before the election, 57 percente polled were against Mitterrand and 53 percent were also displeased with his Grands Travaux. In 1986, however, the tides reversed: 57 percent supported Mitterrand and 56 percent were now in favor of the Grands Projets.

17. Mitterrand also apparently changed electoral policies to favor his party, avoiding the disastrous defeat for the Socialists that had been forecasted. See MacMillan, p. 215.

18. Wiseman, p. 236. See also *Le Grand Louvre: Métamorphose d'un Musée 1981–93,* an official account by Emile Biasini et al. It restates Pei's claims that the pyramid's shape was generated from largely functional demands: lighting the interior with as diminished a volume as possible in the court. Nevertheless, Biasini recalled Pei wanting to mark the presence of the "buried architecture" (*architecture enselvie*) by an "emergent" shape in the Cour Napoléon. See pp. 22–29, partially translated in Bezombes.

19. Noteworthy is the subsequent development of this glass for more typical commercial installations, now commonly known as low-iron or white glass. See Wiggington's technical description of light transmissions in various types of glass, pp. 05.250–251.

20. From an interview with Michael Flynn at Pei Cobb Freid Partners, New York, June 1999.

21. Wiseman, p. 259.

22. See Masheck, "Crystalline Form, Worringer, and the Minimalism of Tony Smith," chapter 10.

23. This historical account is indebted to Bletter's research in "Bruno Taut and Paul Scheerbart's Vision," pp. 268–299.

24. Ibid., p. 324.

25. Giedion, "Nine Points on Monumentality," p. 62.

26. Cassirer, vol. 1, p. 86.

27. Hegel, "Architecture," p. 305. There are more than a few parallels between aspects of Pei's pyramid and Hegel's calls for a truly symbolic architecture free from the externalities of materiality and function. Hegel saw even religious association as detraction. Before settling on the Tower of Babel as the purest example of the "symbolic," he lingered on the possibilities of the Egyptian pyramid to fulfill such a dimension. See also Hollier, pp. 3–13.

28. Halley, "The Crisis in Geometry," p. 112.

29. Chave's "Minimalism and the Rhetoric of Power," makes many associations that have direct bearing on this discussion of the Grande Pyramide, as well as to Dominique Perrault's Bibliothèque Nationale in chapter 5. Whereas much of her critique delves into the naming of various minimalist works, she elaborates on Frank Stella and Donald Judd's efforts to render the work "non-relational," preventing viewers from having any individual reading of the work. See especially pp. 50–54.

30. MacMillan, p. 222.

31. Chaslin, "Grand Louvre, Prisme Changeant de l'Opinion."

32. "Combien de fois a-t-on entendu parler des dépenses 'pharaoniques' de l'ancien président de la République? . . . La fameuse pyramide, tant décriée lorsqu'elle fut dévoilée pour la première fois, n'est-elle pas devenue, au même titre que la tour Eiffel, un symbole universel de la France—une France moderne qui sait mettre en valeur sa propre culture." From Jodidio, p. 5.

33. I. M. Pei was fully aware of the urban amenity offered by opening the Cour Napoléon to foot traffic from the transverse Passage Richelieu. Opening this passage, which had been closed to the public while the Ministry of Finance occupied the pavilion, was a political act, positioning Public Works Minister Emile Biasini against a finance ministry recalcitrant to give up the location and power signified by its former housing in the Louvre. See Biasini et al., *Le Grand Louvre,* pp. 30–33.

34. Rice, *An Engineer Imagines*, p. 63.

35. Fainsilber, in his foreword to Rice and Dutton's *Structural Glass*, p. 5.

36. See Melchior-Bonnet's thorough and fascinating account of seventeenth-century glass-manufacturing processes in *The Mirror*, especially pp. 58–62.

37. See Wiggington, *Glass in Architecture*, appendix 2, p. 05.271. See also Henrivaux, *La Verrerie au XXᵉ Siècle*.

38. Wiggington, pp. 05.272–273. See also Klein and Lloyd, eds., *The History of Glass*.

39. Rice and Dutton's description compares the different support systems in far greater detail than is allowed by the scope of this study. I have paraphrased their thorough descriptions here and below to convey expediently the technical facts to the reader that will be necessary for greater discussions. See pp. 33–36.

40. Wiggington, p. 05.275. Tempering is a process also known as heat toughening.

41. Rice and Dutton, on RFR's articulated bolt system, pp. 37–42.

42. Ibid., on the radisseurs and the cable truss support system, pp. 43–66.

43. Ibid., on the main frame and serre module as a whole, pp. 78–85.

44. Ibid., on climate control systems, appendix pp. 94–100.

45. See Scheerbart, *The Gray Cloth*.

46. Again, this section is indebted to Bletter's historical account of crystalline gardens in "Bruno Taut and Paul Scheerbart's Vision," p. 268.

47. "Alpine Architecture," part 3, in Scheerbart, *Glass Architecture*, and Taut, *Alpine Architecture*, p. 124.

48. Bletter, pp. 300–310. See also Iain Boyd Whyte, ed., *Bruno Taut and the Architecture of Activism*.

49. See Richard Pommer's "Mies van der Rohe and the Political Ideology of the Modern Movement in Architecture".

50. In *The End of the Modern World*, Guardini wrote, "To exercise power means, to a degree at least, that one has mastered 'the given.' Power over 'the given' means that man has succeeded in checking those existential forces which oppose his life, that he has bent them to his will. Today the scepter of power is wielded by the hand of man," p. 109.

51. From Mies's "Architecture and Technology": "Technology is far more than a method, it is a world in itself/As a method it is superior in almost every respect./But only where it is left to itself as in/the construction of machinery, or as in the giant/structures of engineering, there technology reveals its true nature./There it is evident that it is not only a useful means,/that it is something, something in itself,/something that that has a meaning and a powerful form—/so powerful in fact, that it is not easy to name it./ . . . Wherever technology reaches its real fulfillment, it transcends into architecture."

52. See discussion by Schwartzer, pp. 167–209.

53. See Kahn's incisive "The Invisible Mask."

54. The French press was all too aware of the effects of importing commerce into the precinct of the Louvre, universally condemning it. See Guerrin, Laurence, and Brandeau.

CHAPTER 5

1. See François Chaslin, "Grands Projets" for a full account of the bibliothèque competition.

2. Bédarida, p. 33.

3. Chaslin, "Grands Projets."

4. Ibid.

5. Higgonnet "Scandal on the Seine," p. 32. See also Higgonet, "The Lamentable Library."

6. Reported in Bruno Suner.

7. From my interview with Dominique Perrault in July 1997.

8. See description in chapter 4.

9. Frampton, *Modern Architecture,* p. 232.

10. It is noteworthy that the glass used in the Bibliothèque Nationale was the same low-iron glass developed by Saint Gobain Vitrage for Pei's Grande Pyramide du Louvre.

11. From an interview with Dominique Perrault in Jacques and Lauriot-dit-Prévost, p. 48.

12. Much of this account is indebted to Brian Brace Taylor's "Technology, Society, and Social Control," and Reyner Banham's "Machines à habiter," chapter 8 of *The Architecture of the Well-Tempered Environment.*

13. Taylor reports that the inmates of the Cité were not forced to stay at the institute until "recuperated," but they were required by the rules of the Salvation Army to participate in therapeutic programs to be guaranteed housing.

14. Taylor noted Le Corbusier's involvement with Ernest Mercier, leader of the French political movement *le Redressement Français.* The group, in pursuit of an idea of revolution coordinated by a cadre of elite specialists, advocated Tayloristic methods of reorganization of production and relationships with labor.

15. From my interview with Dominique Perrault, July 1997.

16. Foster, "The Crux of Minimalism," p. 38.

17. Examples of these spaces abound, most significantly in the final central temple at the national Shinto shrines at Ise and the Imperial Castle in the central park in Tokyo. These observations have been noted by several authors, notably in Fumihiko Maki in "Japanese City Spaces and the Concept of Oku" and in Roland Barthes's *Empire of Signs.*

18. From the same interview with Mitterrand in Jacques and Lauriot-dit-Prévost, p. 48.

19. In my interview of July 1997, Perrault drew a direct comparison between the bibliothèque and Frank Gehry's Guggenheim museum at Bilbao, which had been recently completed and widely published internationally.

20. An anecdote related on a tour of the Hôtel Berlier by one of Perrault's employees.

21. Krauss, p. 134.

22. From Mitterrand's introduction to Jacques and Lauriot-dit-Prévost, p. 7.

23. Attributed to Dominique Jamet, Mitterrand's original head of the library project. Quoted by David Lawday, p. 22.

24. See Weiss, "Versailles: Versions of the Sun, the Fearful Difference," in *Mirrors of Infinity,* especially pp. 52–78.

25. Revel, "The Court," in Nora, *Realms of Memory,* vol. 2, p. 121.

26. See Baumann-Reynolds.

27. See "A Survey of France: The Grand Illusion," in *The Economist* (June 5, 1999), p. 3.

EPILOGUE

1. See Mitchell Schwarzer's discussion in "Freedom and Tectonics," pp. 167–214.

2. Hartoonian, *The Ontology of Construction,* p. 24.

3. See David Leatherbarrow, *The Roots of Architectural Invention,* pp. 198–204.

4. In his essay "Rappel à l'Ordre: The Case for the Tectonic," Frampton outlined different categorizations of construction, a seminal conceptual structure for his most recent book, *Studies in Tectonic Culture.*

5. See Isenstadt, in a brief but precisely explicated discussion on these issues. See also Fausch.

6. See Schwarzer, "Tectonics of the Unforeseen." In this essay, Schwarzer advocates the same inclusive potential of the tectonic, which he labels postmodern: "Postmodern tectonics takes the critical stance that architecture can neither retreat nor solve the problems of the world. An activity inflected by art and intellect as well as by technology and business, architectural construction must be immersed in the greater cultural wars of its age," p. 65.

References

Aragon, Louis. *Paris Peasant,* trans. Simon Watson Taylor. Boston: Exact Change, 1994.

Auer, Gerhard. "The Desiring Gaze and the Ruses of the Veil." *Daidalos* 33(15 Sept. 1989): 36–53.

Banham, Reyner. *The Architecture of the Well-Tempered Environment. Second edition.* Chicago: The University of Chicago Press, 1984.

Barthes, Roland. "The Eiffel Tower," *The Eiffel Tower and Other Mythologies.* New York: Farrar, Strauss and Giroux, 1979; reprinted in *The Barthes Reader,* New York: Noonday Press, 1990.

Barthes, Roland. *Empire of Signs.* New York: Farrar, Straus, & Giroux, 1982.

Bataille, Georges, "Architecture," *Œuvres complètes.* Paris: Gallimard, 1970.

Baudrillard, Jean. *L'Effet Beaubourg: Implosion et Dissuasion.* Paris: Editions Galilée, 1977.

Baumann-Reynolds, Sally. *François Mitterrand: The Making of a Socialist Prince on Republican France.* Westport, CT: Praeger, 1995.

Bautier, Geneviève Bresc. *The Louvre: An Architectural History.* Paris: The Vendome Press, 1995.

Bédarida, Marc. "The Upside-Down Library: Mitterrand's Testament." *Lotus International* 70 (Oct. 1991): 30–41.

Benjamin, Walter. "On Some Motifs in Baudelaire," *Illuminations,* ed. Hannah Arendt, trans. Harry Zohn. New York: Schoken Books, 1989.

Benjamin, Walter. "Paris: Capital of the Nineteenth Century," *Reflections,* ed. Peter Demetz, trans. Edmund Jephcott. New York: Schocken Books, 1989.

Benjamin, Walter. *The Arcades Project,* trans. Howard Eiland and Kevin McGlaughlin. Cambridge: Belknap Press of Harvard University Press, 1999.

Béret, Chantal. "Le Choix du Réel." *ArtPress* 190 (Apr. 1994): 28–35.

Bezombes, Dominique. *The Grand Louvre: The History of a Project.* Paris: Le Moniteur, 1994.

Biasini, Emile. *Grands Travaux.* Paris: Editions Odile Jacob, 1995.

Biasini, Emile, Jean Lebrat, Dominique Bezombes, and Jean-Michel Vincent. *Le Grand Louvre: Métamorphose d'un Musée 1981–1993.* Milan: Electa France, 1989.

Biln, John. "(De) Forming Self and Others: towards an Ethic of Distance." *Post-Colonial Spaces,* eds. G. B. Nalbantoglu and T. C. Wang. New York: Princeton Architectural Press, 1997.

Blaswick, Iwona, Michel Jacques, and Jane Withers, eds. *Jean Nouvel, Emmanuel Cattani et Associés.* Zurich: Artemis, Arc en rêve centre d'architecture, 1992.

Bletter, Rosemarie Haag. "Bruno Taut and Paul Scheerbart's Vision—Utopian Aspects of German Expressionism." Ph.D. dissertation, Columbia University, 1973.

Bletter, Rosemarie Haag. "Paul Scheerbart's Architectural Fantasies." *Journal of the Society of Architectural Historians* 34 (1975, 2): 83–97.

Boissière, Olivier. "Institut du Monde Arabe." *L'Architecture d'aujourd'hui,* 255 (Feb. 1988): 1–22.

Bonnemaison, Sarah. "A New Landscape for the Capital," *Allegories of Commemoration.* Ph.D. thesis, University of British Columbia, 1995.

Boundas, Constantin V., ed. *The Deleuze Reader.* New York: Columbia University Press, 1993.

Braudeau, Michel. "Le temple et ses marchands." *Le Monde* (December 2, 1993).

Bryson, Norman. *Vision and Painting: The Logic of the Gaze.* New Haven: Yale University Press, 1983.

Bryson, Norman. The Gaze in the Expanded Field," *Vision and Visuality,* ed. Hal Foster. Seattle: Bay Press, 1988.

Buck-Morss, Susan. *The Dialectics of Seeing: Walter Benjamin and the Arcades Projects.* Cambridge, Mass: MIT Press, 1991.

Cassirer, Ernst. *The Philosophy of Symbolic Forms,* trans. Ralph Waldheim. New Haven: Yale University Press, 1953.

Chaslin, François. *Les Paris de François Mitterrand, Histoire des grands projets architecturaux.* Paris: Gallimard, 1985.

Chaslin, François. "Grand Louvre, Prisme Changeant de l'Opinion." *L'Architecture d'aujourd'hui* 263 (June 1989): 8–16.

Chaslin, François. "Grands Projets; Concours de la Bibliothèque nationale de France." *L'Architecture d'aujourd'hui* 265 (Oct. 1989): 184–195.

Chave, Anna C. "Minimalism and the Rhetoric of Power." *Arts Magazine* (Jan. 1990): 44–63.

Cohen, Jean Louis, and Bruno Fortier, eds. *Paris: La Ville et Ses Projets, a City in the Making.* Paris: Editions Babylone, Pavillon de L'Arsenal, 1988.

Collins, Christiane and George. "Monumentality: A Critical Matter in Modern Architecture." *Harvard Architectural Review IV: Monumentality and the City* (Spring 1984): 15–35.

Colquhoun, Alan. "Critique." *Centre Pompidou. Architectural Design* 47, no. 2, 1977, 96–104.

Conrads, Ulrich. *Programs and Manifestoes on 20th-century Architecture,* trans. Michael Bullock. Cambridge: MIT Press, 1990.

Cook, Peter, Warren Chalk, Dennis Crompton, David Greene, Ron Herron, and Mike Webb, eds. *Archigram.* London: Studio Vista, 1972.

Curtis, William J. R. "Grands Projets" *Architectural Record* (March 1990): 75–82.

Debord, Guy. *Society of the Spectacle.* Detroit: Black & Red, 1983.

de Certeau, Michel. *Culture in the Plural,* trans. Tom Conley. Minneapolis: University of Minnesota Press, 1997.

Deleuze, Gilles. *The Logic of Sense,* ed. Constantin V. Boundas, trans. Mark Lester. New York: Columbia University Press, 1990.

de Moncan, Patrice, and Christian Mahout. *Le Paris du Baron Haussmann: Paris sous Le Second Empire.* Paris: Editions Seesam-Rel, 1991.

des Cars, Jean, and Pierre Pinon. *Paris-Haussmann: Le Paris d'Haussmann.* Paris: Editions du Pavillon de l'Arsenal, Picard Editeur, 1991.

Dirks, Nicholas, Geoff Eley, and Sherry B. Ortney, eds. *Culture/Power/History: A Reader in Contemporary Social History.* Princeton, NJ: Princeton University Press, 1994.

Dupavillon, Christian, and Francis Lacloche. *Le Triomphe des Arcs.* Paris: Editions Découvertes Gallimard, 1989.

Ellis, Charlotte. "Prouvé's People's Palace." *Architectural Review* (May 1985): 40–47.

Evans, Robin. "Mies van der Rohe: Paradoxical Symmetries." *AA Files* Spring 1990, no. 19, pp. 56–68.

Fausch, Deborah. "The Oppositions of Post-Modern Tectonics," *Architecture New York* 14 (1996): 48–57.

Ferguson, Priscilla Parkhurst. *Paris as Revolution: Writing the Nineteenth Century City.* Berkeley: University of California Press, 1994.

Foster, Hal. "The Crux of Minimalism," *The Return of the Real: The Avante-Garde at the Turn of the Century.* Cambridge, Mass: MIT Press, 1996: 127–171.

Foucault, Michel. *Discipline and Punishment: The Birth of the Prison,* trans. Alan Sheridan. New York: Vintage Books, 1979.

Frascari, Marco. "The Tell-the-Tale Detail." *VIA 7* (1984): 22–37.

Frampton, Kenneth. "Mies van der Rohe and the Monumentalization of Technique, 1933–67." *Modern Architecture: A Critical History.* New York: Oxford University Press, 1980.

Frampton, Kenneth. "Rappel à l'Ordre: The Case for the Tectonic." *Architectural Design* 60 (March/Apr. 1990): 19–25.

Frampton, Kenneth. *Studies in Tectonic Culture: The Poetics of Construction in Nineteenth- and Twentieth-Century Architecture.* Cambridge, Mass.: MIT Press, 1995.

Geist, Johann Friedrich. *Arcades: The History of a Building Type.* Cambridge: MIT Press, 1983.

Giedion, Sigfried. *Space, Time, and Architecture.* Cambridge: Harvard University Press, 1941.

Giedion, Sigfried. "The Need for Monumentality." *Harvard Architectural Review IV* (Spring 1984): 53–61.

Giedion, Sigfried. *Building in France, Building in Iron, Building in Ferro-Concrete/Texts and Documents,* trans. J. Duncan Berry. Santa Monica, CA: Getty Center for the History of Art and the Humanities, 1995.

Giedion, Sigfried, with Jose Luis Sert and Fernand Léger. "Nine Points on Monumentality." *Harvard Architectural Review* IV (Spring 1984): 62–63.

Gleiniger, Andrea. *Paris Contemporary Architecture.* Munich: Prestel-Verlag, 1997.

Goulet, Patrice. "Institut du Monde Arabe." *Architecture + Urbanism: Jean Nouvel* (July 1988): 30–45.

Goulet, Patrice. "I. M. A.: Le Concours pour l'Institut du Monde Arabe, Paris." *L'Architecture d'aujourd'hui* (Feb. 1982): 81–90.

Guardini, Romano. *The End of the Modern World: A Search for Orientation,* trans. Joseph Theman and Herbert Burke. New York: Sheed & Ward, 1956.

Guerrin, Michel. "Grand Louvre Musée et Centre Commercial au Risque de la Cohabitation le Carrousel des Inquiétudes." *Le Monde* (November 19, 1993).

Halley, Peter. "The Crisis in Geometry." *Arts Magazine* (June 1984): 111–115.

Harriss, Joseph. *The Tallest Tower: Eiffel and the Belle Epoque.* Boston: Houghton Mifflin, 1975.

Hartoonian, Gevork. *Ontology of Construction: On Nihilism of Technology in Theories of Modern Architecture.* Cambridge: Cambridge University Press, 1994.

Hays, K. Michael. "Critical Architecture: Between Culture and Form." *Perspecta* 21 (1984): 14–29.

Hegel, G. W. F. "Architecture," *Aesthetics, Lectures on Fine Art,* trans. T. M. Knox. Oxford: Clarendon Press, 1975.

Henrivaux, Jules. *La Verrerie au XXe Siècle.* Paris: E. Bernard et Cie, Imprimeurs—Editeurs, 1903.

Herdeg, Klaus. *Formal Structure in Islamic Architecture of Iran and Turkistan.* New York: Rizzoli, 1990.

Higonnet, Patrice. "Scandal on the Seine." *New York Review of Books* (Aug. 15, 1991): 32–33.

Higonnet, Patrice. "The Lamentable Library." *New York Review of Books* (May 14, 1992): 43.

Hollier, Denis. *Against Architecture: The Writings of Georges Bataille.* Cambridge, Mass.: MIT Press, 1992.

Isenstadt, Sandy. "Spectacular Tectonics." *Architecture New York* 14 (1996): 44–47.

Jacques, Michel, with Gaëlle Lauriot-dit-Prévost, eds. *Bibliothèque nationale de France 1989/1995.* Paris: Artemis and Arc en rêve centre d'architecture, 1995.

Jay, Martin. *Downcast Eyes: The Denigration of Vision in Twentieth Century French Thought.* Berkeley: University of California Press, 1993.

Jodidio, Phillip. "Comment Chiffrer la Culture?" *Connaissance des Arts* (July–Aug. 1997): 5.

Judt, Tony. "A La Recherche du Temps Perdu." *New York Review of Books* (Dec. 3, 1998): 51.

Kahn, Andrea. "The Invisible Mask," *Building Drawing Text.* New York: Princeton Architectural Press, 1991.

Kaufman, Edgar, and Ben Raeburn, *Frank Lloyd Wright: Writings and Buildings.* New York: Meridian, 1960.

Klein, Dan, and Ward Lloyd, eds. *The History of Glass.* London: Orbis Publishing, 1984.

Krauss, Rosalind. "The Grid, the/Cloud/, and the Detail," *The Presence of Mies,* ed. Detlef Mertins. New York: Princeton Architectural Press, 1994.

Lacan, Jacques. *Four Fundamental Concepts of Psychoanalysis,* ed. Jacques-Alain Miller, trans. Alan Sheridan. New York: Norton, 1981.

Lacan, Jacques. *Ecrits: A Selection,* trans. Alan Sheridan. New York: Norton, 1977.

Laurence, Benaim. "Grand Louvre Rue de Rivoli, chez les marchands du temple." *Le Monde* (November 19, 1993).

Lawday, David. "Foreign Affairs: Paris Is Finished." *Atlantic Monthly* 276 (August 1995): 22–26.

Leatherbarrow, David. *The Roots of Architectural Invention: Site, Enclosure, Materials.* Cambridge: Cambridge University Press, 1993.

Lefebvre, Henri. *Everyday Life in the Modern World,* trans. Sacha Rabinovitch. New Brunswick: Transaction Publishers, 1971.

Levene, Richard C., and Fernando Márquez Cecilia, eds. *El Croquis 65/66: Jean Nouvel 1987–94.* Madrid: El Croquis Editorial, 1994.

Levin, Miriam R. *When the Eiffel Tower Was New: French Visions of Progress at the Centennial of the Revolution.* Boston: University of Massachusetts Press, 1989.

Lipstadt, Hélène. "A Paris of the 21st Century." *Art in America* (Nov. 1984): 104–113.

Lowe, Sebastian. "Design Control in France." *Built Environments* 2(2): 88–103.

Lowe, Sebastian. *Modern Architecture in Historic Cities: Policy, Planning, and Building in Contemporary France.* London: Routledge, 1998.

Maki, Fumihiko. "Japanese City Spaces and the Concept of 'Oku.' " *Japan Architect* (May 1979): 44–53.

Mark, Robert. *Light, Wind, and Structure: The Mystery of the Master Builders.* Cambridge: MIT Press, 1990.

Marrey, Bernard, with Jacques Ferrier. *Paris sous Verre: La Ville et Ses Reflets.* Paris: Editions du Pavillon de l'Arsenal, Picard Editeur, 1997.

Masheck, Joseph. *Building-Art: Modern Architecture under Culture Construction.* Cambridge: Cambridge University Press, 1993.

Martin, Hervé. *Guide to Modern Architecture in Paris,* 1st ed., Paris: Editeur Syros-Alternatives, 1990; 2nd ed., Paris: Editions Alternatives, 1996.

McMillan, James. *Twentieth-Century France: Politics and Society, 1888–91.* London: Arnold, New York: Oxford University Press, 1992.

Melchior-Bonnet, Sabine. *The Mirror: A History,* trans. Katharine H. Jewett. New York/London: Routledge Press, 2001.

Mertins, Detlef, ed. *The Presence of Mies.* New York: Princeton Architectural Press, 1994.

Mertin, Detlef. "The Enticing and Threatening Face of Prehistory: Walter Benjamin and the Utopia of Glass." *Assemblage* 29 (1996): 6–23.

Mies van der Rohe, Ludwig. "Architecture and Technology." *Arts and Architecture* 67 (Oct. 1950): 30.

Mock, Elizabeth. "Built in the USA, 1932–44." *Architectural Forum* (May 1944): 81–96.

Moneo, Rafael. "Recent Architectural Paradigms and a Personal Alternative." *Harvard Design Magazine* (Summer 1998): 74.

Noiriel, Gérard. "French and Foreigners." *Realms of Memory: The Construction of the French Past,* vol. 1. Pierre, Nora, ed. New York: Columbia University Press, 1996.

Nora, Pierre, ed. *Realms of Memory: The Construction of the French Past,* vols. I–III, trans. Arthur Goldhammer. New York: Columbia University Press, 1996.

Panofsky, Erwin. *Perspective as Symbolic Forum,* trans. Christopher S. Wood. New York: Zone Books, 1991.

Pinon, Pierre, ed. *Les Traversées de Paris: Deux siècles de révolutions dans la ville.* Paris: Editions du Moniteur: La Grande Halle-La-Villette, 1989.

Pommer, Richard. "Mies van der Rohe and the Political Ideology of the Modern Movement in Architecture," *Mies van der Rohe: Critical Essays,* ed. Franz Schulze. New York: Musuem of Modern Art, Cambridge: MIT Press, 1989.

Quetglas, Jose. "Fear of Glass: The Barcelona Pavilion," *ArchitectureProduction,* ed. Beatriz Colomina. New York: Princeton University Press, 1988.

Rice, Peter. *An Engineer Imagines.* London: Ellipsis, 1996.

Rice, Peter, and Hugh Dutton. *Structural Glass,* 2nd ed. London: E & FN Spon, 1995.

Rice, Shelley. *Parisian Views.* Cambridge: MIT Press, 1997.

Riley, Terence. *Light Construction.* New York: Harry N. Abrams, 1995.

Rorty, Richard. *Philosophy and the Mirror of Nature.* Princeton: Princeton University Press, 1979.

Rowe, Colin. *The Mathematics of the Ideal Villa and Other Essays.* Cambridge: MIT Press, 1976.

Saalman, Howard. *Haussmann: Paris Transformed.* New York: George Brazillier, 1971.

Sadler, Simon. *The Situationist City.* Cambridge: MIT Press, 1998.

Sartre, Jean-Paul. *Being and Nothingness.* New York: Philosophical Library, 1956.

Schama, Simon. *Citizens.* New York: Vintage Books, 1990.

Scheerbart, Paul. *Glass Architecture;* Taut, Bruno, *Alpine Architecture,* ed. Dennis Sharp. New York: Praeger Publishers, 1972.

Scheerbart, Paul. *The Gray Cloth: Paul Scheerbart's Novel on Glass Architecture,* trans. John A. Stuart. Cambridge: MIT Press, 2001.

Schwarzer, Mitchell. *German Architectural Theory and the Search for Modern Identity.* Cambridge, New York: Cambridge University Press, 1995.

Schwarzer, Mitchell. "Tectonics of the Unforeseen." *Architecture New York* 14 (1996): 62–65.

Scully, Vincent. *Architecture: The Natural and the Manmade.* New York: St. Martin's Press, 1991.

Sierksma, R. J. "Transparent Authority: Reflections of Bentham's Panopticon and Steiner's Goetheanum," presented at "Making Connections," annual conference of the Association of Art Historians of Great Britain, Oxford Brookes University, March 2001.

Silver, Nathan. *The Making of Beaubourg.* Cambridge: MIT Press, 1994.

Silverman, Deborah L. "The 1889 Exposition: The Crisis of Bourgeois Individualism." *Oppositions 8* (Spring 1977): 71–91.

Starobinski, Jean. *The Living Eye,* trans. Arthur Goldhammer. Cambridge: Harvard University Press, 1989.

Starobinski, Jean. *Jean-Jacques Rousseau: Transparency and Obstruction,* trans. Arthur Goldhammer. Chicago, The University of Chicago Press, 1988.

Suner, Bruno. "La Bibliothèque de France, Evolution du Projet." *L'Architecture d'aujourd'hui* 273 (Feb. 1991): 12–24.

Taylor, Brian Brace. "Technology, Society, and Social Control in Le Corbusier's Cité de Refuge, Paris 1933." *Oppositions* 15/16 (Winter–Spring 1979): 168–185.

Trilling, Julia. "Paris: Architecture as Politics," *Atlantic Monthly* 252 (Oct. 1983): 29–35.

Tschumi, Bernard. "Space and Events," reprinted in *Architecture and Disjunction.* Cambridge: MIT Press 1994.

Van Zanten, David. *Building Paris: Architectural Institutions and the Transformations of the French Capital, 1830–70.* Cambridge: Cambridge University Press, 1994.

Vattimo, Gianni. *The Transparent Society,* trans. David Webb. Baltimore: The Johns Hopkins University Press, 1992.

Vidler, Anthony. "*Transparency.*" *The Architectural Uncanny.* Cambridge: MIT Press, 1992.

Weiss, Allen S. *Mirrors of Infinity: The French Formal Garden and 17th Century Metaphysics.* New York: Princeton Architectural Press, 1995.

Whyte, Iain Boyd, ed. *Bruno Taut and the Architecture of Activism.* Cambridge: Cambridge University Press, 1982.

Wiggington, Michael. *Glass in Architecture.* London: Phaidon Press, 1996.

Winterbourne, Erica. "Architecture and the Politics of Culture in Mitterrand's France." *Architectural Design* 65 (March–Apr. 1995): 24–29.

Wiseman, Carter. *I. M. Pei: A Profile in American Architecture.* New York: Harry N. Abrams, 1990.

Zola, Emile, *Paris.* Dover, NH: Alan Suttan Publishing, 1993.

Index

NOTE: PAGE NUMBERS IN ITALICS INDICATE ILLUSTRATIONS.